"Koenig is back with a second installment that blows even more pixie dust off the Magic Kingdom."

– Dennis McLellan
Los Angeles Times

"The sequel to *Mouse Tales* is another behind-the-scenes look at Disneyland, full of much declared love for the Disney ethos. Little boxed features contain 'tales of tourists gone on mental vacations'—an abundant source of humor—and affection permeates much of the rest, whether Koenig is recounting funny situations involving the ungainly costumes park performers wear or the tragedy of the 'first person killed at Disneyland while just standing in line,' which Koenig links to more profit-hungry than quality-minded park management."

– Mike Tribby
Booklist

"Koenig breaks new ground ... offers a sometimes risqué, often humorous and at times insightful look into the workings of Disneyland.

"Koenig stuffs the book with wonderful anecdotes that will entertain anyone who has ever visited Disneyland or worked there. He covers everything from how Pirates of the Caribbean was first envisioned as a walk-through attraction to the tale of a maniacal annual passholder who took it upon herself to use her electric wheelchair to 'protect' Mickey Mouse from perceived threats.

"This second installment in his series makes for a quick and entertaining read about one of America's most famous cultural icons."

– Jerry Hirsch
Orange County Register

MORE MOUSE TALES

A CLOSER PEEK BACKSTAGE AT
DISNEYLAND

by David Koenig

Foreword
by Van Arsdale France

BONAVENTURE

BONAVENTURE PRESS

More Mouse Tales: A Closer Peek Backstage at Disneyland by David Koenig

Published by
BONAVENTURE PRESS
Post Office Box 51961
Irvine, CA 92619-1961
USA
www.bonaventurepress.com

Cover art by Ray Haller
Map art by Chas. Balun

Copyright ® 1999, 2002 by David Koenig

Publisher's Cataloging in Publication Data
Koenig, David G.
    More Mouse Tales: A Closer Peek Backstage at Disneyland / by David Koenig.
        p. cm.
    Includes annotated references and index.
    1. Disneyland (Calif.) — History. 2. Amusement Parks (Calif.). I. Koenig,
        David G., 1962- II. Title.
GV1853.3.C22K   1999   791.0687949   99-073100

ISBN 0-9640605-7-4 (hardcover)

ISBN 0-9640605-8-2 (softcover)

Printed in the United States of America
10 9 8 7 6 5 4

For Zachary,
Disneyland's newest little visitor, who made
writing this book take about nine months longer—
nine wonderful, unforgettable months

Contents

Foreword 11

Preface 13

1. The Happiest Job on Earth 17
   Whistle While You Work … It's in the Contract

2. Fairy Tales in 3-D 31
   Making Dreams Come True in Fantasyland

3. It's a Jungle Out There 52
   Real Life Adventures in Adventureland

4. The Wild, Wild West 84
   Living It Up in the Great Outdoors of Frontierland

5. Southern Spirits 102
   Thrills and Chills in New Orleans Square

6. No Place Like the Future 119
   Trying to Stay Ahead in Tomorrowland

7. Character Witnesses 139
   Mickey and the Gang Squeal

8. The Disney Police 167
   Maintaining the Magic—By Force

9. The Business of Show Business 189
   Managing the Magic for Fun & Profit (But Mostly Profit)

10. Crossroads 213
    Keeping the Magic in the Magic Kingdom

    Notes 219

    Index 234

Acknowledgments

I'LL be the first to admit that *More Mouse Tales* isn't my story. It's the story of the more than 400 past and present Disneyland cast members whom I have had the priviledge of interviewing and, in many cases, becoming friends with over the last twelve years. I compiled the stories. These people lived them.

Those kind enough to share their adventures with me included: Francisco Alanis, Margaret Anderson, Mike Aramaki, Earl Archer, Tom Askew, Earl Baker, Bob Baldwin, Tony Baxter, Eric Beaumont, Bob Beekman, Robby Beeman, Betsy Bonilla, Christopher Borja, Doug Boynton, Don Brown, Gail Brown, Don and Dayna Budde, Craig Carman, Jim Cashen, Jennifer Casteix, Paul Castle, John Catone, Kevin Chaney, Garry Conk, Frank Cozza, Craig Carmen, R. Danberry, Mike DeForest, Janice (Adamczyk, Seibert) Doezie, Leon Duty, Dorothy Eno, John Ezell, Ray Flores, Bo Foster, Van Arsdale France, Gary Fravel, Ken Fujimura ...

... and Mark Gabriel, Cindy Garbino, Glen Garcia, Terry Garrison, Bob Gentleman, Jack George, John Gerlach, Alan Glisch, Mike Goodwin, Chad Gordon, Josh Green, Barry Grupp, Bill E. Hackbarth, Ray Haller, Garth Hamlin, Jim Haught, Elizabeth (Confer, Cooper) Hayes, Dan Healy, Brent Hedman, Kent Helwig, Steve Hendrickson, Kimberly (Hilston) Hensley, Art Herrera, Robert Hill, Cliff Hils, Ed Homola, Cathy Hughes, Darren

Lee Hundley, Sam Hunsaker, Deena (Summers) Ippolito, Bob Januska, Harvey Johnson, Rich Johnson, Diane Judd, Paul Kabat, Larry Kaml, Phil Keen ...

... plus Douglas Keene, Austin Keiser, Mark Keiser, Chris Kraftchick, Jill Marie Landis, Jeff Lenburg, Brian Levine, Heidi Levine, Sam Levine, Paul Lewanski, Yolanda (Garcia) Lewanski, Todd Lidvahl, Wayne Lubke, Kevin Malone, Frank Marter, Don McLaren, Rolf Mendez, Steve Messick, Arlen Miller, Colette Miller, Dick Mobley, Jim Moore, Jason Moy, Sara Moy, Grover Nutt, Dan O'Trambo ...

... as well as Ken Pellman, Tony Pena, Bob Penfield, Chris Perley, Mike Pritchard, Milo Rainey, Sheryl (Dominguez) Ralston, Tom Ravenscroft, Dick Reger, Patrick Robertson, Dane Rowland, Patricia (Vickers) Rudolph, Leonard Russo, Dan Serber, Phil Seymour, Gene Spindler, Tim Stanley, Heather Steele, Greg Stephan, Jeffrey Stoneking, William Stout, Carl Trapasso, Bruce Turner, Eric Vogelvang, Jerry White, Kent Wilson, Dennis Wolf, Cindy Yan, Eric Yang and Mark Zimmer.

Of those, Bob, Liz and Mark were extra helpful in rounding up friends to share their memories with me. I am also grateful to the ever-gracious Van France for kindly providing the foreword.

I was priviledged to work with three fine editors—Randy Skretvedt, Sara Daly and Tom Graves—and two terrific artists, Ray Haller, who created the cover art, and Chas. Balun, who produced the park and attraction maps.

Added assistance came from Don Bertino, Dwight Curran, Carole Mumford, Jerry Hirsch and Marla Jo Fisher of *The Orange County Register*, E. Scott Reckard and Dennis McLellan of *The Times-Orange County*, attorneys Lisa Stern and Neil Newsome, Matt Coker, James Brown and the staff of the Anaheim office of Cal-OSHA, Jane Newell and the staff of the Anaheim History Room at the Anaheim Public Library, the staff at the Orange County Courthouse, and the Disneyland Alumni Club (P.O. Box 3232, Anaheim, Ca. 92803-3232).

Help and support came from past and present associates Chuck Casey, David and Marti Cutler, Dave DelVal, Julie Howard, Autumn Schwanke, Alan, Liz and Julie Wickstrom, and Cindy Wild.

I thank my friends and helpers Bill Bax, Charles Christ, Jason and Shannon Clark, Jessica Haller, Larry, Sheryl, Garth and Mimi Hamlin, David Hayes, Tim Hensley, Bill Jagielski, David, Laura, Jason and Ryan Keefe, Rita and Bob Pipta, Terrie Rudolph, Brent and Chris Walker, and my family, Gerald, Anne, Joe, Paul, Maryanne and Zachary Koenig, Michelle, Paul, Devon and Megan Roden, and, of course, Laura Koenig, who never stops assisting and encouraging me.

Most of all, I am grateful to my Lord and Savior, Jesus Christ, for His love and for everyone He has placed and everything He has allowed in my life.

Foreword

by Van Arsdale France
Founder and Professor Emeritus of the Disney University

IN 1988, when David Koenig first told me he was going to write a book about Disneyland, I thought he was a little crazy. I had been a Disneylander since before the park opened in 1955, and was just completing my own book, *Window On Main Street*. I firmly believed that he couldn't write a book about Disneyland without having worked there.

Well, as it turned out, it took seven years, but he did write the book, and *Mouse Tales* has been highly successful. Ironically, the fact that he never worked there was a major asset.

When one person writes of his experiences, the reader receives the anecdotes of one person. But *Mouse Tales* contains the anecdotes of a whole park-full of people. David spoke to everyone, regardless of status, supervisor or sweeper, as long as they had a good story.

In the early days of Disneyland, everyone, no matter their position, gained status simply from working at Disneyland. Relatives, friends, everyone who knew me was always asking, "Can you get me a job at Disneyland?"

Back then, Disneyland was the only theme park in the world and gave people a chance to work with Walt Disney himself, for goodness sake!

The pay rates at that time exceeded those for equivalent service jobs. Our cast members, often college students, received excellent training that they could use in their profession of choice. Working at Disneyland, even for just one or two summers, was a fantastic thing to put on your resume. Few schools offered graduates as much status as the University of Disneyland.

Best of all, you made friends for a lifetime. Many, in fact, met their future spouses while working alongside them at Disneyland. The Harbor House entrance to the employee parking lot became known as Friendship Point because at the beginning of summer, people would congregate there, evaluating their prospects for dates. You could smell the musk in the air.

There was excitement in being part of Walt's show, because there was always something different. Walt loved trying new things and always added magical attractions or shows or parades for Christmas and summer—in part, because we needed them to get people to try this new form of entertainment.

Nowadays, in every corner of the country and the world there are theme parks (or at least they call themselves theme parks). Things have changed at Disneyland, too. But there's still a lot of pixie dust with not only cast members who honor Walt's ideals, but with guests who grew up with Disneyland. Many are now annual pass holders creating new memories with their children.

After all, dreams never die.

Preface

I NEVER thought I would write a "Mouse Tales II." After seven years researching the first *Mouse Tales*, published in 1994, I figured I'd answered every question about what it's like Behind the Ears at Disneyland.

In fact, at a Disneyana convention soon after the book's release, the first of countless readers asked when the sequel was coming. I laughed. An Imagineer who was within earshot noted that *Mouse Tales* recounted seemingly every major incident in Disneyland's history, including backstage secrets, the best anecdotes, funniest pranks, the strikes, deaths and other disasters. What, he wondered, could possibly be left for a sequel?

Plenty. I've come to realize that unusual things happen at Disneyland every day, and each of the more than 100,000 people who have served as cast members over the years has a tale or two. As such, all the stories and secrets in this book are new.

In addition, things have changed at Disneyland in just the last five years. *Mouse Tales* showed that, despite what Disney wants everyone to believe, Disneyland is not immune to the mishaps that regularly occur in real life. Still, many of the problems weren't Disney's fault. Most of the guests who were injured didn't heed clearly posted warnings. And park management did everything it could to ensure its safety records was as spotless as possible.

Unfortunately, while Disney management clings to the image of "the Happiest Place on Earth" to sell tickets, they no longer strive for perfection. Why go to the trouble and expense of providing a *premium* product if people will pay for *adequate*?

Certainly the first *Mouse Tales* alluded to management's increasing focus on the bottom line. But that was only the beginning.

Because Disney tries so hard to present itself as practically perfect in every way (and often comes close), it has engendered the most vocal of supporters and the most vociferous of critics. Criticize Disney in any way, no matter how constructively, and the supporters instantly cast you into the enemy camp. They fail to realize that many of Disney's critics just want to make Disneyland a better place.

When *Mouse Tales* came out, some questioned whether it would terrify people of the park and keep them away. Hardly. At its heart were a love of Disneyland, an appreciation for its designers and employees, and a fascination for how it all worked. Indeed, countless people have told me the book made them want to visit Disneyland more than ever. They wanted to check out the big green door to Club 33 and all the other things they'd never noticed

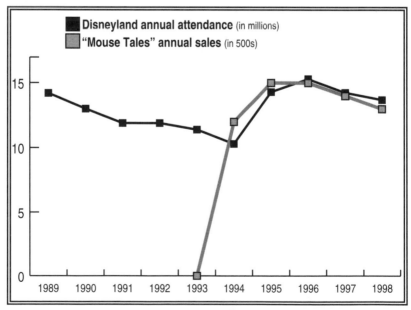

– Park attendance figures from Amusement Business

before. Many bought annual passes.

So, instead of driving attendance down, I am convinced *Mouse Tales* actually increased attendance at Disneyland. Sales figures of *Mouse Tales* back me up (see chart on previous page). Note how Disneyland's popularity parrots the book's. Park attendance was plummetting to new lows before the release of *Mouse Tales*. The experts attribute the sudden turnaround to the end of the recession, a related increase in tourism, new attractions or promotions. But no one has mentioned the Mouse Tales Connection.

Well, park attendance is again on the decline, and there are no fancy, new $100 million attractions coming any time soon. How can we turn things around? It looks like it's time for another book about Disneyland.

– David Koenig
May 1999

1

The Happiest Job on Earth

DON'T call Disneyland an amusement park. Six Flags operates amusement parks. Disneyland is a *theme* park, and, to purists, there's a world of difference. Amusement parks are disorganized collections of carnival rides. But a theme park, especially Disneyland, is a *show*, designed more like a motion picture or a play than a carnival.

Every image is manipulated, each area, or "land," organized into a logical sequence of events or scenes to take the audience from point to point through a story.

The end of the first scene, Main Street, fans out from a central hub like spokes in a wheel to four more scenes: guests can turn west through a cowboy fort facade to Frontierland or through Tiki gates to Adventureland; they can turn east toward the space rockets of Tomorrowland, or walk straight through a storybook castle to Fantasyland.

To support the stories, master designer Walt Disney insisted that every component coincide with the theme of its land—every attraction, every restaurant and every shop, right down to the trash cans. He barricaded his park inside a twelve- to 20-foot-high earthen berm. "I don't want the public to see the world they live in while they're in the park," Walt explained. "I want them to feel they are in another world."

Disneyland even uses the terminology of show business. The crowd is the *audience*, made up not of customers, but of *guests*. Each employee is a *cast member* assigned to a *role*, either *backstage* or dealing with the public *on stage*. The cast doesn't wear uniforms—they're *costumes*, picked up from *Wardrobe*.

Workers are cast like actors in a show. Years ago, your gender, race and physical appearance influenced what part you got or if you got a part at all, especially in the 1960s and '70s, when the park had fewer job openings, comparatively higher wages and less contact with the Equal Opportunity Employment agency. "Until the late 1970s," said one old-timer, "Personnel had a stack of 100 applications, and maybe they'd pick 20."

According to former Disneyland casting director Gary Conk, "We really tried to place people where their personalities would fit, like the Jungle Cruise or Tiki Room. For certain rides, you had only certain size costumes; girls and guys wore slacks on the Matterhorn and had to have the right type of figure. During an interview, we might ask them to recite part of the spiel or go try on a costume to see how they looked in it. You couldn't do that now. You'd get into a lot of trouble."

"In casting now," he added, "they probably view in their minds how someone will fit in the part. They know what they're hiring for. Before, you could choose the cream of the crop. You might interview 20 people and hire one. Now you interview 20 people, and you need 21."

Historically, the employees with the most contact with guests— tour guides and ride operators—were "The Beautiful People." Proper physical appearance was of utmost importance. As an interviewer noted on one prospective employee's application: "Wants to be in Operations, but is too broad in the beam."

Few people apply at Disneyland to flip hamburgers in a hot, greasy kitchen. But interviewers use tricks to fill less desirable food service positions. "Foods positions initially pay the highest wage and offer the most hours per week, with good reason ... the Foods Division has the highest turnover rate and is generally considered to be the worst division to work for in the park," revealed Tomorrowland Terrace manager Eric Beaumont. "Over the years I learned that the interviewers are told to say that only Foods positions are open unless the potential employee makes a specific request. I was far too green to be anything but excited about any position in the Magic Kingdom."

Often, introverted or less attractive applicants are assigned to Foods, where there's less contact with the guests. "Those kids worked ten times harder than any of those ride operators ever thought of," said one foreman.

Another worker agreed: "In Operations, the pay was better, the working conditions were better, and there was the status."

Cast members were stereotyped to not only what they did, but where they did it. The West Side of the park, including Adventureland and Frontierland, has more outdoor areas, inviting free spirits, whether more laid back or more wild. The attractions are more compacted on the East Side; the focus is more on the structures than the trees and open spaces, attracting more conservative personalities.

"There was a vast cultural difference between the lands," recalled long-ago Jungle Cruise skipper John Ezell. "In Adventureland, we hung out, leaned on posts, scratched our navels. In Tomorrowland, everyone was six-foot-one, trim, stood erect."

"The difference between the West Side and the East Side was like night and day," former ride operator Doug Boynton generalized. "It seemed like everyone was typecast. You retired on Main Street. Persons with a proclivity toward the same sex were in Tomorrowland. And, they protected the better looking women in Fantasyland by having the under-developed, less mature men there."

After being assigned a role, cast members undergo intensive training to indoctrinate them into "The Disney Way." The training, applied with equal parts common sense and motivational pixie dust, aims to inject employees with the show biz bug and encourage them to adopt Disneyland as *their* Disneyland. Walt realized that if cast members broke character, the whole illusion would fall apart. They had to buy into his traditions of teamwork, safety, courtesy, cleanliness, and strive to uphold them day in and day out.

Most new hires are starstruck, raring to go. Disneyland's first

Guest Pains

At one time or another, the thought probably has occurred to every cast member: Disneyland would be a great place to work if it weren't for the guests. Asked to suspend their disbelief, visitors often suspend all other normal thought processes, as well. "They walk in the front gates and their IQ drops about 30 points," noted one employee.

The frequency of dumb questions, which cast members would refer to as "Guestions," is astonishing. "The Disney Way" handbook warns cast members to have patience answering questions because guests didn't come to Disneyland to read signs. "We're told, once they walk in, they're not gonna read, even if the signs are right in front of them," said John Catone. "You'll be asked 'Where's the restroom?' 500 times. Or, 'How do I get to such-and-such a place?,' even though the signs are all there. I felt if I *didn't* get asked questions, something was wrong."

Tales of tourists gone on mental vacations appear in boxes throughout the book.

workers also felt a personal, familial connection to Walt; later employees have their own fond childhood memories of Disney movies and Disneyland itself. Guests come to Disneyland to have fun and cast members are a part of their fun.

Despite Walt's meticulous planning, the daily operation of Disneyland can be entirely unpredictable, for Disneyland is a show without a script. And it's a show that invites onto the stage tens of thousands of guests—who haven't taken the "Disney Way" classes. Visitors are creatures of the real world and, like it or not, they will bring part of that real world in with them.

The employees aren't animatronic, either. They can be told to smile on cue, but keeping a sincere smile can be difficult under the pressure of pleasing 2,000 often demanding visitors an hour.

"Disney is so intent on delivering the product to the guest, they want you to leave everything personal backstage," said ride operator Kent Wilson. "They have never addressed the human factor. When you're dealing with human beings, you're dealing with variables. But to keep up hourly counts, Disney wants you to compress them through attractions like meat through a processor. They forget that people may be elderly or disabled."

Park management sometimes forgets that it's difficult to fake being happy. "There was fun in being part of the Disney act, but anything with repetition becomes a job," Wilson said. "You can tell yourself, before you step out on stage that, 'This is a brand new experience for each guest,' but the truth is it's your fifth or sixth year. (Burnout) usually happens in about the fifth year. It's often the last year of your education, you're still working holidays, your focus is elsewhere. One day I was working the Peter Pan ride, it was about my fifth year, and I found myself snapping at a guest. When I got backstage, I realized I either had to quit or change my attitude."

Yet the show must go on. Cast members try their best to maintain their smile and their sanity. Some try often ingenious ways to have fun, occasionally at the expense of the performance. As a result, the "leads" who oversee front-line cast members mostly play babysitter for the typically college-aged workforce, as well as take charge in emergencies.

Still, despite years of planning and practice, occasionally the show breaks down.

Disneyland's show begins before you enter the front gates. It starts at Toll Plaza, the toll booths leading to the parking lot, which serves as the show's exterior lobby. There, guests are welcomed by a smiling attendant, then waved on by other attendants through a maze of orange plastic cones to their parking place and ultimately to a tram ride to the Main Gate.

> **Motorist** (to the toll gate attendant, in a furious storm): "Is it raining inside?"

The lot didn't start out as much. In the park's first years, only the two sections closest to the Main Gate were paved. Attendants would line the dirt with chalk to show cars where to park. "The old trams, there from Day One, never tracked properly," recalled long-time parking lot supervisor Bob Gentleman. "They would pull about four cars, and the tail car never followed the lead car. They'd make real wide turns and sometimes hit a pylon or a car." The troublesome trams were replaced by more reliable blue and yellow vehicles in 1975, which were joined in 1997 by larger, higher powered red and white trams.

Although tram drivers are paid a little more than others in Operations, the parking lot has never been the most glamorous area to work. "In the early days, the parking lot technically was part of Operations, but we were not allowed to rotate into positions inside the park," recalled former parking lot host Paul Lewanski. "In some ways, it was the penal colony of the park, where we were sent for rehabilitation."

Called "field rats," the workers who wave in cars are often isolated from each other and don't have much interaction with the guests either. Visitors usually are in a hurry to get into the park. Once, a couple was so excited they took off on the parking lot tram, forgetting that in their car, with the doors locked, the engine running and the air conditioning on, they had left their baby. Operators had to break into the car and search for the embarrassed parents.

Field rats also have little protection from the hot sun or fierce rain. "The weather conditions could be horrendous," Lewanski remembered. "They gave us these wonderful fleece-lined coats, but then changed the costume to lightweight, non-insulated jackets.

Doctor, Doctor

Originally, the parking lot's handicapped section was called "Medical Parking," but the name had to be changed because doctors constantly tried to park there, arguing that they were on call.

Fortunately, supervision usually looked the other way if we deviated a little from the dress code. We all became experts on thermal underwear and ski caps."

The toll booths sometimes become miniature wind tunnels. Sniffling attendants end up wiping their noses on anything they can find—their sleeves, ticket stubs, "Welcome to Disneyland" brochures. One attendant with a cold vowed to give free parking to the first guest who had a box of tissues. A woman drove up with an opened Kleenex package on her dashboard. The motorist agreed to a swap, but cautioned, "There aren't many left." She handed over the packet, drove through and the attendant reached into the package to discover it contained a single tissue.

Before the park installed counters at the toll booths, it wasn't uncommon for attendants to work out trades. One morning, a group of cash-strapped teenagers drove up to the toll booth and was mortified to see how expensive parking was. "Six dollars?" one asked. "Do we have to pay?" To their surprise, the attendant answered, "Do you have any food?" The kids began rummaging through their car and came up with an unopened box of Strawberry Pop Tarts. The attendants began laughing, high-fiving each other and swapped the pink-frosted Pop Tarts for a parking ticket.

Another toll booth attendant was fond of In 'N Out hamburgers, so whenever someone drove in with an In 'N Out takeout bag, she would jokingly ask, "Where's *my* burger?" Usually, the guests would laugh. Once, a visitor replied, "Well, we do have one left." The attendant said that, no, she couldn't take it, she was just kidding. But her co-workers persuaded her to take the burger. After

Gate Keepers

Guest questions asked to ticket sellers at the Main Gate:

- "Are you open until you close?"

- "Do I have to pay to go in?"

- "Do you give discounts to tourists?"

the party drove through, the lead asked the attendant, "Did you charge her for parking?" "Of course," the attendant answered, to the lead's consternation. So, the lead hopped on a scooter, chased down the car and refunded the guests' parking fee.

Working in the parking lot affords more freedom than inside the park, where cast members might feel always under the watch of a foreman or supervisor. Additionally, attractions typically have a never-ending line of people waiting to get on. In the parking lot, attendants might find free time after the big crowds arrive in the morning.

To pass the time, during the 1984 Olympics, attendants staged their own Parking Lot Olympics. Events included motorized car slaloms through cones, the cone toss, cone shuffleboard, cone bowling, and cone skiing (riding on two cones while holding onto the back of a scooter).

Other times, for fun, field rats might direct all the white cars into one section, driving guests crazy as they desperately try to identify their own vehicle at the end of the night.

Years ago, cast members would make Super 8 movies to show at an end-of-the-summer banquet. Early one morning, a cameraman climbed onto a high platform and filmed the parking lot trams performing close order drills, set to the "Blue Danube Waltz."

Another time, a tram driver warned his passengers that, for a

---

Store Tours

Guest (to Penny Arcade cashier, looking for change so he could view one of the old-time filmstrip viewers): "Can I have $10 in pennies, please?"

Another Guest (after receiving a few brand new pennies in change from an Emporium clerk): "Does Disneyland make you shine the coins?"

Yet another Guest (looking for a stuffed animal, to an Emporium hostess): "I already have a Chip, where can I find a Munk?

cast member film, a friend who was a uniformed policeman was going to stop the tram for speeding. Sure enough, the officer pulled them over and began writing a ticket. Suddenly, the driver kicked the ticket book out of his hand. The policeman yanked the driver out of the tram, threw him against his police car, handcuffed him, shoved him in the backseat and drove off, red lights flashing and siren blaring. The passengers on the driverless tram sat there amused. But hundreds of onlookers, who weren't in on the joke, were aghast. To this day, they probably still tell the story of the day the Disneyland tram driver was arrested.

Guests enter the park's Main Gate into a small courtyard that serves as the show's interior lobby. From there, they pass through one of two tunnels under the Disneyland Railroad tracks, leaving behind reality and stepping into the show itself.

Scene One is Main Street, U.S.A., a fanciful recreation of turn-of-the-century America. Over the years, Main Street appears to have changed little, except for a fresh coat of paint. The shops have changed names. Gone are the Tobacco Shop, Bluebird Shoe Shop, Cole Swimsuit Shop, China Closet and Town Square Realty.

The old stores were as much for show as for selling. Originally, the street featured a showroom for Wurlitzer pianos and organs, an old-time Upjohn apothecary where professional pharmacists handed out free vitamins, and the V-Ette Corset Shop, operated by the Hollywood-Maxwell Co., manufacturer of brassieres, girdles, corsets and other intimate apparel. Designers built a large porch in front of the shop "to keep traffic down," but Disneyland and underwear still didn't seem to mesh; Hollywood-Maxwell mutually decided with Disney to close shop in 1956, a year after the park opened.

By design, most of the attractions on Main Street are sightseeing vehicles: turn-of-the-century streetcars and horseless carriages, sur-

---

Guest (to a Main Street host): "Where is the supermarket?"

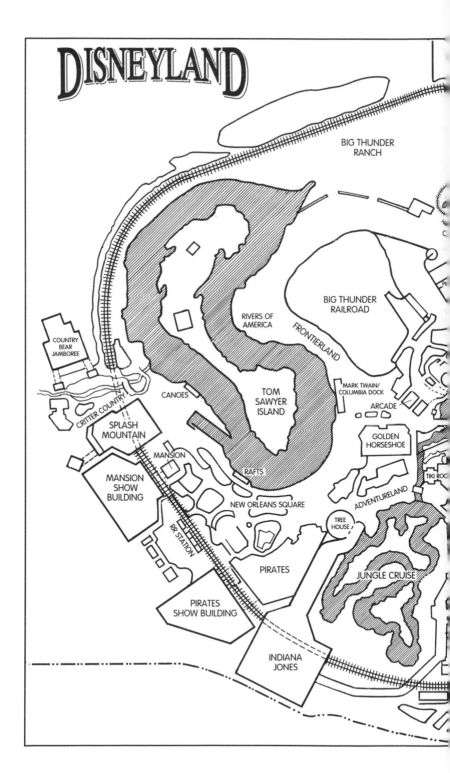

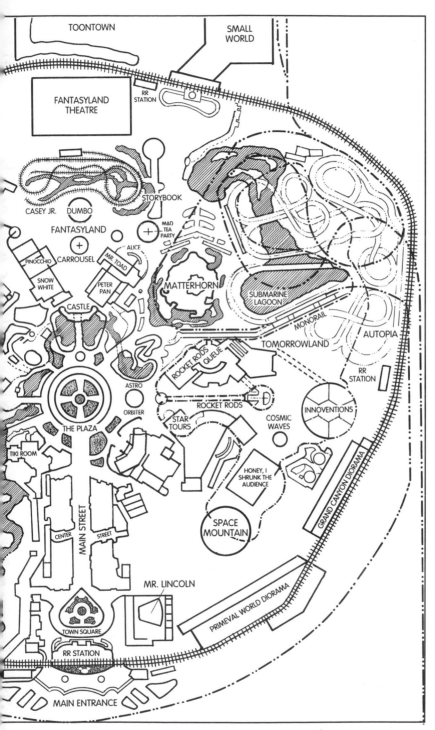

TOONTOWN

SMALL WORLD

FANTASYLAND THEATRE

RR STATION

CASEY JR.   DUMBO

STORYBOOK

FANTASYLAND

MAD TEA PARTY

PINOCCHIO   CARROUSEL

ALICE

MR. TOAD

SNOW WHITE

PETER PAN

CASTLE

MATTERHORN

SUBMARINE LAGOON

MONORAIL

AUTOPIA

TOMORROWLAND

ROCKET RODS QUEUE

RR STATION

ASTRO ORBITER

ROCKET RODS

INNOVENTIONS

THE PLAZA

STAR TOURS

COSMIC WAVES

TIKI ROOM

HONEY, I SHRUNK THE AUDIENCE

GRAND CANYON DIORAMA

CENTER STREET

MAIN STREET

SPACE MOUNTAIN

MR. LINCOLN

PRIMEVAL WORLD DIORAMA

TOWN SQUARE

RR STATION

MAIN ENTRANCE

ALL MAPS NOT TO SCALE

reys, double-decker Omnibuses, an antique fire engine and, circling the park, the Disneyland Railroad. More than entertaining, the attractions help set the stage, drawing people further into the park.

Despite the typically heavy crowds on Main Street, ride operators have a lower key, slower paced job in keeping with the area's relaxed, carefree theme. They often have more time to chat with the guests, even while steering their vehicles. Still, drivers have to keep their eyes peeled for preoccupied pedestrians, who sometimes recklessly rush down the street or wander in a daze. If Main Street gets too crowded, the vehicles aren't used.

Most commonly used are Main Street's four horse-drawn streetcars. The park's sixteen horses work two to four days a week, two to four hours a day, pulling at a leisurely pace. One horse named Jct, though, was used only at night, because she sweated so badly that she looked as if she had been abused. "Jet had the route timed in her head," recalled driver Robby Beeman. "She thought she only had to make so many trips, so she would always try to rush through them to knock off early for the night."

The horses can be temperamental. Drivers try to prevent guests from slapping the horses to make them go faster or from feeding them popcorn, so no fingers get bitten.

One volatile horse, Michelle, hated the Disneyland Band and would rear up and snicker whenever she heard them coming. Once, a child clipped Michelle with a Mickey Mouse balloon and the horse went ballistic, kicking at the front of the buckboard.

Another time, a boy running by the trolley loading area hit the horse with his balloon. The horse, enraged, broke free of its reins and bolted around Town Square. The trolley jumped the tracks and thudded to a stop against a curb. But the horse tried to run into the

---

Tourist from Florida (in a whisper to a Clock Shop hostess, after selecting a Disneyland 30th Anniversary watch): "You know, these watches are going to be very valuable some day because California is going to fall off into the ocean next year."

Main Street Opera House before getting wedged in the turnstiles.

Custodians have the hardest horse-related job: cleaning up after them. Years back, a long line of horses paraded down Main Street during a Western Days promotion. In the middle of the parade, an employee tried to wheel a dolly carrying a barrel of baked beans across Main Street to the Plaza Inn restaurant. A dolly wheel hit the trolley track rut and spilled about eight gallons of beans. At the end of parade, the janitors arrived to clean up after the horses and, staring at the baked bean slick, all wondered, "What happened to the horses?" One brave custodian took a closer look and deduced, "He must have gotten sick from eating baked beans." They ended up hosing down the street.

The only Main Street attraction ever to require an E ticket actually spends more time out of Main Street than in it. The Disneyland Railroad's four steam engines circle the park, transporting guests to and through the other lands.

Attractions hosts and hostesses help guests board and disembark, while an engineer and fireman operate the engine. The engineer controls the movement of the train, while the fireman monitors steam pressure, maintains the fire in the firebox, and ensures the air pressure for braking is functioning properly.

Since the train runs around the perimeter of the park, it doesn't offer as scenic a view as the Monorail. The most unique thing that railroad passengers get to see is a diorama of the Grand Canyon added in 1958 and another of Primeval World introduced in 1966.

Passengers looking extra close might see a little more. For several years, during the holidays, maintenance workers would hang a Christmas ornament on a curved vine over the first Primeval World lagoon. Others tried to top them. One New Year's Eve, an employee put a party hat on a triceratops. Another time, a worker

---

Guest (to the stocky, bald attractions host taking tickets at the Walt Disney Story): "Are you Mr. Disney?"

hung a small sign in the back of Primeval World diorama that read: "If you lived here, you'd be home now."

Main Street's fixed attractions, the Main Street Cinema and Great Moments with Mr. Lincoln at the Opera House, are no longer very popular. When Disneyland discontinued taking individual tickets for each attraction, operators stopped manning the cinema. Working Mr. Lincoln consists of not much more than directing guests into the theater and introducing the show. The only one known to have trouble performing their duties was audio-animatronic Abe himself. The figure first recited his amalgamation of speeches at the 1964-1965 World's Fair in New York, during which the Imagineers thought they had worked out all the kinks. But after he relocated to Disneyland late in 1965, the figure constantly went into spasms in mid-performance. After thoroughly checking the robot's electrical system, maintenance realized that the show's power supply was fed by the same sub station that fed 600 volts to the Monorail. Whenever the Monorail ran in these sections, there would be a power surge, causing Lincoln to spasm. Surge suppressers didn't work, so Lincoln's power line was run under Town Square and linked to another sub station behind City Hall.

Although a more reliable power source cured Abe of the shakes, he still experiences the occasional glitch. In the middle of one performance, the figure suddenly bent at the waist and, hunched over, continued speaking. A group of grade school children in attendance later sent "Get Well Soon" letters to the park. One child hoped Mr. Lincoln could find some help for "his back problem." Another thought Abe had a heart attack. Yet another wrote: "At first I thought he was bending down to tie his shoe, but then he started talking to the floor...."

Guest (exiting Great Moments with Mr. Lincoln): "Who played the part of Mr. Lincoln?"
Cast member: "Uh, no one."
Guest: "Oh my goodness, do you mean that was really Mr. Lincoln himself?"

2

Fairy Tales in 3-D

AT the far end of Main Street sits Sleeping Beauty Castle—landmark, photo opportunity, walk-through exhibit and entrance to Fantasyland, where fairy tale characters and cartoon settings come to life. Walt cited the lyrics to "When You Wish Upon a Star" as inspiration for creating the "land where dreams come true."

Fantasyland's dark rides best recreate Disney's animated features, specifically *Snow White and the Seven Dwarfs*, *Pinocchio*, *Alice in Wonderland*, *Peter Pan*, and the Mr. Toad sequence of *The Adventures of Ichabod and Mr. Toad*. Inside, guests travel in small vehicles past a series of scenes and characters illuminated by glow-in-the-dark "blacklight" paint. The cars are powered by electricity that runs through the track, or "bus bar." By pressing a button on a control board near the loading zone, operators can send power to a particular section of the ride, starting up cars in that area, or can cut power to a section, so cars there coast to a stop.

In the early years, besides a ticket taker, a team of three ran each dark ride—one operator on the control board, one helping guests into the vehicles, and one helping them exit. Originally, the worker on unload manually unlocked the safety bars on each car. The park quickly devised a system so the locks were automatically tripped when the cars entered the unload area, reducing the three-person shift to one.

Peter Pan's Flight, believably soaring over London, is the most popular of the dark rides, followed by the frantic Mr. Toad's Wild Ride. Although it covers two stories, Alice in Wonderland is the most easily overlooked, since it was built two years after and around the corner from the others.

Snow White's Adventures ranks by far as the most intense. In the days of individually ticketed rides, a ticket taker could caution parents that the attraction might be frightening for small children. That didn't stop obstinate adults from insisting their children would be fine, only to have the kids bawling their heads off through the entire attraction. As one angry father climbed out of his vehicle with his wife comforting their crying daughter, he snarled at the ride operator: "Why didn't you tell us there was a *witch* inside?"

When the ride was rebuilt in 1983, it got a new name (Snow White's *Scary* Adventures), as well as an ominous, dungeon-like pre-show area; the Imagineers figured if the children weren't scared away by the queue, they'd survive the ride.

Operators of the open-air rides in the Fantasyland courtyard— King Arthur's Carrousel, Dumbo the Flying Elephant and the Mad Tea Party—instruct guests to board their favorite pony, pachyderm or tea cup, then hit a timer that sends the vehicles circling, usually for a preset 90 seconds.

On the Carrousel and Dumbo, before the vehicles start moving, an operator makes the rounds to ensure all passengers are strapped on. The Mad Tea Party is trickier, because the eighteen cups sit on three large spinning plates, which all sit on a giant spinning master plate. The guests control the spinning of their own Tea Cups.

During the ride's first two years, the Tea Cups had no brakes or clutches—nothing to limit how fast they could be spun. There also was nothing to prevent guests from spinning their Tea Cups before all the guests had boarded. Despite being cautioned, "Please do not

---

Guest (looking for the Dumbo attraction): "Where are the flying pigs?"

turn your wheel until the ride begins," riders usually were too excited to listen. More than once a prematurely twirling cup's giant handle narrowly missed striking a guest who had not yet boarded. Finally, the park installed a braking system that prevented guests from beginning to spin until everyone was safely seated.

For a while, another added chore for Tea Cup operators was checking the vehicles after each ride to make sure guests hadn't lost anything, namely their lunch. All too often, visitors filled their stomachs with junk food, then promptly unfilled them during the ride. Ideally, explained former host Earl Archer, "several of our wonderful custodial staff will be nearby keeping a watchful eye, ready to assist at our beck and call." As a backup, plenty of "pixie dust" is kept in the storage room and ride operators are trained how to sprinkle on the dust, let it absorb the "mishap," and sweep the finished product into a dustpan, all with a smile on their faces.

The Tea Cups have no seatbelts, since the centrifugal force generated by the spinning cup threw people backwards, not forward. Nevertheless, a handful of riders over the years have flown out of their cups.

Perhaps the most serious injury was suffered by an eleven-year-old boy who, in 1991, was thrown out of his tea cup, then struck by a second cup. He sustained a fractured spine, shoulder injury and nerve damage in one arm.

The boy's family sued the park. Their chief witness was a

Going for a Spin

A three-year-old girl began screaming hysterically when her father tried to take her on the Mad Tea Party; she was afraid the giant Tea Cups were filled with hot coffee. Dad finally picked her up to show her they were empty. Hesitantly, she gave the ride a try, and soon it became her favorite attraction. During one return visit, the Tea Cups had been removed for rehab, but before the girl could become distraught, dad soothed her by explaining, "They must be in the dishwasher."

physics professor who claimed that the boy would have risen slowly out of the cup, providing the operator with about 30 seconds to
Emergency-stop the ride. In addition, the family pointed out that
the vehicle had no seat belts, lap bar restraints or basic hand holds,
and there was only one operator.

Disneyland, though, blamed the child for standing up, despite a
warning spiel beforehand to remain seated at all times. Witnesses
said they saw the boy arch his back, push himself out of the cup,
and shout, "This is cool!" before someone yelled at him to sit
down. The ride operator said she hit the E-stop button because she
saw his head tilted back and thought he was getting sick, but she
never saw him ejected from the Tea Cup.

The jury ruled for Disneyland, but the judge struck down the rul-
ing on appeal. His rationale: "The jury obviously gave consider-
able weight to the warning spiel. They asked that this warning
spiel be reread, and returned their verdict shortly thereafter. In the
court's view, the warning spiel was not entitled to any weight (primarily because it) was delivered by the witnesses so rapidly as to
be almost unintelligible against the crowd noise, the music playing,
and the obvious lack of attention given by young riders, such as the
plaintiff, who were primarily concentrating on obtaining a seat in
the Tea Cup. Also, the rereading (in court) didn't accurately reflect
the spiel as given. Each time a witness testified to the spiel it was
necessary for the court reporter to interrupt and ask the witness to
slow down so that she could properly record it. When the reporter
reread the spiel it was at the reporter's speed and not at the speed of
the various witnesses."

The judge, explaining that the boy's actions were not out of the
ordinary, declared a mistrial and ruled for a new trial. This time,
Disneyland appealed.

When the park first opened, Walt knew he wanted a boat ride
in Fantasyland, he just didn't know what kind. That didn't stop
him from opening the Canal Boats of the World, a boat ride past all
sorts of weeds. Unfortunately, the paucity of scenery left little for
the boat operators to do. "Hmmm, will you look at that," drivers
enthused, hoping no one would ask at what.

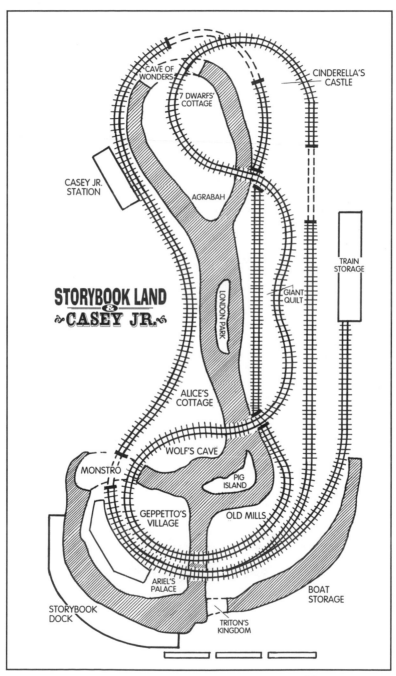

A year later, the Imagineers created Storybook Land by filling the shores with charming miniature settings from Disney's animated films, including London Park from *Peter Pan*, the Seven Dwarfs' diamond mine, the Three Little Pigs' houses, and Mr. Toad's Toad Hall.

To preserve the illusion, maintenance workers must keep the area perfectly groomed and free of gigantic soda cups and popcorn boxes. "It's a real problem," one worker admitted. "A weed that may shoot up can be half as big as a tree!"

Originally, the boats were powered by outboard motors, which often overheated and had to be towed back to the dock. Worse, the gasoline engines were so loud that the passengers could barely hear the spiel. After a few months, the motors gave way to batteries stashed under the seats.

That first summer, the ride was staffed predominately by men, dressed in white shirts and wide brim hats. An all-male closing crew had the arduous duty of manually pulling the boats into the storage area and connecting the battery cables to charge the boats overnight. Eventually, electricians installed a two-way switch on the boats, providing a reverse gear to easily back the boats into the storage tunnel. One by one, more women began being assigned to Storybook, until the only male was the foreman. Finally, Disneyland caught up with the times and—gasp—started having fore*women*. It remained an all-women attraction until 1995, when all the rides went co-ed.

Though politically incorrect today, Walt thought some rides should be run only by men and some only by women. To him, a man working Storybook was like a father telling fairy tales to his children. Still, most males were uncomfortable working the attrac-

---

Bathroom Humor

The Fantasyland restrooms across from the Matterhorn are marked "Prince" and "Princess." A little girl, after being escorted out of the men's room explained, "But I want to see the Prince!"

tion. "The Storybook spiel was for a woman," recalled old-timer John Catone. "As foreman, I'd have to give the girls breaks and do the spiel, and even in 1956 you'd be surprised how many times men asked me for dates." Other foremen gave breaks to just the ticket taker and had her break the spielers.

Among cast members, Storybook became known as the place where the most beautiful women worked. "Unfortunately," recalled former Frontierlander Jack George, "the park was really strict about you not going into one area wearing another area's costume. But the girls on Storybook were always blonde and cute, and we wanted to meet them, so we had to devise elaborate backstage routes to visit them."

Without any obnoxious male co-workers around, the only excitement was when a hostess fell into the water.

There are only so many ways for a young lady to be creative pointing out fairy tale settings to small children, that seemingly never changed—unless a landscaper got his weedwhacker too close to the miniatures. One operator, in particular, always looked for a chance to have fun on Storybook, but rarely found it. It was just the same tour after tour ... until the day she noticed a dead rat lying in the miniature dingy anchored in front of tiny Toad Hall. "Normally there's nothing funny about Storybook, so we couldn't wait to go around," Diane Judd recalled. "I'd drive fast to that area and say, 'Now here's something special, everyone get your cameras ready, it's Mr. Mole's friend, Ratty, sunning himself.' And there was this dead rat, on its back, legs sticking up, eyes bugging out, orange fangs exposed. And it sat there for three days, changing color, losing fur."

A year after the park opened, Fantasyland welcomed its first attraction that had nothing to do with fantasy. Inspired by an aerial

---

Guest: "How many kids do I have to have to go on a Fantasyland ride?"

tram system under construction in Switzerland, the Skyway provided guests with a panoramic overhead view between Fantasyland
and Tomorrowland. A massive drive mechanism buried inside the
Fantasyland Station continuously pulled the 42 cabins along a
cable supported by two 40-foot-high pylons, one of which would
later be hidden by the Matterhorn.

Skyway operators helped load and unload guests, and swung
around the thousand-pound vehicles at the end of the line for their
return trip. Despite the cabins' tremendous weight, swinging them
was more a matter of technique than muscle. The trick was to
smoothly catch and guide the gondolas around the turn. The harder
you threw them, the more they tended to jerk and slow down.

The main challenge was keeping guests quickly unloading and
loading, so the cabins kept moving. Riders during the Skyway's
first years had the option of using two tickets to buy back-to-back
rides, but wait times became so long that Disneyland soon eliminated roundtrips. Passengers who wanted to return to their point of
origin would have to get off and go to the end of the line, a common choice for guests who left their stroller halfway across the
park at the other station. That didn't stop shrewd passengers from
trying to finagle a free return trip. Guests, suspecting that operators probably wouldn't shut the ride down to make them get off,
might pretend that they spilled their purse in the cabin, lost a contact lens or just didn't understand English.

Freeloaders, though, were among the least of a Skyway host's
worries, considering that the gondolas traveled 60 feet in the air,
unsupervised. Riders, alone and difficult to watch, stood up,
leaned over the side, violently rocked the cabins, threw objects or
spit on the guests below, or smoked marijuana.

So operators could instantly communicate problems between
ends of the park, the two stations were linked by a special phone
system. There was no need to dial; just picking up the receiver at
one end of the line caused the phone at the other end to ring.

Of all the problems, spitting was the most frequent and most
infuriating. Discipline was left to the discretion of the ride operators at unload. They might let the perpetrator off with a stern warning, call security to scare him, or devise a more creative punishment. Operators might hand the offender a paper cup and make

Excuses, Excuses

A sampling of the explanations provided by Skyway riders caught in acts of mischief:

- A common excuse from spitters: "Someone spit on me the last time I came to Disneyland, and I was just paying him back."

- Caught expectorating over the Casey Jr. railroad: "I just wanted to see if I could hit the man wearing the engineer's hat."

- Inside the Matterhorn: "I was trying to hit a moving target like at the Shooting Gallery."

- From the oldest of three pint-sized passengers: "My little brother didn't know how to spit, so I was just showing him how."

- From a man who, noticing the professional mountain climbers scaling the Matterhorn, stood up and leaned out of his cabin: "I thought I could get off onto the mountain and climb to the top with those other people. I've climbed mountains all my life. Where is their climbing station, anyhow?"

- Swinging their cabin: "Oh, it's okay. We had a bet on that we could swing the cabin over the cable before we reached the next pole. It sure was a blast! I think we can make it next time for sure."

- Leaning over the edge: "I was looking for the handle so I could get the door open so I could see if there was a wheel underneath our car."

- From a guest who prematurely pulled his own release cord, sending his cabin out over Fantasyland with the door still open and mere feet behind the previous cabin: "We wanted to be close to our friends' bucket so our pictures would come out better."

him fill it up with spit before he could leave. Sometimes, he'd then be ordered to pour the cup's contents onto himself. If there were two spitters, they might be made to stand on a quarter and spit at each other.

Victims also tried to retaliate. One afternoon, a woman was hit by spit as she walked through Tomorrowland. Her husband ran to the station and when the guilty boy's cabin arrived, he reached in, grabbed hold of the kid and cocked his fist back to hit him. Fortunately, a security officer arrived just in time to restrain the man, and then to escort the boy and his friend out of the park—for their own safety.

Once spit struck the engineer's cap of an old Navy veteran working as conductor on the Casey Jr. Circus Train. Incensed, he leaped the train ride's fence and bounded up the Skyway steps three at a time. As the spitter stepped out of his bucket, the engineer spit in his face. Satisfied, the operator returned to the train, and the guest, evidently learning his lesson, never filed a complaint.

Another time, the minute their cabin took off from the Tomorrowland Station, two muscular college students let loose with a chunky gob. Little did they know, standing right below was a top-ranking park official, known for his fiery temper. With fresh saliva streaming off his shoulder, the executive shot up the steps to the station, and barked at the operators: "Get the other side on the horn and tell them to hold those (bleep)ing punks in that red bucket Number Seventeen, and tell Security to get their (bleep)s over there NOW! Tell them if they let them get away, I'll fire the whole damn bunch of them!" With that, he jumped into the next cabin to follow in hot pursuit. Blissfully unaware, the guests continued spewing all the way to Fantasyland, only to be greeted at the station by four uniformed security officers and several undercover detectives, with countless supervisors, foremen and ride operators crowded onto every step out front. Security escorted the culprits

---

Guest (as he disembarked at the Fantasyland Skyway station): "Is this Fantasy Island?"

backstage, likely to experience the most severe punishment ever handed down for drooling.

The most realistic threat to riders was strong winds, which could buffet the buckets. So, the Skyway station was equipped with a large digital meter to gauge wind speed. It usually fluctuated between zero and three knots. If the meter hit twelve knots, employees shut the ride down. Guests often asked, "What's that?" Cast members, gauging their gullibility, might reply: "That's a scale to see if you're too heavy." Or, "It's to let us know when our sandwiches are ready down at the deli." Or, from the slightly morbid: "That's the number of people who have fallen out of the Skyway." During the conversation if the wind picked up and the number increased, the host would add, "There goes another one!" If the number went down, he'd say, "Oh, they found one!"

For dangerous situations, in the mid-1970s Disneyland installed speakers on the Skyway towers and microphones in the stations. By depressing the "All Ride" switch, operators could give announcements or warnings "from on high." Hosts were to use the device for emergencies only, since upon hearing a deep voice suddenly resounding from the sky, guests typically froze in terror. As such, the device became known as "the God Switch."

Emergencies were rare, though. Over the years, the Skyway caused few injuries; still, the *potential* for injury was always there. The concern wasn't for the cable breaking, but rather that kids swinging the buckets might pull them off the rollers or crack the cabin's arm. One time, the arm on a cabin carrying two children did break and punctured the gondola roof. Shakily, the cabin made it back to the station.

In fact, it took nearly 40 years for a guest to file a major lawsuit concerning the attraction. On April 17, 1994, a 30-year-old man from Highland, California, tumbled out the open door of his gondola as it passed from Fantasyland to Tomorrowland. Miraculously, he fell only about 20 feet before landing in a massive tree near the Alice in Wonderland attraction. He suffered minor injuries, and promptly filed suit against Disneyland.

But park officials were suspicious from the start. Immediately after the incident, Disneyland removed the cabin from service and thoroughly inspected it. They found the door's double-lock system

LUCKY CATCH. The guest who "fell" out of a Skyway bucket happened to land in the only tall, wide tree directly beneath the vehicle's path. (1995) *Photo by David Koenig.*

in perfect working order. Operators wouldn't dispatch a cabin until both its outside latch and sliding bolt were secured. Anyone opening a cabin from the inside would have to reach out—way out—to push a button and flip a handle.

By coincidence, the man landed in the only tall, wide tree underneath the Skyway's nearly quarter-mile-long path; had he fallen anywhere else, he probably would have been killed. But Disney's lawyers' case was made when a guest stepped forward who captured on video the Skyway rider reaching out of his cabin and fiddling with the door lock.

Unimpressed, the man refused to drop his case. For two-and-a-half years, he stuck to his story. Then, days before the trial was to begin, he finally admitted he "came out" of the cabin by his own power, apologized to Disneyland, and dropped the suit.

Six months after the man "fell" out of the bucket, Disneyland dismantled the Skyway. Because the closure came so soon after the accident, many people mistakenly deduced that it was shut down because it was unsafe.

Disney explained that the ride just wasn't very popular any more, but the Skyway's ever-lengthy lines belied this excuse. Ridership did drop sharply that final summer, but not due to declining popularity.

To keep the cabins from backing up, Standard Operating Procedure (or "SOP") required four cast members per station when circulating the maximum rotation of 42 cabins. Two worked unload (one receiving the full cabin and opening the door for the exiting guests, the other closing the door and throwing it around to the load position) and two load (one receiving the empty cabin and opening the door for guests to board, the other closing the door and sending it into dispatch). At 34 cabins, each station could drop the second unload position since the incoming cabins were more spaced apart. Anything below 34 cabins allowed for just one person at load and one at unload.

In the morning, Skyway would gradually build its cabin fleet. Usually at 10:00 a.m., there were 32 cabins and two cast members. At 11:00 a.m., they put two more cabins on line and added a third ride operator. By noon, there were 42 cabins and four cast members. The process would reverse at night.

But during the Skyway's final summer, management scheduled only three cast members plus one to give breaks at each station, decreasing the ride's capacity from 42 to 34 cabins.

Do the math. Estimate that the Skyway ran for fifteen hours each summer day. Since it took seven minutes for a cabin to go roundtrip, a cabin saw about eight rotations an hour or about 120 roundtrips per day or 840 trips per week. In a ten-week summer, that single cabin made 8,400 roundtrips. Assume the average load one way was three passengers, or six per roundtrip. That means a single cabin carried 50,400 people a summer. If the Skyway cut eight cabins all summer long, they lost a hypothetical 403,200 riders ... or nineteen percent of the ridership from a 42-cabin summer.

Testified one Skyway operator of that final summer: "We always had a line and rarely sent empty cabins. Even late at night."

In actuality, the attraction was done in by a combination of factors. First, although popular, it was a comparatively low-capacity ride, even stocked with 42 cabins. The aging attraction was due for an expensive overhaul. The park also was under pressure to make the Skyway accessible to handicapped visitors, which would have been prohibitively expensive and, for a ride that shouldn't be stopped, impractical. Finally, as a general principle, whenever a new ride opens at Disneyland, an old ride closes. Ever profit-minded, the park won't keep adding attractions that increase oper-ating costs without ensuring long-term increases in income. In that sense, even though the attractions are located lands away, the Skyway was replaced by the Indiana Jones Adventure.

Fantasyland's other landmark, the 147-foot-high, snow-capped Matterhorn mountain, started as a 20-foot-high pile of dirt. When construction crews were digging up the castle moat, they had to put the dirt somewhere. So, they piled it up to the right of the castle, on the border of Fantasyland and Tomorrowland. To pretend that the dump site was supposed to be there, workers leveled off the top, added a few park benches and young trees, and created a sparse picnic area, called "Lookout Mountain."

Unfortunately, whenever the wind whipped up, the mountain got a little smaller, and dirt was blown all over the rides. Walt wouldn't leave it just dirt for long. He put one of the Skyway pylons on top and considered tying it into the Alpine theme by calling it Snow Mountain. Then, after a trip to Switzerland, he had a better idea: he wanted his own Matterhorn, built to one-one hundredth scale of the real peak and complete with a runaway bobsled ride.

The Hole Truth

Disneyland's Matterhorn was built as a one-one hundredth scale replica of the actual peak in Switzerland, with one glar-ing difference—namely, giant holes in the side for the Skyway to pass through. Know-it-alls were quick to point out the difference. But Walt had an explanation why his Matterhorn had holes: "Because it is a Swiss mountain."

In 1959, the Matterhorn Bobsleds became Disneyland's first thrill ride, and America's first tube-steel roller coaster. Actually, the mountain contains two separate tracks, the slightly faster *A* side (to the left, near the *A*utopia), with the only significant dip, and the slightly longer *B* side (next to the Prince and Princess *B*athrooms).

Like all roller coasters, the bobsleds are powered by gravity. The sleds are pulled by a chain-lift to the top of the mountain and freefall all the way down. Initially, the speed of each ride was determined entirely by the weight in the sled. If a sled wasn't heavy enough, it wouldn't have enough momentum to make it out of certain dips and would stall, rocking back and forth until the next sled rearended it. The only safety feature was a light on the chain-lift that turned green when the preceding sled had a fifteen-second head start.

The signal wasn't enough. Soon, the cracks in the bobsleds' backs began to multiply—as did the lawsuits. Guests involved in the collisions filed six lawsuits that first year; Disneyland settled them all. The park took to court one of five Matterhorn-related suits filed the next year, and lost. Nine bobsled suits were filed in 1961. Disney settled the rearendings, fought and won the rest, but knew something would have to change.

So, all along the track, the park added speed pacers to maintain allowable velocities. The devices resemble automobile tires with large flywheels attached. Constantly spinning "boosters" move the sleds along at slow points, while "retarders" (or "trimmers") spin in the opposite direction to slow the sleds down in fast areas and at the end of the ride. Afterwards, the ride averaged about one rearending lawsuit every two years.

Water also acts as part of the braking system, especially at the splashdown finale. Yet running vehicles through water all day long can make for maintenance nightmares. "It's like driving an automobile in the rain," said coaster mechanic Mike Goodwin. "Everything gets wet. If the wheels aren't inspected or flushed every day, water will get in the wheel bearing and rust it, and you'll have a sled that will run too slow."

Depending on how evenly they are maintained, different sleds run at different speeds. Years ago, employees used a row of stop watches to time the sleds each morning to determine the order of the sleds. The sleds would be positioned so that the fastest sleds were separated from the slowest, so they wouldn't catch up with each other.

In 1978, a computerized emergency braking system, similar to Space Mountain's, was installed to prevent the sleds from getting too close together.

The rest of the mountain has been updated inch by inch. Because of its age and heavy use, the Matterhorn undergoes the longest and most frequent rehabs, usually lasting six to eight weeks. In 1990, maintenance launched a twelve-year rehab program, designed to replace large sections of the track, coaster structure and mountain.

For ride operators, popular attractions such as the Matterhorn provide the challenge of cycling through a never-ending stream of guests without things breaking down. Getting the ride restarted, known as "running a breakdown," can be just as challenging and even dangerous. When the ride shuts down, a crew must run alongside the length of the track, releasing each brake. Employees are encouraged to do it safely, but quickly—potentially perilous on a wet, oil-stained path filled with obstacles. Several employees have been injured.

In 1979, one employee running a breakdown slipped while trying to release a bobsled. His foot went under the track and the sled ran over it, tearing off the top and pulverizing the bones. A co-worker removed his own shirt, wrapped up the injured foot, and called for an ambulance. The foreman, believing he was exaggerating, sent up a nurse with a bag of ice. The victim was finally carried to the bottom of the mountain, where an unmarked white van waited to take him to the hospital. As the victim lay on the stretcher, covered with a sheet, he told the wide-eyed crowd: "It really is a safe ride. Really." The host who called for help received one commendation that day, and a second the next.

Guest (looking for It's a Small World): "Where's the ride with all the small kids?"

Another employee was backstage waxing a bobsled when his electric buffer short-circuited, sending 110 volts through his hands. Screaming, the worker fell to the floor—on top of a metal grating. Fortunately, the co-worker nearby was wearing rubber soled boots and could pull him to safety. The victim missed two days of work due to his accidental electrocution.

The main thing employees do to keep guests safe is making sure each seatbelt is securely fastened and hoping it stays that way. Two guests have been killed after standing in and falling out of bobsleds, and the family of the most recent victim tried to blame the cast members for not adequately checking her seatbelt.

That made workers even more cautious and, for a while, almost paranoid. Not long after the accident, a Skyway rider passing through the Matterhorn noticed a purse and a leather jacket on the bobsled tracks. Reaching the Tomorrowland Station, he notified a ride operator, who relayed the message to a co-worker going on a break. That worker informed his lead and by the time the news finally reached the crew of the Matterhorn, "There's a *purse and* a leather jacket on the track in the Matterhorn" had become "There's a *person in* a leather jacket on the track in the Matterhorn." The control tower has two sets of buttons to stop the bobsleds, the E-stop (which turns off the power) and a power disconnect (which cuts off all power). The dispatcher hit them both—twice. Then a team of nervous operators was sent up to walk the track, dreading what they would find.

If riders remain seated, at worst, they'll get a little wet during the ride's splashdown finale. Well, usually just a little. On Grad Nites, one former Matterhorn operator would hide at the end of the ride with a bucket of water and, when guests would splash down at the bottom of the waterfall, he'd pour the bucket on their heads. The riders just figured they got an extra-wet ride. Once, though, he dropped the bucket. It missed the sled, but got caught in a pump

---

Guest (looking for It's a Small World): "Where can I find the Mad, Mad World of Children?"

that sends water back to the top of the mountain, messed up the water level, and shut down the ride. The culprit earned a well-deserved, three-day suspension.

In 1966, a revolutionary new system premiered at Disneyland that would forever change the way attractions were designed. It's a Small World may look like a leisurely, ten-minute boat ride past more than 350 singing dolls from around the world, but it's much more. It's the park's first continually loading, mass-capacity attraction.

As soon as the operators squeeze at least fifteen people into a boat, an employee in the dispatch tower sends it off through the canal, where water pumps inside carry it along a slow, 1,400-foot-long journey. The faster the boats are emptied, refilled and dispatched, the more boats can be pulled on line from a backstage storage area, increasing the ride's capacity to thousands of guests per hour.

Having more boats, though, does not guarantee a shorter wait. Constantly, boats back up at the end of the voyage, so guests often wait longer to get *off* the ride than they waited to get *on* in the first place. The main problem is that ride operators will bring on line as many boats as possible, forgetting that ride capacity isn't determined by the number of boats, but rather by how quickly they can unload, load and dispatch them. A flume filled with 44 boats sent out every 30 seconds will serve fewer guests than 24 boats sent out every fifteen seconds. The boats stack up at the end because there are too many boats in the flume.

Another change is equally to blame. Back when the park sold A through E tickets, Disneyland made its money with capacity. The operator in the Small World dispatch tower was constantly aware of how long his line was and worked hard to keep wait times down.

Guest (looking for It's a Small World): "Excuse me, young man, can you tell me where the Valley of the Dolls is?"

As his supervisor would remind him, "People standing in line aren't spending any tickets." In 1982, the park replaced individual ride tickets with an unlimited use pass, essentially eliminating the incentive to move guests through attractions quickly.

Thanks to a repetitious, all-too-memorable theme song and simplistic animation, the once hypnotically charming attraction has, for many, become a colorful new form of torture. Many regular visitors avoid it at all costs, riding it perhaps only as a way to punish unruly children.

Some time ago, as their boat returned to port, a group of rambunctious teenagers begged the dispatcher, "Please! Please! Can we go again?" The operator smiled slightly and sent their boat on a second trip. Then, when their boat returned, she let their boat pass through the unload dock for a third trip. After three straight voyages, the teens, on the verge of madness, were begging, "Please! Please! Can we get off?"

Fortunately for the employees, no one has to work inside the ride. Despite the absence of lookouts or security cameras, passengers remain relatively calm throughout the ride, perhaps lulled into submission by the mind-numbing melody.

But one summer it was the employees who needed to be watched. An underground network of sweepers would sneak into the ride and inappropriately dress the figures, adding small hats or putting cigars in their mouths. With custodians all over the park armed with walkie talkies, they could radio a warning whenever they saw a supervisor coming. One sweeper finally did go too far, tying a Mickey Mouse balloon around one doll's mid-section to simulate oversized genitalia.

In Fantasyland, many of Disney's famous animated personalities found a home, but not his most famous characters: Mickey Mouse, Donald Duck, Goofy, Pluto and Minnie Mouse ... until

---

Guest: "Will the Toontown Trolley take me back to my car?"

1993, when Mickey's Toontown opened just beyond It's a Small World.

For the most part, Toontown didn't provide employees with any new challenges—workers manned a trolley, a kids-sized roller coaster, a Roger Rabbit-themed dark ride and a food court, and oversaw tours of Mickey's and Minnie's homes.

The area's least ingenious attractions are Disney-themed versions of activities borrowed from the typical McDonald's Playland: a basin filled with plastic balls, a climb-and-slide activity center, an inflatable bounce room. Toontown, unlike many such playlands, is actually supervised, yet that hasn't prevented the mishaps inherent in letting small children run rampant in a structure impossible to completely child-proof.

Goofy's Bounce House has yielded its fair share of broken limbs. The pint-sized chutes on Donald Duck's Boat had to be boarded up because adults insisted on sliding down them, often with children on their laps. Several children suffered broken legs when they slid down the Chip 'n Dale Tree Slide in their parents' laps and their legs got intertwined or the child's leg stopped against the protective rubber molding on the side of the ladder, but the parent kept going.

In 1995, a 41-year-old woman going down the slide struck her left knee on a decorative acorn on the side railing. After undergoing arthroscopic surgery and while awaiting kneecap replacement surgery, the woman filed suit. Less than six months later, Disneyland dismantled the slide. The park's excuse was that the fiberglass slide was beginning to wear through and they decided not to replace it to save on labor costs (after the injuries, an attendant had to be stationed at the slide to make sure guests obeyed the "No double riders" sign).

Inside the adjacent Acorn Crawl are hundreds of plastic "acorns" that employees must wash every night. "Once, a lady

---

Guest (pointing at steps on Donald Duck's boat): "Do these stairs go both up and down?"

said her son lost something in Chip 'n Dale's Nut House," recalled Sam Hunsaker. "As a general rule, we emptied the balls at the end of the night, and any items that we found were sent to Lost and Found, so we asked people to check there at the end of the evening. But this boy had a tube sticking out of his chest from an operation, and he'd lost the blue plastic clamp that held his chest closed. We cleared everyone out (of the pit) immediately."

Cast members also quickly evacuate the pit upon learning that a child has wet his pants.

Still, Toontown does provide children with guaranteed access to the most popular personality in the park. After touring Mickey Mouse's house and backyard film studio, guests are led onto a mock movie set for either *Steamboat Willie* or *Fantasia*, where they can pose for photos with the mouse himself. Yet one day in the spring of 1997, guests who had posed with the Sorcerer's Apprentice Mickey were told they couldn't buy their photographs. In the background of the scene, a clipboard that was supposed to read "Directed by Donald Duck" had been altered surreptitiously; someone had changed the "u" in "Duck" to an "i." Countless photos had been ruined. The park, unable to identify the culprit, suspended everyone working the attraction.

The Talking Trash Can

One corner of Toontown features a collection of cartoonish props, such as a talking mailbox and manhole cover and crates that make noises when their lids are opened. As a prank, operators have told guests in the area that if they stuck their head in a garbage can and yelled, Mickey Mouse would answer them. Unbelievably, many fell for it.

3

It's a Jungle Out There

IN Adventureland, guests are supposed to forget the 50,000 other visitors around them and imagine themselves traveling far from civilization, to the mysterious, remote jungles of Asia and Africa. Originally developed as "True Life Adventureland," the area was based on Walt's nature film series, especially the then-in-production *The African Lion*.

"It all started from an idea that sprang from our True Life Adventure films," Walt once explained. "We would duplicate in Disneyland Park actual scenes and settings from this nature series."

The heart and, in fact, bulk of Adventureland would be the Jungle Cruise, an *African Queen*-look boat ride along a network of manmade rivers named after the world's most famous tropical waterways. Along the way, guests pass through a jungle inhabited by plastic-and-steel wildlife. The earliest pre-animatronic animals were limited to lateral motion and a few crude mechanical functions: three crocodiles on a track circled through the water, their tails wagging and hinged jaws flapping; a pair of baby rhinos charged forward; two lions opened and closed their mouths in sync with pre-recorded roars; friendly hippos submerged and resurfaced, their ears wiggling.

To fit the profile of a jungle explorer, the first skippers were permitted to wear goatees and earrings. The guides played the part of the narrator in the films, describing the facts (did you know giraffes have no vocal cords?), fun (guests could pet the hippos), even the romance of the jungle (the driver might pause beneath Schweitzer Falls—"named for the famous doctor-scientist"—to give couples a special moment).

And, of course, there was a little humor, the type of puns common in the nature film series. Mechanical monkeys cavorting among the ruins of a Cambodian shrine were up to "monkey business," you made a "nodding acquaintance" with a giraffe, and for Old Faithful the crocodile, seeing that another group had survived a trip through the jungle was "enough to bring alligator tears to this old boy."

Guests also were taken aback by the "hazards and dangers" along the river. A rogue hippopotamus charged the boat, but our intrepid skipper would fire two shots into its gaping mouth. From there, as the boat leaves the Nile and pushes down the Congo into headhunter territory, "the air grows thick with menace and mystery," read the spiel. "Do you notice a tingling in your scalp? Do you feel that danger lurking behind every log?"

To play up the drama and fend off the charging hippo, captains were armed with real Smith & Wessons, with a slight, but easily removed, alteration. Until eliminating them in early 2001, Disneyland had thirteen guns, each registered with the FBI. At closing time, the guns were collected and locked up, and if one was missing, no one was allowed to leave until it was found.

Typically, the pistols were loaded with blanks, but one morning the metal cage that supported the hippo head rose from the waters—with no hippo head. Allegedly, an anonymous skipper smuggled in a real .38-caliber bullet and blew away the hippo.

Even loaded with blanks, the guns when fired at close range have done damage to everything from Jungle Cruise hats and boat decking to human flesh. During his first week at work, one flirta-

---

Guest (entering a Jungle Cruise boat): "Is there a bathroom on board?"

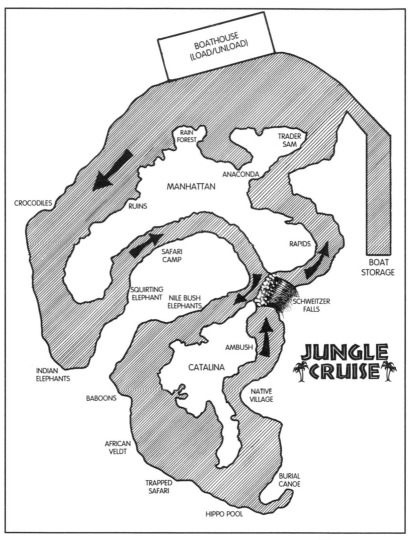

BOATHOUSE
(LOAD/UNLOAD)

RAIN
FOREST

TRADER
SAM

ANACONDA

MANHATTAN

CROCODILES

RUINS

SAFARI
CAMP

RAPIDS

BOAT
STORAGE

SQUIRTING
ELEPHANT

NILE BUSH
ELEPHANTS

SCHWEITZER
FALLS

AMBUSH

INDIAN
ELEPHANTS

CATALINA

JUNGLE
CRUISE

BABOONS

NATIVE
VILLAGE

AFRICAN
VELDT

BURIAL
CANOE

TRAPPED
SAFARI

HIPPO POOL

MAP NOT TO SCALE

tious skipper got dramatic after a female guest rebuffed his advances. Thinking the chamber was empty, he held the muzzle of his pistol to his head and pulled the trigger. The gun fired, severely burning his temple and narrowly missing his eye.

The guns also are used to signal for help in emergencies. For normal use, skippers load the guns with red pellets they affectionately call "candy." To send out a signal, captains fire special black pellets, sometimes referred to as "black licorice," which are several times louder so they can be heard through the whole jungle.

One shot has no meaning. The gun probably misfired.

Two shots (the normal number fired at the hippo) means all clear.

Three shots signals a stalled boat and the driver cannot proceed. Either the river is blocked or the boat has lost power, but is still on the track.

Four shots is for serious emergencies, such as a heart attack or fire. The driver then radios in to explain the emergency, as all boats proceed to the dock as quickly as possible. At the dock, workers clear the queue, take the boats off line, and call Central Communications and First Aid for a security officer and a nurse.

Five shots is not used, to avoid confusion between four and six shots.

Six shots indicates a derailed boat. If skippers drive too fast at certain spots along the route, such as the turn past Schweitzer Falls, the boat might jump off the rail. "You could be fired for that, because the whole ride stopped," recalled Jack George. "But the maintenance guys would cover for you. They got four hours of skin diver pay to lift the guide back onto the rail, and they wanted the extra money, so they would blame it on a faulty guide."

One ride operator's first day was so busy, no one had time to teach him the gun signals. During one trip, he enjoyed shooting the hippos so much that he decided to shoot the rapids as well— five times. Two minutes later, he was back at the dock, where everyone stood silent and motionless, wondering what sort of catastrophe happened in the jungle.

Dock workers were especially confused when playful skippers had shootouts in the hippo pool or at the falls, and twelve or eighteen shots would ring out.

Drivers sometimes employ their firearms to retaliate against bratty passengers, firing their pistol close to a troublemaker's ears, or they might shine their spotlight in his eyes. One driver found himself with a boatload of exuberant Japanese tourists, who weren't paying any attention to his spiel. The guests were standing up, snapping pictures and talking so loudly, that the driver finally stopped the boat and fired two shots into the air. No one moved or made a sound for the rest of the trip.

"In the early days, the Jungle Cruise was very serious," recalled Gary Fravel. "The object of it was to take the guests into the jungle. There was nothing light-hearted about it. It was a three-dimensional True Life Adventure."

Skippers could improvise slightly upon the spiel, but weren't to make light of it. One evening in the late 1950s, a guide came upon Schweitzer Falls, only to realize that the falls were shut off. He announced, "... and here's Schweitzer Falls—oops, I guess Uncle Walt forgot to pay his water bill." A supervisor was on board and fired him.

Slowly, with the addition in 1962 of a humorous elephant bathing pool scene and the aging of the primitive mechanical animals, the atmosphere and tone began to soften. Through the 1960s, the script was rewritten to emphasize the jokes, some clever, some corny. Guides were permitted to ad lib—if preapproved, of course—and the best gags were added to the official script, which grew from eight to the current 24 pages, including several alternate lines for every scene.

Officially, the policy on improvising has always been: "If you have something new, run it by us." Few do. And, as long they're not off color, ad libs add an element of spontaneity most guests appreciate. Skippers might try funny accents, make topical jokes about the scenery, or even tease the guests.

One guide memorized the words to the natives' chant and would get his passengers to sing along. Another jungle boat captain referred to the two guys at unload as "the lovely Lee sisters, Ug Lee and Home Lee," then instructed his passengers that to show their appreciation for a spiel well done, as they exited they should pull the dockhands' leg hairs. They did.

Skippers took pride in thinking up new lines. They were out to impress their co-workers as much as the guests. One captain boasted that he had 20 entirely different spiels. Crews held contests for the best unload spiel, offering free beer for the skipper who got the biggest laugh as his passengers were exiting.

One ride operator would do a historical spiel, made up entirely of Jungle trivia but no jokes, or he might say a single joke at the very end. Guests didn't get it. His co-workers thought it was hilarious.

Most guests found the skippers' sarcasm refreshing. In fact, they came to expect it. "In that costume, people knew what you were like," one captain said. "We could get away with saying what no one else could."

Back in the old days of ticket books, one operator might ask guests to "Please have your ticket in hand, ready to give to the host." The host at the turnstile then would get into a rhythm taking tickets, and, invariably, guests would try to have some fun by pulling their ticket back out of his reach at the last second. One ticket taker, wearing unapproved dark sunglasses, continued reaching out anyway, as if collecting invisible tickets, all the while staring blankly straight ahead. Finally, the woman said, "Ha, ha, I got you." Straight faced, the host answered, "Ma'am, I don't think that's very funny. I'm blind." At first she was stunned, then asked, "If you're blind, how do you know I'm giving you the right ticket?" Without missing a beat, he replied, "Disneyland textures the tickets so I can tell them apart." Embarrassed, her husband said, "Just give him the ticket!" The couple walked away sheepishly, all the while feeling the other tickets in their ticket books.

"Supervision was more lenient on Jungle Cruise," said another captain. "Once you got back behind the wall of the jungle, you were pretty much on your own."

Occasionally, though, some went a little too far. One night, a woman toward the back of the boat covertly began breast-feeding her baby. The driver noticed, shined his flashlight on her and remarked, "Now if you don't have enough for everyone ...." The

---

Complaint Department

A complaint filed at City Hall by a woman upset with her Jungle skipper: "That man said jokes. The whole time. Never stopped. He had a joke every five seconds."

crass host often insulted guests, but allegedly never got into trouble because his girlfriend at City Hall, where guest comments are collected, would weed out any complaints.

Even a spirited captain is not guaranteed a receptive audience, since many passengers, after a day of waiting in long lines, all but dare skippers to make them laugh. Skippers can deliver the exact same spiel, with the exact same delivery to consecutive boats, and one group will sit in stony silence, while the next laughs hysterically from start to finish.

"A boat usually holds 32 passengers," recalled one skipper. "Once I took a group of Sumo wrestlers who were so heavy, we could only hold sixteen people. They couldn't understand me. They just sat there, stoically, not one smile. That was a long trip."

For veteran park employees, the chore of having to be "on" trip after trip after trip can be monotonous. "The Jungle Cruise is probably the most demanding attraction with regard to people skills," said West Side host John Ezell. "It's unlike, say, the (Tom Sawyer) rafts, where if you feel like it you can sit on a rail, catch some sun, and choose to talk to people or to not talk to people."

Jungle captains don't have that option. They have to talk. "We hated to work Jungle Cruise, all that spieling," recalled Ray Flores. "Sometimes we had contests to see how few words we could say. I got my down my spiel to 42 words. Every so often I'd have to comment, 'What ... excitement ....'"

One operator so hated to work the Jungle, all he did the whole spiel was point out the animals: "Elephant. Snake. Hippo." A supervisor rode on his boat one day and was infuriated. After the trip, the supervisor called the driver into his office and chewed him out: "You'll never work Jungle Cruise again!" The operator was ecstatic. "Hooray!" he thought. "It worked."

For many college-aged newcomers, though, the Jungle was the place to be. One envious food services worker used to sell ice cream from a stand in front of the Jungle Cruise, dressed in the same outfit as the ride operators. "I wanted to work the Jungle Cruise so badly that on my breaks, I'd hang out there," he recalled. "I learned the spiel so well, the ride operators started letting me take out boats. They'd get free breaks. If a foreman or supervisor would come by, they'd hide me in the fire hose compartment on the dock."

After filling in for one trip, he was called aside by the foreman and told, "Hey, I don't see your name on my roster." The ice cream vendor explained that he wasn't a ride operator, but had always dreamed of working the Jungle. It took several months, but the foreman finally arranged a transfer from Foods to Operations.

The high-energy requirements usually mean a young staff and, as one foreman remarked, "you put all those eighteen-year-olds together and you're bound to have something funny happen."

Jungle crews reportedly threw the wildest parties and for a while had a summertime Binge Club, an organized opportunity to drink too much. During a July afternoon at an Angels baseball game, one cast member got so drunk, he realized he should call in sick for his evening shift on Jungle. But the park was so crowded that his foreman said he better show up or else. The inebriated ride operator left his car at the stadium and had a friend drive him to work. As he staggered onto the dock, his foreman approached. But before the foreman got close enough to smell his breath, six shots rang out. The tipsy skipper offered to respond to the call. He jumped into a skiff, zig-zagged between other boats along the river, and found his skiff flying through the air. When it came back down, he realized he had run over an animatronic crocodile, putting it out of commission for months. After he helped get the boat back on the rail and the ride restarted, he returned to the dock … just as a woman in line suffered an epileptic seizure. While clearing out the queue, he heard six more shots ring out and again offered to help put the boat back on line. When he returned, his supervisor was waiting. The cast member inhaled, closed his mouth and turned his head, as the supervisor put his arm around him and smiled, "My friend, you are cool under pressure." Convinced his luck must have run out, the skipper said he had to go home. He walked three miles to the ballpark, then couldn't find his car in the parking lot and had to walk home.

Guest (to a Jungle Cruise attendant): "Do you have any insecticide?"

The duties of working the open-air Jungle fostered tomfoolery. "There was a lot of goofing off on Jungle Cruise," Ken Fujimura said. "There were guys standing around. You could disappear for a minute or two and not be missed. You were not standing in a locked position like on Pirates of the Caribbean, for instance."

The fun extended from the dock—where guests would stand four deep to watch the horseplay—to the river. The Jungle Cruise being a boat ride, water was a natural weapon. "The top of Schweitzer Falls was an easy, two-minute run from the dock," one captain said. "A favorite thing to do was to send a guy with a five-gallon bucket of water to the top of the falls to douse a ride operator you didn't like."

Operators also might trip the hydraulics on Bertha the Squirting Elephant to shower a boat or use the hose on the far side of the small island to blast fellow drivers. Another trick was sending out a boat without passengers in front of the intended victim's boat, and a second "deadhead" behind his boat, then boxing him in, so he couldn't avoid being soaked by Bertha.

One evening, the Jungle Cruise supervisor phoned the Pirates of the Caribbean foreman and said, "Grab your biggest fire extinguisher and meet me at the hippo pool." They each grabbed ten-pound extinguishers and ran to the brush behind the hippo pool. The supervisor then called the dock to tell the Jungle foreman that the maintenance dingy had come loose from its mooring behind the big bathing elephant. A minute later, when the foreman arrived in an aluminum skiff to push the little boat back, the snipers jumped out, extinguishers blazing, and turned him into a snowman.

Another evening, three ride operators jumped into a maintenance skiff for a joy ride, but failed to notice that someone had removed the lead weights from the bow. They threw open the motor and the bow shot straight up. The boat spun around a few times, smashed into the dock, flipped over and sank to the bottom of the river. The engine was destroyed, but the culprits got off with a reprimand.

Sometimes, mischief makers will involve the mechanical animals in their pranks. Someone once put party hats on all the hippos. A banana clutched by a mechanized gorilla was replaced with a *Playboy* pin-up. Headhunter Trader Sam has been dressed up with various hats, sunglasses, even a banana stuck under his skirt.

During a series of private parties in 1995, the park hid plush lion cubs throughout the jungle and supplied children with flashlights to "Spot the Lion King." Somehow, stuffed Simbas ended up in the charging rhino's mouth, in the mouth of a lion in the African Veldt, underneath a bull elephant's foot, and on the spear of a dancing native.

Sometimes, ride operators put themselves in the middle of the action. In 1995, the queue was redesigned into a two-story boathouse, complete with mock room settings, which gave ride operators a place to pretend to be audio-animatronic, acting like doctors or playing checkers in robotic motions.

Employees are never to be seen in the jungle scenes. Once, a skipper noticed a smock-clad portrait artist taking a shortcut across the park through the African Veldt and told his passengers, "Ah, a missionary taking art to the natives!" During operating hours, maintenance workers may take a skiff out to the islands to repair a figure. If a boat passes by, the workers head for the brush to hide, but sometimes there's no time so they'll have to freeze or pretend they're picking fleas off a baboon.

Pranksters aren't as shy. They'll ride on the backs of the animals, dance with the natives or tie themselves to a pole as if they've been captured. Skippers have climbed eighteen feet to the top of the Trapped Safari. One guy held a box of popcorn to the mouth of a zebra and waved to the guests as if he were feeding the animals. One stood behind the huge spider web, screaming at the top of his lungs as if the phony spider were eating him. Occasionally, someone would stoop behind Trader Sam's canoe and set his head on top of the pile of skulls. One pretended to have oral sex with the hyenas. Another put on a lab coat and acted as if he were giving a rhino a rectal exam.

Since many of the pranks would qualify as firing offenses, ride operators often reserve the most outlandish for their final day of work. One night passing by the African Veldt, a skipper shined his spotlight on the zebras to discover one had a rider on its back—a stark naked co-worker. For another guy's parting shot, he sneaked into the Trapped Safari scene, wearing mouse ears and holding the two hyenas on leashes, screaming "Sic 'em" as the boats passed.

Others have joined the Elephant Bathing Pool for a communal shower.

On one skipper's last day, his co-workers rerouted the ride's railing system into a complete circle, so he couldn't get back to the dock, forcing him to take a second straight trip through the jungle.

As a decades-old Jungle Cruise tradition, departing skippers, after their last shift, were thrown into the hippo pool. After his last trip, one brawny foreman refused to get back into the boat. It took six guys to throw him in. When the group arrived at the hippo pool, the foreman put up such a fight, he was strong enough to throw in three of his captors before being pushed in himself. Just as the boat returned to the dock, its remaining crew of three soaked, a supervisor walked up. A minute later, the four guys who were dunked swam up, one doing the breaststroke. Everyone in sight received a reprimand.

Such horseplay, noted a former skipper, "was before the necessity of clamping down. Every time a union contract came up, things seemed to get a little stricter. Things became more and more litigious."

Over the years, park management grew less tolerant of the antics. Still, tradition is tradition, so when Larry Kaml turned in his notice in 1996 after more than eleven years in the jungle, he wasn't going quietly. As he neared the dock with his final boatload of passengers, mostly co-workers, he announced that it was a custom to get thrown into the water on one's last day—but he wasn't going to stand for it. He removed his shirt and shoes, and dove into the water.

Cold Feet

Nights can get cold on the river, so in the early 1970s one skipper bought a pair of electric socks. He ran the cord up his leg, out of his pants, and plugged it into the 12-volt outlet in the front of the boat. Wide-eyed guests, noticing his plug, would ask, "Are you animatronic?"

🏰 **Disneyland.**	GOOD FOR CHOICE OF ONE	"**F**" ADULT ADMISSION
MAIN STREET	WALK DOWN MAIN STREET (ONE WAY)	
TOMORROWLAND	DRINKING FOUNTAIN ATTRACTION TRASH CAN ATTRACTION	
FANTASYLAND	MEN'S ROOM ATTRACTION (CLOSED AT DUSK)	
FRONTIERLAND	VIEW BIG THUNDER WORKERS EATING LUNCH POPCORN WAGON GUEST CONTROL	**F**
ADVENTURELAND	INHALING AND EXHALING OXYGEN RIDE	
BEAR COUNTRY	SIT DOWN ON REAL WOODEN BENCH	
C418905	or any other "F" attraction	COUPON

THE F TICKET. Jungle Cruise skippers poked fun at management's attempts to increase profits in this 1979 cartoon from "Jungle Drums," one of several unofficial newsletters that cast members began producing in the early 1970s. Other "land papers" included Tomorrowland's "The Tom Crier," Fantasyland's "Mouse Tracks," Frontierland's "Smoke Signals," and the Haunted Mansion's "Now That You Mansion It."

"I had my mind set on swimming the entire length of the river, but once I got by the Indy queue I realized I wasn't as young as I used to be," Kaml said. "So I jumped into a boat leaving the dock, but we only got about as far as the falls because the ride had shut down and boats were all backed up. A supervisor from another area heard about me jumping in and, not realizing it was a tradition, freaked."

When Kaml's boat finally returned to the dock, security officers were waiting to escort him to the security office, where he was held for an hour waiting for a policeman, who arrested him for criminal trespass, a misdemeanor. Disneyland refused to drop the charges, intent on prosecuting Kaml for attraction down time.

Kaml maintains that the ride closed for only ten minutes and disputes the wild rumors that have since surfaced—that the ride was down for nearly half an hour as he swam the entire river, waving to guests in bypassing boats and calling out, "Can you call for help? I fell out." That near the hippo pool he had stashed an inflatable raft that he used to hand-paddle back to the dock. Or, that it wasn't a raft, but a floating lounge chair that he sat in, tipping his sunglasses to the crowds and sipping a tropical drink. Or that, most far fetched, on his last day, mysteriously, an animatronic baby baboon disappeared.

Although Kaml had been a long-time, well-respected cast member with "a stellar record," the park refused to back down. Then, about a week before Kaml was to appear in court, the Anaheim city attorney dropped the charges due to insufficient evidence.

The Jungle Cruise had always made park management nervous because it was the one ride where ride operators were encouraged to be creative, rather than smiling, nodding caricatures. The park wanted more control.

In 1995, the year before the Kaml Incident, the Jungle Cruise came under new supervision. Previously, attractions were grouped together geographically. Yet Disneyland was beginning to realize that operating different types of attractions requires different skills. Roller coasters, for instance, need operators who can handle a fast pace and think on their feet.

The problem of mismatched ride operators was most acute on the spiel rides. Many workers with no interest in or talent for spieling often were assigned shifts on spiel rides because they worked in the area. But, especially with Jungle Cruise, the spieler would make or break the ride. A proposed new system of management would group attractions by type. There would be a "roller coaster complex," "a dark ride complex," "a water ride complex," and so on. The first, experimental complex would be Narration Attractions, composed of spiel rides.

Narrations began with Jungle Cruise, Storybook Land and Circle-Vision, and eventually grew to include the Enchanted Tiki Room and the temporary Toy Story Funhouse. Great Moments with Mr. Lincoln also was considered (but the hostesses protested), as was the Sailing Ship Columbia, but that seemed impractical, since the Columbia rotated crews with the Mark Twain, a non-spiel attraction.

Each complex would have one supervisor during the day, with accountable leads filling in at night. Heading the Narrations

On Lines

There's an old saying at Disneyland that, "A line attracts a line." Have a few people form a line and, it doesn't matter what it's for, soon others will line up behind them. One Spring Break morning in the early 1970s, the park was about to open with the Matterhorn, Haunted Mansion and Pirates of the Caribbean all temporarily down. With no other comparable draws to siphon off the crowds, the foreman of the Jungle Cruise knew everyone would head for his attraction. He positioned every available stanchion in front of the Jungle Cruise and past the adjacent Treehouse. Sure enough, guests poured in by the thousands. Within an hour, the line wrapped through the bullpen, around the Treehouse, past the Tiki Room, out of Adventureland and out of sight. Incredulous, the foreman decided to see how long the line was. He discovered the end all the way down Main Street, past the Emporium, and joined the end of the line. "These people have just come in the Main Gate," he thought. "They can't have any idea what they're in line for." So, he finally tapped one woman on the shoulder and asked, "Excuse me, what are we standing in line for?" She turned, looked back down the line and answered, "I think this is the line for pancakes." The foreman, figuring it was an orderly line, headed back to Adventureland without saying a word, as the hours-long line extended closer and closer to Town Square.

department was flamboyant supervisor Bruce Kimbrell, who got his start fifteen years before on the Jungle Cruise.

For each Narrations attraction, Kimbrell assembled two people who were very intimate with the ride and recommended by their previous supervisors. Paul Hersek and Larry Kaml represented the Jungle Cruise, spending two weeks in a conference room discussing how to improve guest interaction, courtesy and show. The park had just replaced the queue with a rustic, two-story boathouse and redesigned the boats to coordinate with the adjacent new

Indiana Jones attraction. "So," recalled Kaml, "we decided that if they're going with Indiana Jones theming, the only thing missing was the skipper. We wanted to move away from the skipper as narrator to being a part of the action. We were trying to make something good better."

The group recrafted the Jungle Cruise spiel, to carry over Indiana Jones' 1938 theme. Removed were all modern day references, such as reaching "the most dangerous part of our journey: the return to civilization and the Southern California freeways." Skippers were encouraged not to make any non-spiel jokes, especially any topical remarks. The committee created a new training manual, "The Jungle Cruise Survival Guide," that, in addition to the new SOP script, contained a 1938 fact sheet listing the year's top personalities and events. The guide also included detailed descriptions of all the jungle animals and the legendary history of the Jungle Cruise (a trading company that turned tourist operation when guests visiting the newly-uncovered Indy Temple were willing to pay for jungle tours). Finally, it described potential characters that skippers could become, from nerdy scaredy-cat to arrogant, over-confident know-it-all.

To staff the attractions, Kimbrell circulated a sign-up sheet for volunteers throughout the park. His philosophy was: "I do not want anyone to work Narrations attractions who does not want to." All Narrations workers, whether they had experience on the attraction or not, had to take a four-hour class on increasing guest interaction and improving show. The class outlined the five points of Fantastic Spieling: Show awareness, Presentation, Interaction, Enthusiasm, Language (S-P-I-E-L), and showed cast members how to become better communicators and more interactive with guests to support "the guest-driven performance."

During one critique session, Kimbrell noted how at Disneyland the attraction is the focus, and the cast members are merely background. The exceptions to that, he said, are Narrations attractions, because the cast member is part of the show, as much as Bertha the Squirting Elephant or Monstro the Whale.

"We really tried to work with skippers and have them develop different deliveries," said Kaml, himself a theater arts major. "By the time I left I had five characters: a very conceited, hard-driving river captain named Spike, a dim-witted mechanic, the resident bush pilot whose plane went down in the jungle and seems to be preoccupied with finding it, the accountant in desperate need of a map, and a German zoology professor stuck in the jungle because his funding was cut."

Skippers were encouraged to accessorize their outfits as wacky as they wanted, so long as Kimbrell approved. Disneyland went so far as to buy hats, canteens and other props that skippers could check out from the foreman for the day.

Management attempted to create a "do as I do" not just a "do as I say" partnership between itself and the workers. All working leads were placed in a regular rotation once each week. As well, Kimbrell accompanied most of them on trips to demonstrate his style and help captains with theirs.

That summer, most of the crew got squarely behind Kimbrell and the Narrations experiment. "Bruce *was* Walt Disney brought back-to-life," recalled Mike DeForest, who transferred to the Jungle from the East Side. "He got to know us personally, he rode on our boats, he gave us critiques of our performances, he held parties, made 'Narrations Team' watches and T-shirts with all our names on it, printed weekly newsletters announcing who got guest compliments, presented awards, had team fund raisers like 'Have your picture taken with Bruce wearing an ugly toupee,' he held Jungle Cruise 'costume accessory' contests, and most important to me, he always quoted Walt's philosophies. All other supervisors were a far cry from Walt."

In memos to employees, Kimbrell quoted Walt or wrote "in character," very atypical of a Disneyland supervisor. Read one early memo: "Just a note to the crew regarding our recent operation and its sudden change from transportation of cargo and goods to the ever more popular tourist cruises. We have record breaking compliments from our passengers who have returned unscathed, all commenting on our expertise as navigators and our unique narra-

---

Guest (at ticket booth): "May I have some postage stamps?"

tive skills as guides. But try to avoid taking short cuts through known headhunter territory while transporting passengers. Remember, we will only make a profit in the future if we bring back all of the non-paying passengers."

The memo even had a playful way to encourage skippers to stick to SOP and the 1938 theming: "There has been much concern about Jungle Cruise guides misleading their passengers. Believing that several of our skippers have been purchasing and consuming large quantities of Trader Sam's homemade distilled Jungle Juice, there have been many documented reports of guides telling departing passengers of an unmapped and fabricated land just past our surrounding jungle region referred to as 'Disneyland' where there are light parades, automobile parking areas and other unbelievable, hallucinated foolishness. Remember, *it is 1938* and Trader Sam's Jungle Juice has been recommended for medicinal use only!"

Kimbrell urged skippers to stick to the SOP script, not for fear that they would get in trouble, but to maintain the integrity of the ride. "Andrew Dice Clay can say something funny," he told them, "but that doesn't mean it's appropriate for the Jungle Cruise." And with Kimbrell's personal attention, for the first time, skippers felt comfortable trying out non-SOP jokes for his approval.

The public loved it. After the experiment's first two months, City Hall had received 39 unsolicited guest comments for the three Narrations attractions: 27 written compliments, twelve verbal compliments and no complaints, reportedly a first. Unbelievably, even Circle-Vision received a couple of compliments for its interactive spiel built around the state decorations in the waiting area ("Raise your hand if you're from IOWA!"). The cast members succeeded in pleasing the guests because they were doing a job they enjoyed amidst a pleasant work environment.

The pleasantness would not last. Even before the summer began, opposition had formed against Narrations. Cast members who didn't want change had circulated petitions hoping to stop the experiment before it started. Many old-timers transferred to other attractions for the summer, and looked down on the newcomers as "Narrations sissies."

Ride operators are assigned to a set schedule on a particular attraction during the summer, when the park consistently operates at maximum capacity. But after the summer, the weather and crowds become less predictable and attractions begin to go down for rehab. To improve flexibility during the off-season, cast members return to random scheduling, possibly working different shifts and different attractions. So in late August, old school skippers, who spent the summer on the canoes or rafts, began returning to the jungle, now a very different jungle.

Tension also surfaced in middle management. When veteran Jungle skippers joined Narrations, all ties were cut between them and their former West Side supervisors. "They would not help me with any problems, they would not do my reviews, etc.," recalled Sam Hunsaker. "They said, 'You belong to Bruce now, go and ask him.' But officially I was not transferred to Narrations and could not be, nor could anyone else until contract negotiations with the unions were over for that year. This would not happen until November 5. But, on November 2, I was called up to West Side supervision and fired for poor attendance. I had worked a sixteen-and-a-half-hour day on the Cruise and had no voice left. West Side refused to allow me to trade shifts and work a non-spiel attraction; they told me I had to take a sick day and set up my dismissal."

At least seven workers were terminated for similar, amorphous reasons days before they were to be transferred to Narrations. Kimbrell attempted to intervene on behalf of some of the workers, but, since they were not officially in his department, he was told it was "not his business."

But the deadliest blow to Narrations came from upper management. Although guest compliments on Narrations attractions skyrocketed, efficiency went by the wayside. Jungle captains, in fact, bragged about giving twelve minute cruises rather than the standard seven to nine minute trips and about loading boats well below capacity to increase guest comfort. Ride counts fell to new lows.

First, upper management cut Kimbrell's employee pool, forcing the remaining cast members to work harder and longer. The "P.R." positions, Jungle Cruise and Storybook workers whose only duty was to chat with guests, were cut. Next, leads were eliminated on attractions parkwide, removing experienced coaches and leaders.

Most significantly, upper management put intense pressure on Kimbrell to increase the numbers. Seemingly unable to find a happy medium, Kimbrell began pushing for efficiency, at the cost of earlier gains. Officially, through the next two summers, Narrations still supervised the Jungle Cruise, but as a shell of its former glory.

By the summer of 1997, few of the Jungle crew remained who were steeped in the Narrations philosophy. As before, skippers were told not to deviate from the script, but now they weren't told why. There was no one to instruct them on how to improve their delivery or to develop a character. By telling spielers what they couldn't do without providing an alternative, management basically was trying to make drivers less a part of the ride, not more.

Newcomer Josh Green sensed that the changes began at the time the Indiana Jones Adventure was built alongside the Jungle. "When they added Indiana Jones, they tried to make a new Jungle Cruise, to clear the playing field," he said. "Before Narrations, the skipper would make or break the ride. Now they've shifted the emphasis onto the surroundings, like on Storybook."

Indeed, a giant, atmospheric boathouse had replaced the unassuming bamboo and thatch bullpen. The old boats, with striped canvas tops that looked like circus tents, gave way to themed, more serious looking vessels. The old boats had swivel seats, so skippers could maintain eye contact with the guests and not turn their backs on them. The new boats took the focus off the skipper by replacing the chair with a large, cumbersome crate.

As well, old-timers who didn't work Jungle in the summer of '95 figured they'd always been told to stick to the script (wink! wink!). So, they kept referring to the dancing natives as the original Village People, calling the new attraction "Indiana Jones and the Temple of the Three Hour Line," and making disparaging remarks about It's a Small World. To them, the monkeys would always be "Pat Baboon, Debbie Baboon and Vidal Baboon"—despite their non-existence in 1938. And new hires followed their lead.

As the summer wore on, the mood in the jungle grew darker. Popular skippers began to be fired for seemingly petty offenses, such as isolated instances of tardiness. According to the Jungle grapevine, supervision was promising promotions to brown-nosers who collected incriminating evidence on certain co-workers. Teammates turned into adversaries. Operators began worrying about their spiels and tightening up. Some stopped trying to be funny.

In mid-July, the park received a letter from a guest who said she was thoroughly depressed because her recent ride on the Jungle Cruise was absolutely boring. Management posted the complaint for all to see.

To boost morale, Kimbrell and his assistants once again began accompanying skippers on their trips, to show them how to do it. But, according to several witnesses, Kimbrell used many of the supposedly taboo jokes himself.

Still, one by one, notorious ad-libbers continued to get the axe. Chad Gordon, an outspoken veteran skipper who returned to the jungle after a four-year hiatus, could see the writing on the jungle wall. "They fired all the best comedians," he said. "I knew I was next."

He knew undercover agents had stowed away aboard his cruises and videotaped his spiel. He had seen managers spying on him from behind trees, rocks and animals. He'd just point them out to the guests and incorporate them into his spiel: "Everybody see that guy hiding behind the antelope?"

Gordon returned to work from a short vacation in early August to see his name wasn't on the schedule. Kimbrell called him into his office and said he was firing him for a non-1938 spiel. Gordon, incredulous that they would can someone with "a file thick with guest compliments," said he first wanted a union representative. After a fellow cast member arrived to stand in as union rep, Gordon, a law school student, tried turning the questioning on Kimbrell. "Is it not true that you took a boat out recently with guests and told some of the same exact same jokes that you're firing me for?" he asked.

Gordon said he repeated the question three times before Kimbrell finally answered, "I've been here a long time."

"That's selective termination," Gordon replied.

"Well, you're getting combative," Kimbrell reportedly said, and called in a security officer. Gordon replied that he was fine, but that he was upset because he cared so much about the attraction, the park and his co-workers. "It's sad to get fired for the very thing you were hired for: to bring smiles and laughter to thousands of people," he remembered. "I'm proud of how many home videos I'm on. A couple of years before, I was approached for a promotion to an administrative position. I said, 'You mean I don't get to take out boats? Forget it.'"

According to Gordon, as he was led out of the office, he saw another manager lean over to his witness and warn him to keep his mouth shut and stay out of it. When a supervisor walked Gordon out, a co-worker asked what was up. "They fired me," Gordon answered. The supervisor corrected him: "If anyone else asks, could you please say you were *terminated* rather than *fired*?"

Gordon's ouster caused an uproar in the jungle. "When Chad got fired everyone took a step back," said friend and fellow skipper Josh Green. "We thought, 'If he can get fired, so can I.'"

The jungle paranoia intensified. Four skippers faked laryngitis or sore throats to get doctors' notes so they could transfer to a non-spieling attraction like Big Thunder Railroad.

About two dozen current and just-canned Jungle Cruise skippers began holding meetings at a local restaurant to decide what could be done. Gordon, with his legal training, realized it didn't matter if the firings had violated the law since those terminated were temporary, at-will employees. "The law is black and white. Disney broke the law," he said. "But the most at-will employees are subject to is compensatory damages—lost wages. No lawyer wants to take a case to win someone $5.50 an hour."

Hoping to improve conditions by rallying support from employees throughout the rest of the park, the group decided to write a letter from "the collective voice of the jungle." The letter, penned by Gordon, was attributed to animatronic headhunter Trader Sam and headlined "Beware! Jungle Virus Spreading!" It began: "Many years has your good friend Trader Sam been offering his two-for-one special on his bounty of heads here in the Jungle—never have my eyes beheld the level of hypocrisy and underhanded tactics that are now before me." The flyer attacked co-workers-turned-backstabbers and especially "the head adventurer of the Jungle," a thinly veiled reference to Kimbrell.

Jungle captains secretly distributed copies of the letter, printed on red paper, throughout the park, posting it on employee bulletin boards, leaving it in breakrooms, slipping it into lockers, and handing it out from Main Street to the parking lot.

By then, most skippers had toned down their spiel. Josh Green

BEWARE!!!

Jungle Virus Spreading!

Trader Sam Speaks . . .

Many years has your good friend Trader Sam been offering his 2 for 1 special on his bounty of heads here in the Jungle - never have my eyes beheld the level of hypocrisy and underhanded tactics that are now before me.

"No Man's Land" is a place of no spieling - Trader Sam does not reside in "No Man's" - there is no one to keep me from speaking . . . my voice will be heard. Sam is a voice older than any of those employed by Disney. He is the voice of the Ancients, the wise ones . . . all are instructed to listen and heed Sam's observations and advice.

It weighs heavy on my heart that the furtive nature of a few have eroded the family and community for us all. Just the other day, I saw somebody sneaking up behind me, hiding behind my basket of heads trying to find out if somebody was telling non-SOP jokes.

I've seen many different skippers come and go, many different changes of administration - but I have never seen such clandestine tactics employed by a couple of people. It seems as if suspensions and terminations are being handed out at the rate I move my arm up and down. I have new competition in my trade - someone in the Jungle is offering two old heads for just one new one - I'm thinking about relocating my business - Sam doesn't want to compete with a monopoly.

For many seasons has the Jungle been regarded as an honor to work. In fact, many skippers took great pride in their employment. Pride - now lost to the turbulent and murky waters which so many confused skippers now navigate. How can pride be nurtured in an environment that encourages skippers to backstab each other and then promote them to leadership positions? A true leader earns his respect through trust and honor; not through his ability to deceive and plot against his fellow co-workers. After all, a leader leads by example. If the only leadership shown is through deceit and treachery, what are we to expect in the future for the Jungle? In fact, Trader Sam has been thinking about a career move. Changing professions from Head Salesman to Team Leader wouldn't be much of a change - I am unapproachable, no one can talk to me, my feet are planted in the ground, I will be here my entire life, and I enjoy bragging and showing my trophies . . .

The future looks grim my friends . . . After all, the head adventurer of the Jungle feels he has the liberty to say off-color jokes, while he may terminate others for the same infraction. The natives are restless!!! Just the other day, I saw a skipper I haven't seen since the 70's asking guests if they wanted a twist of lime in their drinks with the baboons on the rocks . . . After all, all he's had to survive on is nuts.

The Anaconda is the third largest snake in the Jungle - to see the first, you must trek to the offices above the River Belle Terrace, the second works among you . . . slithering, sneaky, conniving - he is your trusting friend until the moment he strikes - sneaks up on you - strikes from behind.

My beloved home has now become a burden to work in. After all, skippers must now be wary of curious figures dodging across the Veldt wondering if all video cameras on a boat are for the guests' enjoyment, or simple clandestine tactics for management. Don't worry my fellow skippers - I understand management wants to celebrate the summer with a banquet. What a celebration indeed! A celebration of deceit, underhandedness, and hypocrisy. If you can't make it - don't worry . . . I hear videotapes will be available for all. Quite a PROfessional production.

A neighbor of mine, Trader Sallie, suggested that Jungle Cruise skippers plant hidden recorders in managerial offices to catch conversations. After all, don't skippers have a right to know which team leaders will be plotting against them next?

Ahhh . . . the days of old are still fresh in my mind . . . the legendary skippers of the past . . "Larry the Legend," "the Dossman" . . . true skippers, true entertainers. All gone. Bye now, bye now, most of the caring skippers have been fired by now . . . Indeed, I would leave as well if it weren't for my legs welded into the ground here. Yes, my friends I used to be the envy of all in the park - now I wish I could join some of my transplanted brethren on that high misty mountain where the bears play. There at least, I know where the cameras are on me.

There seems to have been an influx of throat problems for skippers recently. The local Jungle doctor informed me that this mysterious "Jungle virus" has resulted in many skippers visiting the Jungle infirmary to request never to come to the Jungle again. Curious that the mysterious "BK virus" has only had such drastic effects in the past year.

If you fire enough people, it still does not become funny. So long, so long, what's taking management so long to figure out that you can't deceive and treat skippers like dirt and expect them to maintain a high morale. Perhaps a few gift certificates will appease your battered trust. Note to management on the morale tanks of the skippers: Check the level - we're getting close to a 3 shot.

Trader Sam knows all and sees all. For years I've guarded the safety of skippers with my shield of lights . . . . letting skippers know that all are safe to proceed. Be wary my fellow skippers - the winds have changed. Two greens no longer mean all are safe - proceed with caution for the myriad lost souls of past skippers, loyal skippers, are piling upon and blocking the track - switches within the now murky waters of the Jungle - a 101 waiting to happen. Yes friends, in order to see something bazarre in the Jungle these days, you don't need to look across the street.

Until next time, your friend - *Trader Sam*

was one who wouldn't. Working the Jungle was the only reason he
had hired on at the park. He wasn't surprised when he heard that
management had been asking if anyone had any dirt on him.
Unable to find anything substantive, they resorted to make believe.
A co-worker said that she heard him singing on the mike while he
was working the queue. The next day, Green's superior gave him a
verbal reprimand and his walking papers. "This is the time of year
we decide Casual Temporary to Casual Regular conversion," the
manager said, "and we've decided to end your assignment." The
manager refused to provide a reason why and, since Green was a
Casual Temporary, the union was not there to back him up.

Ironically, on Green's last day, Disneyland president Paul Pressler
was on the unload dock, investigating the hubbub, when Green's
boat pulled in, rocking with laughter. One guest from the Midwest
pointed back at the skipper and smiled, "That guy's hilarious!"
Pressler nodded at Green in approval. "I thought it was funny I got
paid," Green would say. "I would have done it for free."

The gang figured it was time for another letter from Trader Sam,
this one more pointed, citing specific alleged violations by park
management of the National Labor Relations Act. After the second
letter, Narrations department managers began interrogating skippers trying to discover the identity of Trader Sam. One cast member said he was grilled for three hours during which he was sub-
jected to profane language and threatened with his job. Since he
was a casual regular, a union rep eventually arrived to back him up.
Allegedly, the last thing he heard was, "If you think this is over,
you're stupid."

The park continued firing skippers they thought were involved.
One ride operator was so disgusted with the plummeting morale
and witch hunt, he quit. After one girl was fired, she started to cry.
"Pull yourself together," her manager snapped. "We're going on
stage."

The Trader Sam group realized it had to go to the press. Gordon
contacted a reporter at the *Orange County Register*, who turned it
into a front page article. Other newspapers, radio and television
stations across the country picked up on the story.

Larry Kaml, who had left the park a year earlier, lamented what
had become of his beloved Jungle. "On Jungle Cruise, there's

always been a large amount of personal expression," he said. "Narrations was to provide a better experience for the guest; the intent was not to force a 1938 spiel down skippers' throats. It was never either it's 1938 or you're fired. Before, we took that person aside and tried to work out the problem. If you just fire ride operators, you're treating them like pieces of machinery."

In time, the controversy cooled. Early the next year, Narrations was disbanded, and Kimbrell reassigned to the new Innoventions attraction in Tomorrowland. In late 1998, the park fired the succeeding Jungle Cruise manager, who had several complaints lodged against him by cast members. Two weeks before, he had terminated seven Big Thunder Railroad operators, including long-time cast members and trainers, for taking a train on an after-hours joy ride.

"Things are status quo, nothing good, nothing bad," says one skipper. "The (secret video) taping hasn't gone on for awhile—at least we don't know of it. There still is, of course, back-stabbing. Jungle has just turned into one of those rides ...."

Adventureland was not much more than a background for the Jungle Cruise, until the area's first expansion brought in 1962 the audio-animatronic musical bird show, the Enchanted Tiki Room, and in 1964 the Swiss Family Treehouse, a 60-foot-high, manmade recreation of the hardwood hearth from Disney's 1960 movie *Swiss Family Robinson*.

During the park's early years, the Treehouse was operated by two or sometimes three hosts—one took tickets, another roamed up and down the stairs to make sure everyone was safe and well behaved, and, if there was a third, he positioned himself on the upper bridge between the two bedrooms to answer questions. They also made sure no one took food or drinks on the attraction, since

---

Guest (after standing at the turnstiles, staring at the 60-foot-tall concrete tree for a full five minutes): "Is this the Swiss Family Treehouse?"

spills could create a slippery hazard.

Many youngsters, uninterested in examining the attraction's intricate details, saw the tree more as an obstacle course, making it a contest to see how quickly they could fly to the top of the stairs and then back down again. Others, to save a precious B ticket, would sneak in the exit gate and walk through the exhibit from finish to start.

Originally, guests could enter the Robinson boys' bedroom through a doorway in front, walk through the scene and exit through a doorway on the right. Walt thought that being able to step into one of the rooms allowed visitors to better feel the part of the shipwrecked sailor. Unfortunately, guests started getting a little too comfortable. First, hand towels began disappearing, then a pillow from one of the hammocks came up missing, then wax fruit from the baskets and a pistol last seen lying on the dresser. The dresser had a glass window on the side so you could see the clothing inside. Someone cracked the window, then someone broke the spyglass. Finally, the doors were bolted and guests rerouted around the outside of the room. That, though, didn't stop guests from tossing straws, candy wrappers, popcorn boxes and other litter through the windows and all over the beds and furniture.

Disneyland eventually installed locks in place of the latches that were intended to keep guests out of the other rooms. All too often, visitors would be spotted relaxing in the Master Bedroom or pretending to play the self-playing pipe organ in the Map Room. One boy, caught in the Map Room spinning the large ship's wheel, explained he was "steering the tree" down the Jungle river.

A common prank was played by kids who would sabotage the Treehouse's water pulley system by overturning the half-coconuts that carried the water, so they'd leak on other visitors.

Over the years, the unique structure has also brought the self-professed Disney historian out of the woodwork. Many experts

---

Guest (to Swiss Family Treehouse attendant): "You know, we Swiss people do not really live in trees."

have been overheard spinning the tale that the tree is real and that it was the reason that Walt decided to build Disneyland here. He's usually a Southern California resident escorting out-of-state relatives through the park. As one self-made tour guide told his friends: "Many, many years ago, this tree was on an island off the California coast, similar to Catalina Island. The natives would make trips to the mainland to trade goods and take back their purchases. After a long time, they became tired of doing this over and over and thought there must be an easier way to travel. So each day they would spend hours throwing dead trees and other debris into the water between their island and the mainland. After a long, long time, the debris began to grow in massiveness and actually formed a bridge that they could walk on. The island has since become part of the mainland and when Mr. Disney saw it he decided to build Disneyland around it, just so he could use the tree for his Swiss Family Robinson Treehouse."

In recent years—until a 1999 remodeling to tie in with *Tarzan*—the Treehouse was left unattended. Earlier, it had been on the same rotation as the Tiki Room. Usually two ride operators run the Tiki Room, although there's not much for them to do. The man-made cast of 225—including 54 orchids, four Tiki poles, twelve Tiki drummers, 24 singing masks, seven birds of paradise, eight macaws, twelve toucans, nine forktail birds, six cockatoos and 20 tropical birds—runs automatically, originally controlled by a full-time soundman in the basement. The ride operator lets the people into the theater and pushes a button that gives him eighteen seconds to tap on José the parrot "to wake him up" in time for the show to begin. Sometimes, hosts would encourage audiences to stomp their feet supposedly to wake up the bird, but actually to upset the soundman down below.

The most challenging part of working the Tiki Room probably is convincing temperamental guests that there's not a bad seat in the

---

Small girl (after visiting the Tiki Room): "Why don't the birds fly away?"

house. No matter where they sit, they won't miss any of the show since every movement, light and effect is duplicated on all four sides of the room.

Not that they'd be missing much. As innovative as the Tiki Room was when it first opened, it soon grew outdated and lost its novelty. Now, as the performance goes on (and on and on), guests begin squirming, trying to work up the courage to sneak out of the theater before it's over. Usually, as soon as one person makes his move, others will follow, until half the crowd remains.

More often, guests just nod off. For exceptionally drowsy audiences, during the climactic thunderstorm sequence, operators turn up the volume by 30 decibels to wake everyone up. Once, for an extra special finale, cast members filled the head of Pele, god of fire, with firecrackers.

Young children seem to enjoy the show the most, entranced by all the motion and especially intrigued by a thunderstorm effect, achieved by streaming water between the windows' two panes of glass. As they exit, kids inevitably touch the window outside and can't understand why it's dry. Explained one quick-thinking dad: "Things dry very quickly in this tropical heat."

As the attraction continues to dwindle in popularity, ride operators have had to try even harder to find things to keep themselves occupied. One summer, to pass the time, Tiki Room operators played cards—with the guy working at the Treehouse. "We'd play Spades over the phone with a dummy third hand, to relieve the boredom," a former host recalled. "The trick was the shuffling. After I let the people into the theater, I'd walk to the Treehouse with all the cards, so for about two minutes, there was nobody in the show. I did it before every show for an eight-hour period. One summer we must have played over 1,500 games."

Most pranks were silly and harmless—until the infamous summer of '78. Since Imagineers originally intended to make the Tiki Room a dinner theater, they attached the attraction building to two

---

Guest: "Is this the Haunted Tree House?"

restaurants, the Plaza Pavillion at the end of Main Street and the luau-themed Tahitian Terrace. Tiki Room operators with too much time on their hands used the strategic location to their advantage. Unlike the staff of the Tiki Room, a cook, food server or counter person couldn't leave his post. Arming themselves with pineapple spears from the adjacent Tiki Juice Bar and E tickets they collected for admissions, the Tiki Room staff became the middle men.

"We were commodities brokers," recalled one devious foreman. "We traded E coupons for rice and chicken or steak teriyaki from the Tahitian Terrace. The guys at Oaks Tavern (snack bar) had hamburgers, fries and Cokes, and wanted chicken dinners. The girls at the Pit (employee cafeteria) loved the E-coupons. The guys in Foods fed us like kings. We never paid for a meal the entire summer."

The next step was to turn a profit, hopefully enough to bankroll an end-of-the-summer party. The operators had seen guests tossing coins into the fountain in the Tiki Room waiting area, so they got the idea that the opening worker on Treehouse would go up to the Master Bedroom and "salt" the bed with a few coins and dollar bills. It got people throwing money all day long. At night, one employee would retrieve the money, while a co-worker stood watch downstairs, explaining that the Treehouse was closed for about five minutes due to a water leak.

Each evening, a fellow ride operator recorded the day's profits in the Tiki Room log book. One afternoon, a supervisor caught the

---

Mind Your Manners

A cast member working the Treehouse volunteered to babysit a lost child. When the girl's brothers and sisters found her, they started beating on her. Finally, the mother arrived but, instead of breaking up the fight, she yelled, "That's right, kids, hit her again! Let her have it for leaving us!" As the happy family walked away, the woman shouted at her freshly battered daughter, "Say thank you to the nice man for watching you."

foreman and the recorder eating pineapple spears in the Tiki Room office when they should have been watching the audience and taking tickets. When he heard they had been called into the office, the recorder panicked. He tore all the incriminating pages out of the log book and stuffed them into his shirt. The supervisor gave them both three-day suspensions

Meanwhile, the Juice Bar workers had seen all the money the ride operators were making and decided to make a little of their own. Occasionally, guests paid for their juice and left before the clerk could give them their change. According to SOP (Standard Operating Procedure), clerks are supposed to put the extra money in the till. But the clerks began putting it in their pocket—sometimes netting all of 50 cents or more for a full day's work.

The supervisor, though, heard about the pocketed change and called one of the juice servers into his office. Shocked that he was being reprimanded over a handful of pennies and nickels, the juicer cracked: "I can't believe you're writing me up for this and you don't do anything about the guys who are making over $200 a day off the guests!" The supervisor went to the log book, only to discover dozens of missing pages. "Tikigate" had begun.

One by one, the supervisor called the suspects into his office, grilling them in front of a tape recorder. He set up a polygraph test in the next room. When he finally got to the foreman, the supposed ringleader, the supervisor sent an operator to fill in at the Tiki Room, presumably for the rest of his shift. The foreman lied through his teeth, refused to take the lie detector test, and said the whole story was a folk legend, "like about people having sex in the wheelhouse of the Mark Twain." Unable to uncover any proof or coax a confession, the supervisor reluctantly sent the foreman back to the attraction, where, with an extra operator, the crew enjoyed double breaks the rest of the day. The ride operators stopped salting the bed, but were never caught and made enough money to finance a raging end-of-the-summer "Crime Does Pay" party at a bar in Newport Beach.

For 30 years, Adventureland experienced few changes beyond the brush growing thicker. Then, in 1995, the peaceful terrain changed forever with the addition of the area's first thrill ride: the Indiana Jones Adventure. For the $100 million attraction, the Imagineers pulled out all the stops, combining the storytelling of a dark ride, the physical sensation of a roller coaster, and the exaggerated realism of Star Tours' flight simulator technology.

With "Indy," the designers played to the park's demographics; unlike at Disney's other theme parks, a huge percentage of visitors to Disneyland are local Southern Californians and other repeat visitors. That's one reason why ridership is low at static, unchanging attractions, especially theater-style shows such as the Tiki Room and Great Moments with Mr. Lincoln. Every time you see them, you receive basically the same experience.

Flight simulator technology would enable the Imagineers to vary the twists and drops on every trip. Indy's sixteen "troop transports" travel along an electric bus bar, like on the dark rides, reaching a top speed of 13.6 miles per hour. The rugged, off-road sensation is simulated by on-board computers, which jerk and dip riders in any of 160,000 randomly generated combinations.

From the outset, guests realize that each trip can be different. The ride begins in the Chamber of Destiny, where guests purportedly enter one of three different portals offering future knowledge, earthly riches or eternal youth. Actually, there's only a single entrance, with two phony doors on each side of it; the side walls and a panel above the doors move, covering up two of the phony doors and changing the real door's position relative to the other exposed doorways.

The jeeps then enter the Hall of Promise, which can look like three different rooms depending on the lighting.

Then comes the real ride, one so bumpy that it had to be toned down twice after employee testing. Said one cast member who previewed the ride: "During the cast member preview, Indy was extremely wild and turbulent. Your knuckles were almost bleeding after that first ride!" Another swears that she would have gone flying out of the car if her husband hadn't held onto her.

In the attraction's first two years, guests lodged more than 200 complaints, including letters, lawsuits and First Aid reports, claiming they were injured on the ride and urging the park to tone it down.

Injuries ranged from bruises, split lips, chipped teeth, cut arms, strained muscles and pinched nerves to herniated and ruptured discs. Among the most seriously injured was 43-year-old Zipora Jacob, who claims the then-four-month-old ride jostled her so vio-

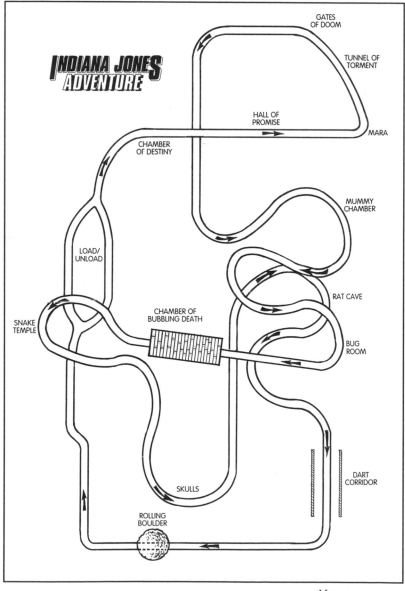

MAP NOT TO SCALE

lently that she suffered a brain hemorrhage. She felt ill during the ride and after staggered out of the vehicle, vomited and collapsed. She was taken to the hospital, treated and sent home, where she lapsed into a coma. After a series of surgeries to treat a subarachnoid hemorrhage (bleeding resulting from extreme shaking), doctors implanted a permanent shunt in her brain. Reportedly, she has been unemployed since the accident and lives in constant pain, with only a few lucid hours a day.

Disney eventually settled the Jacobs case out of court. Soon after, a second woman filed suit, claiming the Indiana Jones ride caused bleeding in her brain.

Designers continued to modify the ride in reaction to guest injuries and complaints. In the months after opening, they added padding to the vehicles' grab bars, contoured seats and foot rests to "reduce rider movement," and eliminated the roughest combinations of twists and dips. Unfortunately, the attraction's thousands of possible combinations made it difficult to determine which part of the ride might be the most dangerous.

Park officials, meanwhile, noted that three signs throughout the queue warn visitors that the "fast off-road journey that includes sharp turns and sudden drops" is not intended for anyone with a weak back or neck. So any injuries, they reasoned, were the guests' own fault for disobeying the signs.

4

The Wild, Wild West

IN Frontierland, guests return to the pioneer days of Davy Crockett and frontier America, from the Revolutionary War era to the final taming of the great Southwest. The original designers tried to duplicate the romance and realism of the Old West, and in the early days, Frontierland could be a little too realistic. Visitors in the 1950s could ride live pack mules, horse-drawn stagecoaches and covered wagons, a real paddlewheeler, tall ship, keel boats and canoes, or participate in authentic Indian Village ceremonies.

Real life, though, can be more unpredictable than Disney's duplications. The stagecoaches and covered wagons were prone to tipping over and quickly abandoned.

The temperamental pack mules were even less reliable. They liked to eat guests' hats and were easily spooked by flash photography, balloons or sudden noises. Caps, bags and cameras had to be hung on a nearby clothesline. The mules also would stage group sit-ins or urinate in tandem.

"We would always stop on the incline at the old arched bridge, because that's where the mules would all like to take a leak," recalled mule skinner Robby Beeman. "Later, a scene of animatronic elks fighting was added, to give the guests something to watch."

The smaller burros were up front, with the bigger ones in back. The largest and feistiest, such as an infamous jack mule named Jarvis, brought up the rear. "There was a weight limit of 190 pounds, and women always lied about their weight," remembered Rolf Mendez. "So we'd call the foreman over. He'd say, 'I'm sorry you can't ride ... or you can wait for Jarvis.' When you sat on Jarvis, you couldn't wear anything around your neck, no purses, no cameras, no bags, nothing, or he'd start bucking."

Over the years, riders fell off mules, were bucked off or dropped to the ground when their saddle straps broke. Once in a while, the saddles slipped, leaving guests hanging upside-down underneath the mule.

Said one old-timer: "By the end of the summer, if there was no blood on the trail, that'd be a successful summer."

"The mules had the best union in the park," recalled one old-timer. "They worked four hours a day, then they'd bring in new mules."

For most ride operators, working the pack mules was a low point. "We all started off on the mules," Mendez said. "They wanted to make or break you as soon as they could. It got hot, it would smell, the mules would simultaneously decide to pee and you'd have thick streams running down, splashing up on your boots. Either you enjoyed animals or you didn't. It wasn't a problem for me. I grew up on a dairy farm in Norwalk, and was a cowboy at heart."

Although summertime on the dusty pack mule trail could be the hottest spot in the park, one foreman arrived every morning with a heavy wool jacket. Whenever someone asked why, he'd answer, "By the end of the day, I'll need it." Inevitably, a girl wearing ultra-tight jeans wanted to ride the mules, and park regulations prohibited anyone from riding side-saddle. So, at least once a day, the foreman would hear "rrrrriiiipppp," grab his jacket and head for the loading area. He'd cover up the girl's freshly ripped jeans and escort her to

---

Guest: "Are the horses real?"

First Aid, so a park seamstress could stitch up her pants.

Regular ride operators helped guests on and off the mules. It was up to professional "wranglers" to ride the lead mules. These dyed-in-the-wool cowboys took care of the mules, cleaned them up, and led them to and from the Pony Farm.

The pack mules were popular, but low in capacity and dangerous, and were sent packing in 1973.

When the park first opened, the Frontierland Shooting Gallery was much more realistic, using real rifles that fired lead pellets. At first, the rifles sat on a cradle, but that left the guests with too much room for error. Next, the guns were locked in a bracket that extended to the ceiling. Later, the park switched to compressed air guns and finally in 1985 to electronic guns that fired harmless beams of infrared light.

In the early years, for the weary attendants, their hands black from the lead, the gallery was not a favorite work spot. "We had a hell of a time getting anyone to work it," recalled Frontierland area manager Jim Haught. "Ricochets of the lead pellets hit several employees and cut them. One kid got shot in the head. And it was so loud, we tried having (the attendants) put cotton in their ears, but then they couldn't hear the guests. We finally got some aluminum ear plugs. Eventually, they put carpet all around to deaden the sound and stop the ricochets."

One time, a bird flew into the gallery and two kids opened fire on the unfortunate visitor. The host hurried to shut down the air on one boy's gun, and as he explained that what the lad did was wrong, the other kid continued firing on what remained of the bird.

By 1956, the conestoga wagons, yellowstone coaches and stagecoaches began disappearing from the Disney landscape.

Guest: "Is the restroom a C coupon?"

Instead, the pack mules would share the backwoods of Frontierland with a Mine Train Ride.

The electric-powered train provided a leisurely paced trip. To keep it from going too fast, conductors braked the train by releasing sand onto the wheels. But during moist evenings and winters, many feared that the trains would travel too fast and slide off the track, especially at the bottom of a steep drop that curved into the Painted Desert.

In 1960, the train's surroundings were transformed into "Nature's Wonderland," mimicking scenery and animals from Disney's western nature films. The more than 200 birds, beavers, bears and other assorted wildlife represented the park's first use of its audio-animatronic technology.

But unlike the sheltered figures that performed at the Tiki Room, Great Moments with Mr. Lincoln and other attractions, these animals were subject to the elements 24 hours a day. "We had birds out in the open, and every bird had his own sound," remembered John Gerlach, maintenance man in charge of the old Living Desert. "The sound room was about 50 feet away. But what would happen is the beaks would get out of sync; over night, dew would get in the hingepins and corrode them. So, we had to go in early in the morning and oil the beaks with an eyedropper."

Other times, a soundman might put in the wrong audiotape. "You'd have one bird's track synchronized to a different type of bird," Gerlach explained. "It's amazing; people would complain, 'Hey, your cactus wren sounds like a mockingbird!' People were smarter than we thought."

Direct sunlight also highlighted the harsh weathering the critters took, exposing badly shedding coats of fur and the occasional missing appendage.

Guest: "Where's the restroom?"
Cast member: (wanting to direct him to a facility in the direction that he was headed) "Which way are you going?"
Guest: "Well, I'm gonna pee."

After the mule ride closed at dusk, the Mine Train had the back-woods to itself. The slow, dark, isolated trips encouraged romance. Especially on Grad Nites, it was the place to neck—or more. "Mine Train was way in the back (of the park), very dark, very secluded," recalled Ray Flores. "There would be about eight cars with a couple in each car, and towards the middle of the ride, I'd look back and wouldn't see any heads. I'd turn off the spiel, and have a Moonlight Train Ride. At the end, I'd go unlatch the doors for the guests to leave, their hair would be mussed, some buttons unbuttoned. That was every trip."

Many nights, couples wouldn't even stay on the train, jumping out of their car to find a private spot in grass. Security guards regularly patrolled the mule trails, often accompanied by ride operators so they wouldn't get lost. In the morning, the mule skinners sometimes found undergarments along the trail and would tack them on the employee bulletin board to let the patrolmen know what they missed.

Since the Mine Train was a comfortable, casual attraction, drivers had the option of clicking off the corny pre-recorded spiel and instead talking to the guests. "Mine Train was a great attraction," remembered Gary Fravel. "Going through the desert and the woods, it was so secluded. The woodland smells, everything worked right into my fantasies of the West. Bear Country, Beaver Valley, Painted Desert, you could really get into it. And it fostered a lot of camaraderie."

The all male, slightly older crew developed a close bond that extended into a fraternity, the Order of the Red Handkerchief, named after the hankies worn by Mine Train operators and, in particular, the hanky worn by club co-founder Frank McNell. A running feud developed between McNell and management, who wanted everyone to wear their hanky around their neck. McNell, though, would always stick it in his back pocket, because he had to

---

Guest (outside the Golden Horseshoe Revue): "What's the Golden Whorehouse?"

use it to clean the oil and grease off the track. Management didn't care, evidently reasoning that a dirty neck fit in with the ride's image of "raunchy coal miner."

Membership in the Order of the Red Handkerchief, founded in 1964 by 36 cast members as a social club, originally was limited only to ride operators who had worked the Mine Train. Since then, the club has loosened its membership restrictions, realizing that since people can no longer operate the Mine Train, the group eventually would become extinct.

The old-fashioned Mine Train took its last trip in 1977, replaced more than two years later by a high-speed roller coaster, the Big Thunder Mountain Railroad. Like Tomorrowland's Space Mountain, Big Thunder is controlled completely by computer. Still, computer malfunctions have caused collisions. Attendants also have made mistakes, such as throwing the switch too quickly while cycling out cars for the night and derailing a train. And, at least once a tow bar connecting two cars separated, sending a car flying off the track—with guests inside.

"Big Thunder is a higher tension ride," admits one ride operator. "If you do something wrong, somebody can get killed."

Frontierland swings around the Rivers of America, home to all manner of western-themed watercraft. On a busy day, you might see three rafts, two keel boats, eight canoes, a huge paddlewheeler, and a similar-sized sailing ship. The majestic Mark Twain has precedence on the river. Since it rides on an underwater track, it can't move out of the way and once it gets going, it can't exactly stop on a dime.

"There was a right-of-way on the river," said old-timer Milo Rainey. "It was unwritten, but understood. You got out of the paddlewheeler's way."

Employees rate "the Mark" as one of the best and easiest attractions to work. It carries up to 390 passengers at a time, so workers are not constantly loading and unloading. Trips last about fifteen minutes, not counting load time, during which one ride operator walks the deck and another sits in the wheelhouse as a lookout. And, with only three working positions (load, deck, wheelhouse), breaks are more frequent and longer.

Despite the giant ship's wheel in the wheelhouse, an unseen member of the steam fitters union actually drives, manning a real steam engine and giant boiler in the ship's bowels. When all the passengers are safely aboard, the ride operator in the wheelhouse buzzes the steam fitter to start the engine, then rings two bells to signal other boat drivers. For emergencies, operators ring one long bell, and have access to an intercom and a radio. For the most part, the wheelhouse is for show—a place for ride operators to invite children or pretty girls.

What the Mark Twain doesn't have are water fountains and a bathroom. It's not uncommon for desperate guests, trapped at sea, to urinate in the trash cans.

The most frustrating thing about working the load dock is the popcorn stand located a few feet away. Every day, guests buy popcorn, then run to the turnstiles to catch the boat. Not only are food and beverages forbidden on the boat, they're not even permitted in the queue. One tourist from France who had just bought two bags of popcorn became irate when the cast member wouldn't let him join his family on the ship. Incensed, the man finally threw the popcorn in the attendant's face. The host, noting the bags were now empty, responded cheerily, "Okay, now you can come in!"

Years before, Walt had tried allowing food on board. In fact, he even had the Citrus House concoct a non-alcoholic mint julep to serve on the riverboat. Unfortunately, guests would throw their empty cups into the river, and the experiment was soon abandoned.

When Disneyland first opened, the Mark had the river to itself—but not for long. By the park's second summer, three other types of watercraft joined the fleet. Most unique were the guest-powered boats: the Indian War Canoes. Walt insisted only authentic Native Americans operate the canoes and adjacent Indian Village, where they created colored sand paintings and performed ceremonial dances. He even went to a Navajo reservation to recruit them, unaware that Navajo Indians are from the desert and none had the slightest idea how to paddle or steer a canoe.

What Disneyland's Indians could do was drink. They became

notorious for their wild parties and for arriving late to work the next morning with bloodshot eyes.

Reportedly, the Indians complained constantly, especially about the heat. "You're gonna have to give us some kind of hat," they would moan. Management, though, would tell them that real Indians of the Old West didn't wear hats, just a headband with a feather in it.

By the mid-1960s, Disneyland realized it didn't have enough responsible Native Americans to go around. So they got Hispanics, Hawaiians, anyone "who looked the part," and dressed them up like Indians. Within a few years, the look requirement became less strict and a team of "The White Indians" was assembled, and by 1971, the Indian War Canoes became the Davy Crockett Explorer Canoes.

For paddle-bearing guests, the canoes provide a unique opportunity to be active participants. With one employee at the front of the canoe and one at the tail, guests outnumber crewmen 20 to two.

For employees, the canoes provide good exercise, sunshine and light interaction with co-workers and guests, away from the crowds. But it is a physical attraction. Workers are usually college-aged, over six feet tall and 200 pounds. Often, new recruits train so hard, the next day, they call in sick to recuperate from their sore muscles. Others, after an especially toilsome training session, have quit. "Man," they bemoan, "this is work!"

An empty canoe weighs 2,000 to 2,500 pounds. Then add six-

Water Foul

Canoe passengers often slip a hand into the Rivers of America, then remark with surprise: "Hey, it's real water!"

One rider spent most of her trip drinking water she scooped out of the river. Near the end of the trip, she noticed a crewman watching her, and asked him, "Is it okay to drink the water?" "Ma'am," he answered, "animals make love and poop in that water. I wouldn't drink it if I were you." She stopped immediately, looking as if she would throw up.

teen to 20 guests who may or may not be assets in the paddling department. It takes practice to learn to control the canoe, to let it do the work. Besides helping to row and steer, the crewmen encourage the guests to paddle and not to splash the guests behind them, often getting into races with other canoes. Only trouble is, if a canoe gets going too fast, it might have trouble making the turns. And if it stops too fast, guests' kneecaps jam into the backs of the seats in front of them.

Worse is the occasional overturning or sinking. Air bags help keep them afloat, which have to be periodically drained of water, usually at the end of the day. One afternoon, one particular canoe was taking a lot of water. Since it was a busy day, the lead didn't want to operate without the canoe. He just had the operators pump the water out after every third trip. The waiting line grew so long, that the lead sent the paddlers on an extra trip before draining, with a boatload of elderly Japanese tourists. Making the turn past the Mark Twain dock, the canoe began listing to one side, when a man stood up to take a picture of the paddlewheeler. The boat flipped. The crewmen helped all the passengers wade to the island, then went out for the canoe. They rerighted it, but the craft had taken so much water it had become "negative buoyant" (rightside up but just below the surface). So, the two operators climbed into the submerged canoe and paddled back to the dock. Guests looked on in amazement, as the two workers rowed across the river, water up to their chests, seemingly without a canoe. Management considered giving the crewmen five-day suspensions, but instead gave them commendations after the lead took the blame.

Geronimo!

One hot afternoon, a young woman riding in a canoe asked one of the operators: "What would you do if I jumped in the water?" Thinking she was kidding, he replied, "Well, unless you can't swim, nothing." So, relieved to hear she wouldn't get into any trouble, she removed most of her clothes and jumped in.

The canoe's first summer also welcomed to the river a pair of keel boats, the same ships used in a Davy Crockett television show. Keel boat drivers had to be the most careful because they had the most control over their crafts; the boats were motorized and not on a track. "It can be hard to see, you're standing in the back, it's top heavy," said Jack George. "At night, you had a spotlight in one hand, a mike in the other hand and you basically sat on the tiller, driving it with your butt."

The first lesson for keel boat drivers was "Don't shoot the rapids," host Rolf Mendez added. "They can be difficult to operate through the rapids. They'd bounce off a rock once in a while. Or, if you turn too late, you could nose into where the Indian campground is and get stuck in the mud."

The park mothballed the two keel boats, the Gullywhumper and the Bertha Mae, in 1994 due to low capacity. They returned in 1996, but disappeared again about a year later, after the Gullywhumper tipped over during an early evening trip.

The park's second summer in 1956 also introduced a mode of transportation more functional than entertainment-oriented: rafts to transport guests to the island in the middle of the river. Early on in the design of Disneyland, Walt realized that without an island he'd have a lake not a river. After all, the boats had to circle around something.

The island itself also could be an attraction. One early idea was to hide buried treasure in various places and call it "Treasure Island." Another thought was to dot its shores with miniatures of American historical landmarks, such as Monticello and Mount Vernon.

Finally, looking to the Mark Twain for inspiration, the Imagineers settled on the name "Tom Sawyer Island." Here, unrestrained by lap bars, children could run along dirt paths and a swaying barrel bridge, explore caves, climb a treehouse and play in a fort.

But as the park soon discovered, the more freedom you give guests, the greater the chance they'll find a way to hurt themselves. Visitors have slipped on the rough terrain, knocked their noggins in the caves, and even been thrown off the pontoon bridge into the water.

Interestingly, more lawsuits have been filed for adults than children. Maybe kids are more resilient or, more likely, adults are more likely to seek retribution when injured.

A half-dozen Tom Sawyer Island injury cases have made it to trial, and Disneyland has won them all. One unsuccessful plaintiff, finding herself beginning to slip on the gravel, reached out for a rock to regain her balance. But the rock was actually a teeter totter shaped like a rock, so she fell.

A 64-year-old woman and a 72-year-old woman jointly filed suit after they fell while crossing the barrel bridge. It seems that when they had made it about halfway across, two boys jumped on, making the wobbly bridge, well, wobbly.

In another case, a four-year-old flew off the merry-go-round rock into the bushes, cutting his chin so that it required stitches. The scar on his chin, according to the lawsuit filed by his father, was the least of his injuries. "My son has seizures, he is unable to sleep, has periodic trances and is very difficult to control," dad reported. His long-term analysis? Possible brain injuries, retarded learning capacity, hyperactivity, speech defects, post-traumatic epilepsy, and chronic brain syndrome with post-traumatic personality disorder. But since the hyper child's own actions caused the injury, the jury ruled for Disneyland.

A constant source of injuries was a fence wrapped with barbed wire that kept guests away from a burning cabin on the northwestern end of the island. "Behind the fort there was a fence with barbed wire, and kids were always getting hurt," recalled security officer Dennis Wolf. "It was poles linked by sticky, greasy, rusty barbed wire, surrounded by hard mud that would get wet, making it easy to slip. I could just see someone getting impaled. They had a suggestion program, so I pointed this out, but they never did anything. Finally a little girl punctured her hand, and as I was taking her and her family to First Aid, I suggested they file a complaint at City Hall. They did, but wrote on it: 'Security guard said I should file a complaint.' (Management) reamed me up one side and down the other, but within two weeks there was a new fence with a sign that said, 'Off Limits.'"

For guests able to sneak through, the area provided the perfect hiding place. Years ago, a ten-year-old runaway was living out of one of the Indian tents near the cabin. The boy would mingle with the crowds during the day, then paddle a canoe out to the island after dark and dine on treats from the snack bar.

Too much food was going unaccounted for. At first, security suspected the island's notorious rat population, but then realized that the rats wouldn't dispose of the wrappers when they were finished. Next, security blamed the janitors, who steadfastly denied it. Then, one night, the boy sank a canoe. Security sent a custodian to clean out the tents and, sure enough, he found the kid fast asleep in his makeshift home.

The motorized rafts transport guests to and from the island with neither track nor keel. Drivers use a throttle to control their speed and a rudder to steer clear of the other ships. The trickiest part is docking, since a full load of 65 passengers makes it difficult to see the dock. Instead, drivers listen to the engine and feel for the dock. First, they bring in the bow, gently bumping one corner, then letting the side squeeze alongside the dock. Occasionally, ducks might get between the raft and the dock.

If a raft comes in too hard, guests can be knocked around. One prankish raft driver, when nearing the dock, would ask his passengers to stand on one leg. When the raft hit the dock, all the guests would tumble over.

Another challenge is avoiding the other boats. The rafts can accelerate to four miles per hour, but if they go too fast, their noses dip and water can creep up and soak guests' feet. A plate eventually was installed along the rafts' edges to keep back the water.

During one trip, a raft driver, trying to get out of the Mark Twain's and canoes' way, cut sharply toward the island and struck a piling at full speed. The passengers fell on top of each other,

---

Guest (at an E ticket ride): "Can I use two Bs and a C?"

including a tourist trying to snap the driver's photo. He ended up with a picture of the sky. Fortunately, everyone burst into laughter; they thought it was part of the ride. Most of the guests at the dock, though, decided to wait for a different raft back.

In 1958, less than three years after Opening Day, the park christened its final addition to the Rivers of America. The Mark Twain was so popular that Walt added another huge craft, the Sailing Ship Columbia, modeled after the first American ship to sail around the world. Disneyland's three-masted, 110-foot-long, full-rigged version, in fact, is a full-scale replica of the original commercial sailing vessel built in 1787.

The Columbia sails when the Mark Twain is down (using the Mark's dock) or on extremely busy days (boarding farther down the dock with a sliding gang plank), when it's usually the last one on the river and the first one off.

Usually a crew of three works the Columbia: one on the dock and two on board. A captain at the wheel mans a joystick for forward, reverse and neutral, while a lookout roams the deck. The lookout spiels along with the captain and climbs the riggings to spot the burning cabin and other sights along the riverbanks. He also fires loud, twelve-gauge shotgun blanks from the ship's large black cannon, as a salute to the island's Fort Wilderness. Years ago, the fort had its own black cannon and would fire back.

As period entertainment, in the Columbia's first years, a trainer and his live chimp, both in sailor outfits, performed near the ship's bow. To add authenticity, six years later a maritime museum was added on the lower deck, showing what life was like for a seaman of the 1700s. Since the Columbia spent most of its time docked, the museum would provide something for guests to see on the many days she was inactive, then be closed when the ship sailed. Eventually, as a cost-saving measure, the museum would be open only when the ship sailed.

Yet, as time went on, the costumes and spiel grew less time specific. The ship's historical significance, in fact, always has escaped most guests. Many mistakenly think it's a pirate ship, and the park unwittingly promotes the confusion by using it as Captain Hook's pirate ship in the river show Fantasmic.

Eventually, Columbia crewmen stopped spieling altogether and just played the pre-recorded narration. Then, in the spring of 1996, Paul Hersek was made assistant manager of Rivercraft Attractions, and he drafted former Jungle Cruise Narrations committee mate Larry Kaml. Their intention was to rejuvenate the Columbia by adding a Narrations-style emphasis on improving show and guest interaction.

The first things to go were the inauthentic costumes, which consisted of blue-striped shirts, deck shoes and ski caps. Kaml went to the wardrobe department and pieced together a new outfit consisting of white shirts, knickers, knee socks and buckled shoes. Next came the spiel.

They created "The Sailor's Guide," patterned after the "The Jungle Cruise Survival Guide." The manual focused on 1787 and included a glossary of terms, sail plan, personnel profiles, and detailed history of the original ship, the Columbia Rediviva, based on extensive research from the Grays Harbor Historical Seaport, a nautical museum in Washington State devoted to the vessel and her sister ship, the Lady Washington.

The revised 31-page spiel was to be performed entirely live, without any pre-recorded portions. On the Columbia, proper spieling is doubly important. "My favorite attraction to work as a ride operator was Columbia," Kaml said, "because there are two who spiel: the captain and Hawkeye, the lookout. They play off of each other's spiel. It was a great challenge for me as a performer."

Finally, an additional cast member was assigned to the Columbia to interact with the guests below decks, answering questions and helping with photos.

Unfortunately, apart from the costumes, few changes lasted, done in by the same politics that doomed Narrations park-wide.

Guest: "Now that I've been on A, where's B?"

Aside from storefronts being repainted and dirt paths giving way to dirt-colored concrete, the look of Frontierland at the river's edge changed little for nearly 40 years. Then, in 1992, the area was transformed to double as a stage and theater for Fantasmic. The special effects-laden show is so popular that guests mark off their viewing territory around the river four or more hours early. Then, after the show, thousands of guests simultaneously cram onto the walkways and mill towards the exit.

Occasionally during the show, the fireworks sprinkle guests with ashes. During the attraction's first three years, at least seven guests complained that they were struck in the eye by burning firework projectiles. During one performance in 1993, a four-year-old and a 21-year-old got it in the eye, and a sixteen-year-old said a bright blue light came toward him, and people started shouting, "Get it off! You're on fire!" He arrived at the First Aid station with red, swollen eyes, purple burn marks on his neck and holes "just like acid burns" in his jacket, according to the accident report.

Another guest evidently was on acid when during the show's psychedelic Pink Elephants on Parade sequence, he dove into the river. The show had to be stopped because it was nearing the scene where the river bursts into flames. The man swam to the Mark Twain dock, where he was apprehended, mumbling racial slurs and something about pink elephants.

Some time later, a pirate performer swinging on a rope on the Columbia swung too far off the side of the boat—and smacked into a lightpost on the shore.

The river also serves as an Equipment Graveyard. When a flashlight or other device doesn't work, it might conveniently disappear ... into the river. One custodian wanted a new Cushman scooter, but the park refused to replace it. So one night he took the scooter to the backside of the river and drove it into the water. No one could find it, so the park had to get him a new one.

Guest (noticing the crowds reserving spots along the river to watch Fantasmic): "What time is Fantasia?"

One West Side tradition is for sweepers, on their last day, to try to throw their brooms and long-handled pans from the mainland to Tom Sawyer Island. It's unknown if anyone has ever made it, but the periodic draining of the river for rehab reveals the many who didn't.

To get in on the fun, on his last day, a worker from Foods threw a trash can in the river.

Due to the physical nature of operating many of the Frontierland rides and the rugged image of the Old West, most were originally run only by males, primarily college aged. So, like on the Jungle Cruise, the area soon became known for its wild "River Rats."

Horseplay and pranks were not uncommon. Early one morning before the park opened, a worker smuggled in a trick ski and attempted to water-ski behind the keel boat. Another working lookout on the Columbia tried to shoot river fowl with the cannon.

On their final day of work, Mark Twain operators seemingly have an affinity for flashing: one, an avid photographer, set up his camera atop the wheelhouse of the Mark Twain and snapped a photo of himself baring his rear for the crowd; another, wearing shirt, tie and boxers, roller-skated across the deck of the paddle-wheeler; a third, wearing his boxers *over* his Mark Twain costume, jumped over the side of the boat and did a cannonball into the Rivers of America.

In 1972, the Indian Village at the far end of Frontierland was replaced by Bear Country, a small collection of shops and snack bars built around a single attraction, the Country Bear Jamboree. The show, starring animatronic bears, harkened back to the Tiki Room in presentation ... and audience response. The popularity of both gradually waned. In fact, one of the few lawsuits surrounding the Country Bear Jamboree involved a man who claimed that he tripped, fell and broke his wrist while exiting the brand-new show because of the huge crowds—a condition that was soon remedied.

Placing the ride at a far, dead-end corner of the park eliminated cross traffic, so crowds grew even more sparse. So in 1989, the area received a *Song of the South*-themed log ride, Splash Mountain, and a new name, Critter Country. With a steep 52-and-a-half-foot drop at a 47-degree angle, Splash Mountain is Disneyland's wettest ride, especially for the rider sitting in front.

To capture riders' expressions of terror, a camera snaps a photo of them just as they go over the falls. The photos are projected onto screens at the end of the ride. Sometimes, though, the expressions of terror are real. One evening in 1994, a photo was displayed of a nineteen-year-old woman who had turned purple, after suffering an aneurysm during the ride and died.

The camera caught another guest screaming, with his shirt wrapped around his hand. Just as his log reached the base of the lift, his gold engagement ring caught on a screw protruding from an overhead hatch. The lift jerked his vehicle forward, twisting and tearing his ring finger from his hand. After the log returned to dock, a ride operator retrieved the ring and mangled finger from the screw.

Once Splash Mountain riders discovered that they were being photographed, they started posing—making silly faces, pretending to read a book, turning around and playing cards, even making obscene gestures or baring some skin. Operators are supposed to screen out the photos before displaying them for all to see. But one attendant saved the images of women lifting their tops and posted the breast-baring women on his Web site, nicknamed "Flash Mountain," where visitors can vote for their favorite picture.

Disneyland launched an internal investigation, instituted security precautions, and, determined to prevent further additions to the Web site, spent a year overhauling the computer system.

Hidden cameras throughout the ride help prevent such monkey business. An operator in the control tower watches a wall of monitors and can make announcements or warnings over public address

---

Guest: "I've been to Fantasyland, Adventureland and Frontierland—where's Disneyland?"

speakers in various scenes. Such power came in handy one afternoon after a rude guest got into an argument with the loading crew. The supervisor, predisposed to take the guests' side of any argument, allowed the party to ride anyway. But the hostess in the control tower watched their boat from monitor to monitor and held the PA button down, muting the music and dialogue as they entered each scene. So, the guest did get to ride—entirely in silence.

5

Southern Spirits

THE fringes of Frontierland always had a distinct Southern flavor, from its majestic Mississippi riverboat to the Plantation House restaurant and Aunt Jemima's Pancake House. Walt soon realized that centuries-ago New Orleans would make the perfect backdrop for several attractions, and had Imagineers design a Thieves' Market, a haunted house and a pirate wax museum.

Even by the furthest stretch of the imagination, such concepts didn't lend themselves to the Old West, so the area would be spun off into an entirely new land. Workers began construction on New Orleans Square in 1961, leveling the entire area, then digging a giant basement. After dining and shopping in a perpetually moonlit Blue Bayou area, guests could go downstairs for a walk-through tour of the pirate museum.

But, after the initial subterranean steel framework was installed, work on the area stopped. Walt had far more strategic plans in mind for his Imagineers. Several large corporations had commissioned Disney to produce exhibits that they could sponsor during the 1964-1965 World's Fair in New York. The move had two advantages. First, the companies all wanted something special and state of the art, so they would, in effect, be subsidizing Disney to make advancements in theme park technology. Second, as part of the deal, when the fair was over, Walt could bring the exhibits home to keep as attractions at Disneyland.

When the Imagineers finally finished work on It's a Small World, Great Moments with Mr. Lincoln, the Carousel of Progress, and the Primeval World exhibit, they returned to work on New Orleans Square, which, by now, seemed rather primitive. So, Walt threw the old plans out and ordered the Imagineers to incorporate what they'd learned while working on the fair exhibits. The breakthroughs in audio-animatronics made on Mr. Lincoln would allow the wax pirates to move and sing and swashbuckle. And, to

UNDERGROUND PIRATES. Initial steel members for the Pirates of the Caribbean (dead center) sat untouched for several years as the Imagineers devoted their energies to the World's Fair. Note the exterior of the Haunted Mansion also under construction to the left. (c. 1961) *Courtesy Anaheim Public Library.*

increase capacity, the attraction became a boat ride, using the system developed for It's a Small World.

The more ambitious plans, though, produced an attraction that no longer fit inside the basement. In fact, it wouldn't even fit inside the park's perimeter berm. So, the original space was transformed into a tri-level structure, stacking not only the beginning of the attraction, but also shops and three restaurants: the Blue Bayou, members-only Club 33 and an employee cafeteria. A separate show building outside the berm would house the bulk of the attraction.

In Pirates of the Caribbean, vessels begin their journey in a moon-lit bayou, illuminated by a projection that mimics the movement of the real moon. Lightbulb-tipped wires, blown by unseen fans, appear to flicker like fireflies. Each boat sails to the edge of a downramp, where it's held in place by paddle brakes until the dispatcher in the control tower is sure the preceding boat is a safe distance ahead. When the coast is clear, the boat plunges down two ramps, sailing underneath the railroad tracks and gaining the momentum to begin its journey.

Before security cameras were installed in the early 1970s, the attendant in the tower had to guess when it was safe to release a boat at the top of the first ramp and occasionally sent a craft smacking into the rear of a vessel backed up at the bottom. He might even send a third boat before receiving word of the first accident from a lookout at the bottom, resulting in a string of rear-end collisions as well as expensive lawsuits.

When the ride first opened, passengers regularly got soaked. When their boat hit the bottom of the first ramp, the water, with no place else to go, came back at the guests in a wave. The Imagineers finally thought to build a false wall that the water could rise up behind.

Guest (to a cast member wearing a brightly colored pirate costume and a Disneyland name tag): "Excuse me, do you work here?"

Guests still can get wet, especially if their boat is loaded too heavily in front. Loaders try to distribute the weight evenly throughout a boat and, when things are slow, only load the middle row to keep the boat level. Many passengers prefer the front seat and often switch. It's up to the dispatcher to hold the boat at the top of the falls and ask them to return to their original seats.

Leaks are another problem. Occasionally, the membrane-covered cement flume pops a leak or water spills over the side, which might drip through to the floor below. Once, the subfloor of the Blue Bayou restaurant flooded, causing intermittent rain showers in the Captain's Quarters scene. Another time, plumbing from an employee restroom sprang a leak directly over the ride's shootout finale, showering guests with waste water.

Similar to the Small World system, the 46 flat-bottomed boats are nudged along the way by 44 submersible Jacuzzi-type pumps. The faintly buzzing pumps push water downstream that takes the boats with it. Over time, some of the pumps have conked out, making for a slower ride.

Sensors throughout the ride trip the dialogue and sound effects, as over 120 audio-animatronic figures loot, plunder and pillage an unsuspecting seaport town. Especially in the early years, the figures leaked red hydraulic fluid, so the maintenance crew put cafeteria lunch trays underneath them to catch the drippings. Each tray had a "float," triggering an alarm when the fluid reached a certain level. Occasionally, the red fluid dripped onto a pirate's clothes, shocking guests; it looked like a blood-bathed buccaneer.

At the end of the attraction, a chain-lift with a 40-horsepower motor transports the boats back up to the bayou. Water is constantly pumped from the bottom level to the top, where large flapper valves help maintain the water level at 256,000 gallons. Occasionally, a worker accidentally leaves down a gate at the edge of one of the downramps, allowing all the water to flow downstairs. The main show building can accommodate the extra volume, but the water level rises high enough for the boats to float out of the flume and through the animation.

Once up the chain-lift, the boats reenter the load area, Laffite's Landing. There, a series of belts and rollers lift the crafts about five inches, working as a conveyor belt and steadying the vessels

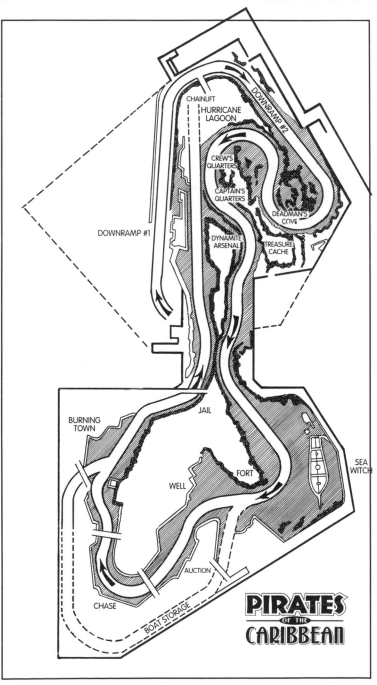

two at a time for loading and unloading. Several guests have sued the park, falsely claiming that they slipped while boarding because their boat moved—impossible since it was not free-floating.

Once, a five-year-old boy was jumping around on the wet back seat of a docked boat, slipped, fell into the water and went under. His mother screamed at the load operator to pull the boy out by his hair, so the attendant obliged. Mom grabbed the boy, who was gasping for air, and barked: "I told you if you kept jumping around this would happen!" The cast member suggested rushing him to First Aid, but mom replied, "No, I was expecting this. I've got a change of clothes in a locker."

The water averages only two feet deep; a greater fear is that someone will get tangled or mangled in the conveyor belt hardware. "The potential for tragedy was there, especially at the load dock," remembered former Pirates foreman Ken Fujimura, surprised that after more than 30 years the attraction has yet to claim either life or limb. "The person in the control tower is supposed to be watching the boats, then, while they're loading and unloading, monitor the security cameras. When the boats stop, you wait until everyone's seated, a counter times through to ready, a green light goes on, and if everyone's ready, you dispatch. But you'd get into a habit of punching dispatch buttons, sometimes when people weren't ready yet and they would fall over into the boat or the water."

During the park's first summer, a woman slipped while climbing out of a boat, fell in the water and her leg caught in the underwater machinery. She escaped with various minor injuries plus serious harm to her knee, and sued. Disneyland settled out of court.

In one of countless close calls, Fujimura was half-carrying a man with crutches into the back of the second boat at the dock, as a worker on the opposite side helped people out. Out of the corner of his eye, Fujimura noticed the first boat leave. Realizing that the second boat would dispatch in less than two seconds, he yelled at the tower to hit the brakes and literally threw the disabled guest across the boat into the arms of the attendant at unload.

Another time, a security officer tried to run across the front boat from unload to load, but the operator in the tower missed his signal. The guard stepped into the boat just as it was dispatched, and fell out the back. He had two seconds to grab hold of the bow of the second boat and rode it out of harm's way.

The attraction can prove equally dangerous for passengers who stand up during the ride or, worse, jump out. Since the boats travel relatively slowly, guests all too often jump out along the way—to take pictures of their friends, to try to pilfer souvenirs from the scenes, or, most often, to escape after the first waterfall because they are so frightened.

One day, a woman seven months pregnant was sitting in the back seat of a boat with her mother. She was so scared after the first downramp, her mother told her she didn't think it was safe for her to go down the second ramp, since she mistakenly thought it was even steeper. So the daughter climbed out of the boat, slipped and fell out the back into the water. She climbed out of the flume a split-second before the next boat arrived.

To watch over unruly guests, the attendant in the dispatch tower keeps an eye on a wall of nine closed-circuit television monitors linked to infrared cameras hidden at strategic points along the route, such as the top of the falls. Since the cameras pick up only heat, the images on the monitors are black and white. A button underneath each monitor activates a speaker near each camera, so the dispatcher can instruct guests to sit down. Stashed in dark corners behind the guests, the cameras are visible to guests only as dull red lights.

Although the show area looks remote, it's actually surrounded by an intricate, three-level network of tunnels. The backstage

---

Dissatisfied Customers

The soundtrack music and dialogue on Pirates are more for atmosphere, allowing guests to drop in on any scene at any time. Nevertheless, one disgruntled guest demanded a refund because he could not hear the "running narration all through the attraction."

Another unhappy guest, who had asked to seat in the front row, was enraged when water splashed on his $1,000 camera. His suggestion: "Put up a (bleep)ing sign!"

labyrinth provides maintenance workers or other employees with quick access to any point in the attraction—if they know their way around. "It's like a maze back there," recalled a former cast member. "When things were slow, you'd give two rookies flashlights, send them to separate destinations, and see how long it would take them, like laboratory rat races. Typically they'd get lost and you'd have to send someone in after them."

Once in a while, guests do get a peek backstage, when accidentally diverted into the boat storage area behind the auction scene. Pirates is such a high capacity attraction that when the crowds lessen in the evening, operators have to cut down on the number of boats to avoid a back up of empty boats. An operator goes down behind the Sea Witch pirate ship, pushes a button to stop the boats, raises a black curtain to boat storage, flips an electrical switch and reroutes the empty boats backstage. Unfortunately, the operators sometimes forget to flip the switch back and provide guests with a cook's tour of the back area.

One evening, two marijuana smokers attempted to take their own unscheduled ride. The young men climbed over a fence near the ride's exit, jumped into a wooden flatbed boat moored by the bayou, untied the rope and pushed off. Before they could reach the downramp, a ride operator spotted the glow of their smokes and shouted, "Hey, get out of there—and put out those cigarettes!" Fortunately, a security officer was nearby, and jumped into the teenagers' boat. The guard rowed them back to shore and led them to the security office. There, they were berated, then allowed back into the park—only to later overdose on pills.

Yet Pirates' most frustrating problem is a smaller critter: cockroaches. The insects love the damp, warm and dark environment, and despite regular fumigation, they keep reappearing, scampering along the floors of the boats. Fortunately, the staff usually catches them by surprise before opening the ride in the morning.

Guest: "How do I get to Carrots of the Pyrobbean?"

Most employees enjoy working Pirates, because the steady pace makes time go by quickly, without the constant pressure of a potential shutdown, like on the Matterhorn. Best of all, the dispatcher, loader, unloader and grouper (the position that groups guests into sets and assigns them to a row) all work near each other.

In the evenings when the crowds thin, there's also time for horseplay. One slow evening, two operators, under the guise of asking for a break, approached their foreman, who was working dispatch, and emptied a pair of fire extinguishers into the control tower. The booth and everything inside it, including the foreman, were blanketed in white.

On his last evening of work, ride operator Bob Dotts was pleasantly surprised to see his co-workers had brought in two elaborately decorated sheet cakes. During breaks and after their shifts, the employees would enjoy the going-away party, not realizing that the guest of honor had disappeared. A short time later, Bob reappeared at the load dock—in the front seat of an otherwise empty boat, hogtied to the bow, handcuffed behind his back, and with whipped cream applied liberally to his head and down his shirt and pants. His friends then sent him through the ride over and over again. Each time his boat came around to the dock, the crew was waiting to douse him with a bucket of strawberry sauce, then with ice water, and finally to affix a crown of watermelon to his head. Guests even got into the act by splashing the helpless hostage.

The ride's supervisor, recently promoted from foreman of the attraction, took one look at the mayhem, turned around and left. The supervisor at the Blue Bayou, though, reported the incident.

The foreman did come clean, in his nightly entry in the Pirates log book, blaming the incident on Dotts: "Efforts to talk him out of the boat were futile. He kept insisting on 'one more trip.' One unknown ride operator tried to clean him up by pouring five gallons of water over his head. Bob was most appreciative. Finally, we insisted his fun stop, so volunteers pulled the boat off ... and cleaned it up." The victim, though, left covered in crud.

Friendlier cast members have made one backstage site on Pirates the most intimate area in the park: the infamous Mylar Table. Technicians use the secluded table, located behind the fortress in the center of the main show building, to cut the shiny sheets of Mylar used for the ride's fire effects. Other cast members use the private spot for more amorous activities.

Along with the Pirates basement, the earliest New Orleans Square construction included building the outside of the haunted house attraction just up the shore. But when the Haunted Mansion first appeared in 1963, it was nothing more than a hollow shell. Work didn't begin inside until after Pirates was completed, by which time the Imagineers had learned several lessons in capacity. Like Pirates, the Haunted Mansion was transformed from a walk-through into a ride-through attraction that would employ a separate, larger show building on the other side of the berm.

The attraction finally opened six years later, then briefly closed. To lower guests so they can walk underneath the railroad tracks to the main show building, the Haunted Mansion uses a pair of elevators. But, about six months after the ride opened, the elevator stopped going down. Somehow, water had seeped into the elevator pits and caused the lift mechanism to fail. By putting green dye in the water, repair workers were able to trace its source to the Rivers of America. Maintenance pumped the entire river, then resealed the elevator pits.

Possibly because the brand new ride was closed so soon after opening, or maybe because it sat there, exterior completed, seemingly ready to open for six years, rumors began circulating that the ride closed because it was so scary it was killing people of heart attacks. Supposedly, the Imagineers toned down the scares, such as retiming the screams in the graveyard to tip off riders that a skull is about to pop up.

In reality, the Mansion has yet to claim its first victim. The attraction is more humorous than haunting. Yet many employees claim otherwise, convinced the building really is haunted. Some swear that while working unload, they have heard the ghostly Little Leota ("Hurry back... hurry back...") call out their own name. "There have been rumors of things happening that can't be explained," said Haunted Mansion mainstay Bob Gentleman. "People say they see strange things, or are tapped on the shoulder, turn and nobody's there. Some people refuse to work the ride."

Working the Haunted Mansion is neither as social nor as spirited as working Pirates. The mood is more somber and, although at least six employees work the attraction at a time, they're spread throughout the attraction. Operators are expected to smile on other attractions, but a more serious, even grim, visage is welcome on the Haunted Mansion. Once a woman asked a Mansion host to smile. He stared at her straight-faced and replied, "I *am* smiling."

One afternoon, remembered Mark Zimmer, "I was feeling really bad and looked terrible. The people loved it—they thought it was part of the show."

The first position stands on the porch and leads groups into the foyer. There, eerie music begins, helping to scare off the too young or timid before it's too late. The surroundings were too much for one fifteen-year-old who, high on drugs, freaked out. The teen began screaming, running around the foyer and throwing himself into the walls. He kicked a hole in a fake doorway and tried to crawl through on his hands and knees. Finally, a ride operator trapped him alone in an adjacent room until security could arrive.

In the foyer, wall panels slide open into two identical rooms that appear to stretch. Actually, the expanding rooms are the elevators that lower about 85 guests at a time below the level of the railroad tracks. As the elevator descends, a sinister voice notes that there are "no windows and no doors..." and the lights suddenly go out, inevitably triggering an onslaught of overdramatic, high-pitched screams. Hosts who operate the elevators often wear ear plugs.

Once, a large contingent of mentally handicapped children boarded the elevator, accompanied by two Haunted Mansion attendants. Upon hearing that they were trapped, several children panicked and started running around the room screaming. Other kids joined in, until the entire elevator was complete pandemonium. Quickly, the screaming turned into vomiting, and the park host and

---

Guest (to a black-gowned Mansion hostess): "Are you supposed to be a nun?"

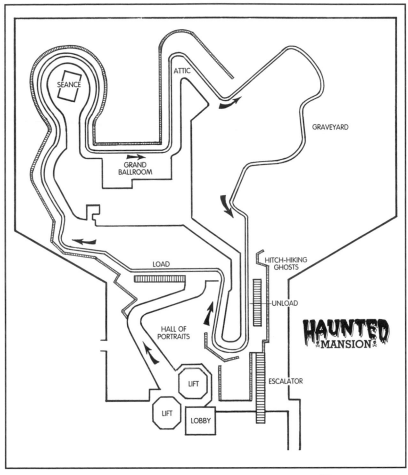

MAP NOT TO SCALE

hostess found themselves under attack. As soon as the lights came back on and the elevator doors opened, the barf-covered cast members hurried backstage to hose themselves off.

The area's confined quarters can be dangerous, as well. A few years ago, two guests got into an argument on the elevator. After they exited, one of the men pulled out a can of pepper spray. The ventilation system drew in the spray and infected the whole group. Security, police, paramedics and six fire engines responded. More than 50 people were sent to the hospital. The culprit was arrested, convicted of misusing pepper spray, and received a bill from Disneyland for the use of the ambulances and fire engines.

In 1996, several women complained that after the crowded elevator went dark someone grabbed their breasts. Two weeks later, the molester returned. But, because the elevator wasn't crowded, the second woman he assaulted that day was able to identify him when the lights came back on. He pushed people out of the way and fled. She chased him down the Hall of Portraits and onto the Doom Buggies. At the end of the ride, she found a security guard to nab him. In the security office, the suspect confessed, apologized and, crying, blamed his behavior on being "sexually frustrated" because of problems with his ex-wife. He was arrested and the victim filed suit—against the park, alleging inadequate security.

The next two positions are Load One, who helps guests board their Doom Buggy from a moving walkway, and Load Two, located about at the end of the walkway, who makes sure everyone is safely inside. Each of the 131 two-passenger vehicles is linked by a tow bar into an endless loop, constantly rolling along a hidden track on rubber tires. The cars' clamshell shape helps not only to direct riders' attention, but to conceal mischief inside the vehicles, from smoking to lovemaking. Some guests, realizing they only have seven minutes, are so anxious, they're already undressing by the time they pass the operator at Load Two.

One hostess working Load Two was standing entirely still, as a passing twelve-year-old reached out of his car and grabbed her breast. She was shocked and asked her foreman what she could do. Since he had no applicable Standard Operating Procedure to refer to, she went down to the unload area and waited for the boy's car. When the car arrived, she slapped the kid in the face. The boy complained, and management reprimanded both the hostess and her foreman. "We got in trouble," the foreman said, "because we'd had ten minutes to think it over."

A backstage operator mans the "tower," watching security monitors that flip through the different scenes surveyed by infrared cameras stashed throughout the attraction. Unlike on Pirates, he's not in an actual tower, but in a hidden control room. The door on the right side of the lobby leads to black velour curtains that conceal the room. Before the hidden cameras were installed in the early

1970s, operators would work "utility positions," standing behind the cars in high mischief areas, such as the Grand Ballroom.

The Ballroom's illusion—of transparent ghosts engaging in a merry wedding feast—is the attraction's most spectacular. Yet the effect is a simple one: guests travel over a balcony viewing through a series of pillars that hold a ten-and-a-half-foot-high by 50-foot-wide plate of near-invisible glass. Mannequins directly below the balcony are reflected onto the glass, creating ghostly images that appear to dine and dance in the furnished, yet otherwise empty, ballroom. Turn up the house lights and the ghosts disappear.

Nowadays, the glass is easier to detect, thanks to an armed guest who, in the 1970s, opened fire inside the Haunted Mansion, Monsanto's Adventure through Inner Space and the Primeval World diorama. Recalled security guard Mark Keiser: "We were on a train going through the diorama and noticed spalling in the second-to-the-last window, where the triceratops are hatching. Three bullet holes were easily noticeable. The trains ran all day, and they repaired the pane of glass over night. They also traced the bullet, and discovered it was the same guy who shot up the snowflakes in Monsanto and the glass on the Haunted Mansion."

The Haunted Mansion glass, though, wasn't as easy to replace. Evidently, the window is so large, that originally it had to be lowered through the roof by helicopter. To replace it, then, would entail removing the roof. Disneyland had a simpler solution. First, they hid the crack with a curtain. Then they covered it up with a spider web decal, still visible between the second to the last set of pillars.

Sharp-eyed riders also can tell that the Mansion's ballroom images are reflections by looking at the dancers. The women, not the men, are leading; no one told the model makers the figures would be seen as reflections.

Workers in the tower are most concerned that during the ride no

---

Guest: "Can we rent the Haunted Mansion for a Halloween party?"

one gets out of their car. Beneath the cars is a fake floor, hiding the drive mechanism and an average eight-foot drop.

On a Grad Nite several years ago, two teenage girls got out of their Doom Buggy in the graveyard scene and proceeded to destroy everything they could get their hands and feet on. "They went kicking over tombstones," recalled maintenance man Mike Goodwin. "By the singing busts is a thin scrim, a see-through gauze they project the ghosts on. They tore that up. They got caught, but they ruined the show. We had to shut it down."

Curiously, the part of the ride causing the most injuries turned out to be the conveyor belt walkway at unload. Women in particular tended to step out with their right foot first, crossing their legs, and stumbling onto the moving walkway. Designers made several modifications to the car and even considered scrapping the walkway altogether.

One precaution was stationing an attendant at unload to walk the belt and make sure everyone exited safely. Yet, not even she was safe. Late one night, the hostess at unload, her feet tired, removed her shoes and so she walking on the belt in nylon stockings. Just as her replacement arrived, the hostess began screaming—her nylons had gotten caught between the teeth combs in the floor and the rubber belt. Inch by inch, the moving floor pulled the stocking down her legs, until it built up between the combs and belt and stopped the belt from moving. The host called to shut down the ride, then grabbed the tool normally used to manually open a Doom Buggy and wedged it under the tooth comb to free the bunched-up stocking. By the time the supervisor arrived, the ride was back in operation. The host explained that "something" had gotten caught in the conveyor belt and he used the lever to remove it. Fortunately, no one asked about the hostess' now-bare legs.

The Mansion's final effect is also one of its most memorable: the Doom Buggies pass a series of mirrors showing that each car

---

Caller (to the Disneyland switchboard): "What day is your Fourth of July party on?"

has picked up a "hitchhiking ghost." The special one-way glass reflects not only the cars and riders before it, but also reveals what's behind it, when those objects are illuminated. Behind the mirrors is a loop of white animatronic ghosts, dimly lit in green and circling in sync with the cars, so that their faint, almost ghostly images can be seen through the mirror. Guests constantly try to take pictures of the hitchhikers, but since they're shooting at a panel of glass, all they get is a picture of their flash.

Cozy shops, stylish restaurants, jazz musicians and sidewalk artists make New Orleans Square perhaps the most atmospheric area of the park. For ten years, though, from 1976 until 1986, the pastel and watercolor street artists were nowhere to be found. Earlier, caricaturists and portrait artists could be found throughout the park—from the Art Festival on Center Street halfway down Main Street and in the lobby of the Opera House to Davy Crockett's Arcade and the old Art Corner in Tomorrowland.

In the old days, the smock-clad artists worked solely on commission, so the faster they painted, the more money they made. "Another artist and I would race a lot," confessed William Stout. "We might have 30 people waiting to have their portrait drawn and we'd race to see how many of the 30 we could get. Eight minutes apiece was the usual time; we could do them in three. We did about 45 each, then stood up and stretched to take a break. I looked at the portraits drying and this one was terrible: a baby's head looked like a misshapen potato with one eye half up its forehead and this curved lip—and then I noticed I had signed it. I didn't even remember doing it. So I asked the cashier, 'What did those people say when you showed it to them?' She said all they

> **Caller** (to the Disneyland switchboard): "I'd like to have my brother paged."
> **Operator**: "Is he a guest in the park?"
> **Caller**: "No, he's not a guest. He paid his way in."

said was 'Oh, my God ....'"

In the early 1970s, the artists joined a union and demanded a base wage as well as vacation pay. "For years we worked completely on commission, which was illegal," recalled Main Street portrait artist Colette Miller. "We unionized, so Disney closed down the place and let all the artists go. We filed a class action suit and for about ten years after, Disney sent us checks for back pay."

6

No Place Like the Future

OF all the lands of Disneyland, none has seen as much change over the years as Tomorrowland. The other areas don't need to be constantly updated—Adventureland is meant to look primitive, Frontierland rustic, and Fantasyland timeless. But Tomorrowland embodies the future, and once-trendy designs and technology ultimately become dated. A land of tomorrow doesn't just have to keep up with the rest of the world; by definition, it has to stay constantly ahead of its time.

Ironically, from Day One, Tomorrowland always has run a little late. It was the last of the original lands to be designed, due to time and money constraints, opening with only a handful of attractions and filled out with a smattering of decidedly unfuturistic corporate exhibits, such as the Dutch Boy Color Paint Gallery, Kaiser's Hall of Aluminum Fame and Monsanto's Hall of Chemistry.

On Opening Day, the most visible attraction in Tomorrowland had more to do with today than tomorrow: a kids-sized freeway. The purpose of the Autopia was to teach youngsters the rules of motoring. Any guest over seven was allowed to drive, but only after he or she passed a driver's test. They then qualified for a souvenir driver's license. And to make sure kids got the message of safety, the original fleet of 40 cars included two black and whites complete with flashing red lights and sirens.

Unfortunately, the track, more than the width of two cars and without a guide rail, proved too great a temptation for recklessness. Mischievous drivers would sideswipe each other, make sudden U-turns and head the wrong way, even hop the curb and go off-road. To direct the cars back on track, operators at various places along the course had stashed special tools, consisting of a curved bar welded to a pair of wheels.

Even after Disney engineers narrowed the width of the track, drivers still found ways to make trouble, sometimes wedging their car sideways and then abandoning it.

To withstand the punishment, broad wrap-around bumpers encircled the early Autopia cars. Occasionally, the hooked end of a bumper caught a light pole and, before a ride operator arrived on the scene, 20 or 30 cars might be backed up, nose to tail. The pressure created by dozens of cars pushing forward prevented backing up the front car and unhooking its bumper from the pole. So, the operator went to the last car, shut it off, pushed it back a few feet, and did the same to every car until he reached the first car.

At long last, in 1965, a steel guide rail was installed along the center of the roadway, keeping drivers on track.

The cars are governed to seven miles per hour, but capable of doing 25. Once in a while, a guest will try to reach under the hood to override the governor, but, ungoverned, the engine makes so much noise, his joy ride is easily detected and short-lived.

To keep an eye on disobedient drivers, a ride operator stands watch on a bridge in a back area of the ride known as the "Back Bridge." Unlike working load and unload, Autopia lookouts lead a lonesome, monotonous existence. One employee, banished to Back Bridge for a full day's shift by his lead, Mark Saunders, spent the entire eight hours retrieving small rocks from near the Disneyland Railroad tracks and rearranging them into giant letters.

Guest (after climbing into an Autopia car and staring blankly down the one-way track): "Now where do I go?"

By the end of the day, sharp-eyed guests riding overhead on the Monorail could look out their window and see, spelled in pebbles: "Saunders Must Die."

As a rite of initiation, new hires often are assigned to Back Bridge as their last position of the night—and never told when their shift is over. Unaware that their fifteen minutes is up, some rookies have spent hours standing watch, even after the park closes.

For employees, Autopia can be like working in the middle of a racetrack, and the attraction soon earned the nickname "Blood Alley." Accidentally and not so accidentally, drivers have bumped, thrown, even chased and run down ride operators. The trickiest maneuver is jumping onto the back of the moving cars as they return from their trip, hoping the driver doesn't veer sharply to throw you. Eventually, a wide concrete divider was built along the unload area, preventing drivers from veering to the right or left.

Children must be at least four-feet-four-inches tall to drive their own car, a requirement not to ensure the car will run safely, just that the car will run at all. Drivers must be tall enough to reach the gas pedal. Still, most kids want to drive the cars themselves. One father, told that his child was too small to ride Autopia by himself, had a fit. He ranted about how much money he had spent that day and how long he had waited in lines. The exasperated hostess finally said, "Fine. Let him in." So the boy climbed in and, unable to reach the accelerator, just sat there. After a few embarrassing moments for father and son, mom finally climbed into the car and gave Junior a hand—or rather a foot.

So smaller children could drive their own cars, in 1956 Disneyland added a Junior Autopia, which used the same cars, only with booster seats and a block of wood on the accelerator. A year later came the automatically powered Midget Autopia, restricted for children eleven and under. The stock amusement park ride ran on an electric bus bar.

In 1957, in the middle of all the little roadways, Fantasyland

---

Autopia driver: "Where are the headlights?"

received an aquatic version of the Autopia, the Motor Boat Cruise. Although billed as an adventure through "white water rapids and rock-filled currents," it was among the park's tamest. Each boat had a steering wheel, but it was just for show; the boats were automatically powered and led on an underwater guide rail. Kids still found ways to make mischief—standing on the bow, trying to leap from boat to boat, or jumping onto the lagoon's many rocks and running onto shore. Of course, the abandoned vessel returned to the dock on its own, leaving the operator to wonder if the guest had fallen overboard. Just in case, a co-worker had to go check things out and fill out an incident report for recall later.

In 1959, the Submarine Lagoon opened along the Tomorrowland edge of the Motor Boat pond. Although Disney's fleet of eight submarines ran on a track and maintained only a partially submerged level, they did provide guests with a unique underwater experience. It wasn't so much the plastic sealife, duplicated for viewers on both sides of the ships, as the type of attraction. Guests got the feeling of being on a real submarine, claustrophobia and all. Some children felt so uncomfortable, they would scream for the entire eight-minute, fifteen-second ride, with no way to escape or turn back.

Workers didn't have it any better. Cast members variously describe working subs as "obnoxious," "the worst" and "a dungeon." Recalled Submarine Voyage pilot Tim Stanley: "There was no good position on subs. Inside, it was claustrophobic and up on dock you were bending over, picking up hatches and ramps. You spent the day sucking diesel fumes and chlorine."

Drivers stand on a platform in the middle of the vessel, the top half of their bodies in an upraised "sail," where they can see the course ahead above sea level. The air conditioning system drew in

---

Guest: "I see the Monorail goes back to the Disneyland
   Hotel. What about the submarine?"

every smell from within the sub, then blew it into the guests' faces through vents beneath each porthole. The main vent was in the sail, behind the pilot's head, and drivers regularly got sick from the recirculated, germ-infested air constantly blown on the back of their necks.

"We'd wedge a penny in the deadman's switch so we could sit or position ourselves forward to avoid the air behind us," said former pilot Mark Zimmer. "Saturday was one of the worst days because some Europeans tend to wash only once a week, generally on a Saturday night."

Once, while driving a sub through the caverns that hid the machinery used to operate the mermaids and other effects, Zimmer detected an unusual odor. A woman was changing her baby's diaper—and it was no secret to the rest of the increasingly irritated passengers. The driver called his foreman to ask him to shut off the falls, then popped the hatches to let some fresh air in. Then, after the ship docked and the guests began to exit, the ride operator noticed that the woman had left her diaper. So, he grabbed a large cloth towel, wrapped her diaper up in it, and hurried off the sub, telling the loading crew not to load the passengers yet. He ran after the woman, calling, "Ma'am! Ma'am! You left a package on board." She turned and held out her hand, into which he placed a neat, towel-wrapped bundle, to the applause of everyone within smelling distance.

For some, the only advantage of working subs was that, once the ride started, there was no contact with the guests. Drivers hit a button for the pre-recorded spiel and were on their own, hidden in the sail. They might bring along text books, flash cards or a secret snack.

Since they were above sea level, pilots were the only ones on board who could see the catwalks that the staff walked on inside the caverns. There, co-workers hung signs, underwear, anything they could think of to amuse the pilots. Occasionally, maintenance left an under-repair mermaid on the catwalks and a daring ride operator would sneak into the caverns and hoist the mermaid onto the front of a sub. When the submarine came out from under the falls, it looked it had picked up a dead mermaid.

Another favorite prank for pilots was stopping the recording midway through, so the next operator would start up the ride with the spiel in the wrong place and have his passengers vainly searching out their portholes for mermaids and sea serpents.

Occasionally, an operator phoned maintenance or supervision to report that Unit Nine was sinking. More often than not, they fell for it; there were only eight subs.

Another time, a cast member sneaked into the sail of a new hire's sub and shoved a whistle in the vent. The rookie suffered through this shrill noise the whole trip.

The subs made their final trip around the lagoon September 8, 1998. Disneyland management attributed the closure to the dated show, with its hokey fiberglass fish visibly suspended by strings. Certainly the attraction needed a serious modernization, but, in truth, the closure came because the attraction took up a relatively large area and was low in capacity (38), labor intensive (requiring about 25 operators a shift on a busy day), and expensive to operate and maintain.

Most of Disneyland's outside bodies of water are interconnected—with water flowing underground from the Motor Boat pond to the castle moat past the Frontierland and Adventureland entrances to the Jungle river and finally to the Rivers of America, where it is pumped back to Storybook Land and the Motor Boat pond. The Submarine Lagoon, though, has its own separate water supply, which had to be chlorinated so guests could see through it to view the show. The chlorine quickly bleached the plastic fish, so to keep up show standards, divers constantly had to replace and repaint the fish.

And the lagoon leaks. Badly. During the last dry rehab of the attraction, an eight-week overhaul in 1988, maintenance determined that the lagoon was losing about 300,000 gallons of water *a day*. The lagoon, which holds about eight million gallons of water, is concrete with Gunite around the edges. Although it's thick concrete, countless cracks had developed due to settling and earthquakes.

Reportedly, the vast volumes of water loaded with chemicals seeping into the earth wasn't dangerous—the park claimed the water was safe enough to drink—just expensive.

Even after the rehab, the lagoon was still leaking about 50,000 gallons of water a day. "We managed to slow it down," said Jerry White, who oversaw the 1988 rehab. "There was no way we could seal all the cracks. There could be cracks under the scenery. They'd have to strip the insides to totally clear the floor and walls."

Above the queue for the subs is the boarding area for the Monorail, which debuted on the same day in 1959. Since the Monorail was one of two attractions personally owned by Walt Disney and training was more advanced, Monorail operators historically were hand-picked. With no rookies or slackers, operations typically ran smoothly.

Since driving the Monorail consists merely of pushing a control

COMING ATTRACTIONS. Sign promises major additions to the park in 1959, including the Monorail, Submarine Voyage and Matterhorn. Note the early Skyway buckets in the background. (1958) *Copyright Anaheim Public Library.*

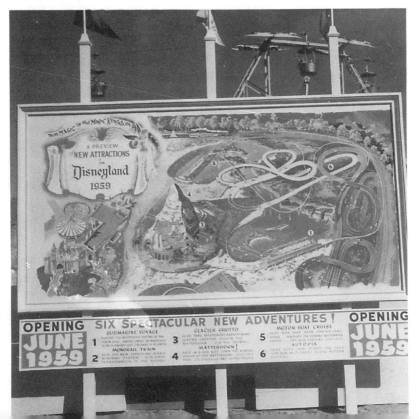

lever into gear, guests wonder if anyone's actually driving. Others, possibly forgetting the ride is on a rail, ask, "Do you have to steer the Monorail?" "Yes," a joker might reply. "I have to lean into the turns."

Since the trip from Tomorrowland to the Disneyland Hotel is more level and has more straight-aways, drivers can run the Monorail at full speed, 35 miles per hour. The return trip, though, has several curves and a seven-degree grade near the Submarine Lagoon, so drivers are instructed to maintain a speed of fifteen miles per hour.

On his last day, in the fall of 1994, one operator decided to make the return trip at full speed, laying on the horn the whole way. He tore around the track and didn't ease until he pulled into the station. There, security and police were waiting to arrest him for endangering the guests. Management also interrogated every Monorail employee, demanding to know why no one hit the button at the station that would have killed power along the track. The breakneck trip slightly damaged the vehicle, spreading the chassis that surrounds the rail and resulting in rougher rides until maintenance could repair it.

The Monorail's slower moving Tomorrowland counterpart, the PeopleMover, tore along at about two miles per hour. The continuously moving tramway was so efficient, it became dull to work. Operators spent their time waiting for something to break down, since once the cars lost their momentum, they had to be evacuated before they could be restarted, to make sure they didn't crash into each other. Operators would help guests exit the cars and walk along the track, 30 feet over unforgiving concrete walkways.

The ride was far more dangerous when it was running, beguilingly so, because it traveled so slowly that guests were lulled into a false sense of security. Several guests were seriously injured on the ride—and two killed—after climbing out of their vehicles.

Guest: "Does the Monorail have a line to Knott's Berry Farm?"

Eight cameras were hidden along the route. Yet, even from the ride's first months, sneaking out of the vehicles, according to one worker, "was fairly common. They had two and sometimes three safety positions along the route. They added extra bars on the cars and installed foot pads along the track that would trip an alarm."

The first intrusion system featured pressure-sensitive mats containing two layers of wires. If the wires touched, the whole ride shut down. The wires were so sensitive, they were often triggered by guests dropping objects out of their vehicle. The mats were later replaced by an infrared beam system. The systems, though, were installed only inside buildings, to protect them from the weather, and on the door side of the vehicles.

Equally uneventful were the Astro Jets (which became the Rocket Jets and finally the Astro Orbiter), a Dumbo-style attraction with circling rockets instead of elephants. To add some excitement, operators would try to break records of hourly ride counts. During one Grad Nite, word spread throughout Tomorrowland that one operator was running up huge numbers on Rocket Jets. It turns out he had gotten into the ride controls and reset the timer so instead of 90-second rides, guests were getting ten-second rides.

Although it was nearly identical to Dumbo, the old Rocket Jets attracted a slightly older clientele, because they were located not in the kiddy-oriented Fantasyland but in Tomorrowland on top of the PeopleMover station, whirling about 90 feet in the air. Guests took one of two elevators up to the Rocket Jets boarding area. One night, the elevator doubled as a holding cell. A group of large, scowling teenagers were spitting over the side of the Rocket Jets boarding area. "Don't spit," advised the pint-sized hostess. "You might hit someone." The guests were unimpressed and started walking toward the hostess. Though nervous, she somehow found the courage to bark, "Just get in the elevator." She was convinced the guests were going to pick her up and toss her over the side. Amazingly, they obliged, she locked them in the elevator and held them hostage until security could arrive.

Hosts and hostesses could have more fun working audio-animatronic-based attractions like Mission to Mars, the Carousel of

Progress and its successor, the musical revue America Sings, where moving, talking props were at their disposal. In Mission to Mars' command center scene, hostesses might decorate animatronic host Mr. Johnson with a Santa hat or Groucho Marx glasses, or litter his console with trash to make him look like a slob.

Or, operators might join the scenes themselves, singing along with the America Sings critters or sneaking into the Carousel of Progress family's kitchen for a drink. One prankster sat in an always empty seat in front of Mr. Johnson, acting like another robotic member of the team at Mission Control. During the show, she mechanically turned to her right to see a supervisor watching her, then turned to the left to see a second supervisor. She kept her job only because as she exited the scene, one guest turned to her friend and said, "Oh, Marge, look! She's real!"

Another hostess sat in the chair, blending in with the action, until the scripted part when a seagull tripped the emergency system, triggering sirens and flashing warning lights. The non-animatronic hostess pretended to freak out and ran out of Mission Control screaming.

Sometimes, the mechanics went funky, and operators didn't have to add a thing. America Sings once ran without any sound. The characters moved their mouths, but had no voices. For some reason, the guests found the silent musical revue hilarious. During another performance, the storks' necks gave way and their heads dipped forward, so it looked as if they were singing their songs drunk. One of the seated robots in Mission Control regularly knocked her phone off the hook.

After the seagull set off the alarms at Mission Control, Mr. Johnson would turn, raise his arm and exclaim, "Oh, no, not again!" During one show, the figure turned, raised his arm and his whole arm fell to the floor, then he exclaimed, "Oh, no , not again!" One guest turned to the hostess and asked, "Does that happen every time?"

Another time, Mr. Johnson turned away from the audience and his arm began twitching and jerking uncontrollably. No one could understand why this clean-cut Disney character was making obscene gestures.

Light years beyond Mission to Mars, Tomorrowland's first thrill ride owes its beginnings to the park's first, the Matterhorn Bobsleds. The Magic Kingdom at Walt Disney World in Florida opened in 1971 without a Matterhorn. Instead, four years later, the park added Space Mountain, a similar roller coaster incorporating the Matterhorn's twin intertwined tracks, long sleds with single-file seating, and tubular steel track construction. Florida's Space Mountain was so popular that six months after it opened, construction began on a version in Anaheim. But the space confines of Disneyland's Tomorrowland ruled out copying Disney World's blueprints. At Disneyland, there would only be one track, but wider sleds allowed people to sit side by side, making room for twelve instead of eight passengers each. With a faster lap bar loading system and a track that was nearly ten percent longer, the new version accommodated up to twelve cars at a time instead of eight per track, providing the same overall ride capacity as the original.

Twelve sleds could run simultaneously on the same track due to the ride's high-tech braking system. A computer opens and closes individual braking zones to maintain a safe distance between each set of cars. Air pressure-controlled brakes along the track slow the rockets if they get too close. Since heavier loads travel faster, a scale weighs each rocket as it is dispatched. The computer automatically determines the needed interval between cars and gives lighter cars a head start. To ensure proper spacing, an operator in the tower can set the rockets to dispatch every 50, 40, 30 or, if all twelve rockets are running, 20 seconds.

Two PLCs (Programmable Logic Controllers) report to the computer, using electronic sensors to monitor the location and speed of each vehicle. If the computer doesn't receive identical input from both PLCs, it shuts down.

Although the technology proved so valuable that it later was installed on the Matterhorn, Big Thunder and other attractions, it

---

Guest (to an attendant near the Space Mountain exit): "Can I enter the exit?"

Things We Hate
About Working Space Mountain

(drawn from notations made by cast members
in an old Space Mountain log book)

(1) Asking for the front row

(2) Singles who say they're single, but with the people behind them

(3) People who say, "Huh?"

(4) People who jump back into moving rockets for guide books

(5) Baby switches at the load dock

(6) Melodramatic acting at unload

(7) Postal holidays

(8) Parties of sixteen who ask for the front

(9) When all six in the group tell you they have six

(10) People who stand in front of an empty rocket (a.k.a. comatose victims)

(11) People who don't hold onto small children

(12) People who touch you

(13) Zippers that scratch your lower abdominal area

(14) Flash pictures in the station

(15) People who tell you to smile

(16) Farts at console

(17) Premature anxiety at load when the bars do not lock

(18) Asking if their glasses will come off

(19) When they say, "But we're together"

(20) Groups of six or more who all stand in the same row

was so advanced that problems were inevitable. During Space Mountain's first year, the system constantly malfunctioned. A warning light might go off, but there was no problem. Or, a problem might occur, but not trigger the warning light. Other times, the computer might misread a rocket's location, and send a second train of cars crashing into it from behind.

An apparent design flaw didn't help any. The ride's boarding area, called the spaceport, has only six sled positions, and if a sled stops in the last position, the ride shuts down. Operators couldn't load and unload fast enough. So, they started running fewer sleds, but capacity suffered. Then, additional operators served as "pushers" to manually push the sleds forward to clear the brake zone. Finally, catapults were added to speed the movement of the rockets in the spaceport.

"Employees had to load at double the speed because there should have been nine slots and due to a design flaw there were six," said host Kent Wilson. "You ended up with ride operators yelling at guests. People tend to be gawking on the downramp, so you'd have to yell, 'Come on down! Right this way!' That ride turned the most friendly and gracious ride operators into the most annoying."

Space Mountain's opening crews were hand-picked, and considered it an honor to be on the opening crew. But the ride's intense noise and high tension soon had them begging for the relative tranquillity of the Matterhorn. "Space Mountain's so loud and noisy," said one worker. "You come off of a nice, quiet break and you walk onto a stage that is chaos."

"On Space Mountain, you got the best ride in the back," said one loader, "but everyone wanted us to give them the front seat. If they were rude enough, we wouldn't load anyone else behind them, so there was no weight, and they were sure to have a bad ride."

Employees turn away riders who are too short or, since the ride is so turbulent, expectant mothers. "Some ladies," remembered one worker, "you couldn't quite tell. I had to ask, 'Are you pregnant?' I was wrong a couple of times."

Passengers without legs also are not allowed to ride Space Mountain, because they might slip out of the lap bar. Once, the crew prohibited a Vietnam veteran from riding because he had no legs or arms. The man's friend complained so fervently, that the supervisor said if they returned at the end of the night, they could take the final trip, in case the ride broke down. During their ride, the vet's head kept smashing into the restraint bar, but his friend

was too busy holding on to his own bar to help. By the time the
rocket returned to the station, the vet's face was covered with cuts.

Rockets, trams, monorails, cars, submarines. Most
Tomorrowland attractions had their roots in the transportation field,
including Circle-Vision 360, the circular movie theater surrounded
by nine screens for 360-degree viewing. It opened in 1955 as
Circarama, sponsored by American Motors, and the movie, a trav-
elogue across America, was filmed with cameras mounted to the
roof of a Rambler.

For the filmmakers, the greatest challenge was ensuring that
something interesting was happening on every screen. Sometimes
there might be beautiful scenery on one side of the road, and nothing on the other. Full-round vision also made it difficult for the
director to ensure that unwanted images stayed off the screen.
Inconsistencies in the 1966 film *America the Beautiful*, for example, included tissues blowing across the battlefield during the
Battle of Gettysburg, a child picking his nose and cattle jumping
each other. Near the Liberty Bell, an elderly man trips on a crack
in the sidewalk, and quickly looks around to make sure no one saw
him. Across from Independence Hall, a mother holding a cigarette
lowers her hand and accidentally burns her young daughter's wrist.
Since the cameras were assembled in a circle, there was no place
for people to hide to watch the filming. Consequently, Walt can be
spotted in about a half-dozen scenes, watching the action from the
shadows.

In 1960, Bell Telephone took over sponsorship and operation of
the attraction. Telephone company employees escorted guests into
the theater, delivered the introduction and exit spiels, and were on
hand to answer any questions as guests exited the theater into a
telephone exhibit.

Since working the attraction was such an honor, Bell employees,
unlike the often rascally Disneyland employees, did everything by
the book. Then, in 1982, Bell announced plans to discontinue
sponsorship of the attraction. Since anti-trust regulators were
breaking it up into three companies (Pacific Telephone, Western
Electric and AT&T), Bell would no longer be involved in joint pro-

motional ventures. So, Bell employees spent the next year training Tomorrowland hosts and hostesses to take over Circle-Vision.

"It was a special job for telephone company employees. They did the spiel word for word," recalled Diane Judd, one of the first park employees assigned to Circle-Vision. "It was half Disney workers, half Pacific Telephone. They didn't know how to handle us. We used to take the gist of the spiel. We liked (working Circle-Vision) because it had free telephones for us to use."

Employees on Circle-Vision, as on most of the Tomorrowland rides of the 1960s, wore tight polyester jumpsuits. One particular outfit quickly became the talk of the attraction after one hostess complained that the suit had given her crabs. The rumor was that she would wear the costumes without underwear. Naturally, no one wanted to wear any costumes that she had. To gross out her co-workers, one hostess removed a clump of hair from her hair brush and stuffed it up her pant leg. She would tell fellow employees that she thought she was wearing a contaminated costume, then shake a pant leg, so the hairball would fall out.

Circle-Vision was typically a calm, uneventful attraction, but employees had fun when they could. And, occasionally, unplanned mishaps occurred. One hostess, a prim and proper girl, delivered the opening spiel in her sweet, demure voice: "On behalf of Pacific Telephone, we're proud to present *America—the—Beautiful,*" and as she descended from the podium, with each step she loudly passed gas. The audience burst into hysterical laughter, and the red-faced hostess hurried for the exit doors—only to discover that her co-workers were holding it closed from the outside. For the entire eighteen-minute show, the guests couldn't stop laughing, and when the doors finally swung open, the hostess ran off without delivering the exit spiel.

Tomorrowland's other theater was built in 1986 to show the 3-D movie *Captain E-O* starring Michael Jackson. For operators, the

Guest (searching for Adventure Thru Inner Space): "Where's Dr. Shrinko?"

attraction was an easy one to work. They announced, "Ladies and gentlemen, sit back and enjoy *Captain E-O*," then pressed a button.

Due to the intense noise, employees were encouraged to wear ear plugs. "We received a lot of sound complaints. It was very loud, just a hair under dangerous," recalled hostess Elizabeth Hayes. "If you worked on rides with a lot of noise—Space Mountain, *Captain E-O*, Autopia, America Sings, they gave you regular hearing tests."

Hayes added: "We wouldn't let any balloons into *Captain E-O*, especially a Mylar balloon because the lasers would bounce off it. They were real lasers."

More troublesome was a dark ride that closed a year before E-O opened, Monsanto's Adventure thru Inner Space. A constantly moving attraction like PeopleMover, the voyage into an atomic nucleus was known by employees as "a vacation from blood pressure and consciousness." The poor souls who worked load walked a giant turntable, constantly, mindlessly. The turntable itself acted as a giant static generator, creating noticeable sparks whenever polyester-clad cast members touched the metal railing.

Also, as on PeopleMover, operators lost direct control of the

---

Shrinkage Problems

To give the illusion that guests were being miniaturized, figures in tiny Omnimovers were seen riding through the Mighty Microscope. Some guests were a little too convinced:

Panic-stricken woman (to Inner Space host): "What happened? I told my son when he got to the small part to wave!"

Another elderly guest (to Monsanto host): "Do you have a *written* guarantee that after I come out of this ride I will come back to my exact size?"

guests once they stepped inside the car. Occasionally, passengers climbed out of their cars into the dark. "Monsanto got to be more of a problem as kids got to know the ride better, where the walkways were alongside the track all the way down," explained long-time lead Dick Mobley. "Kids would realize there was enough light in there. One girl got out of the car, fell down the steps, and landed in the machinery that ties all the cars together. She got caught in the machinery and mangled."

More often, guests made mischief inside their car, beating up on the scenery, having sex, smoking, drinking, doing drugs. "Eventually they had to close Inner Space on Grad Nites," recalled another cast member. "It was Adventure Thru Marijuana. Kids would trip out on the shrinking atoms."

Lookouts, bearing flashlights, hid in the dark to catch trouble-makers in the act. One rookie was given a tally sheet and told to count up by category the number of violators he spotted. Even though the sheet listed all sorts of deviant behavior from smoking to spitting, it didn't cover half of the kinky acts he witnessed.

Inner Space closed in 1985, replaced sixteen months later by the *Star Wars*-themed Star Tours. Four actual flight simulators, called Star Speeders, shake, jerk and whip passengers around as if they're on a poorly navigated trip through space.

The ride is so turbulent, the Speeders occasionally get cracks in them. Guests get the most exciting ride in the back row toward

---

Close Encounters In Inner Space

More sex probably took place on Adventure thru Inner Space than in any other area on the Disney property. As one young man attested to his date as they got off the ride, "What do you mean? There's plenty of time! Let's go again!"

Its closure in 1985 upset both the nostalgic and the erotic. One man stood despondent outside Star Tours, crushed to discover that Inner Space was gone. For years, he had been promising his son that once the boy got older, he'd show him the place where he was conceived.

either end, since the seats are the most off center.

Thrill-seeking employees have discovered an even rockier ride. "We would surf the Star Speeder," said Heidi Levine. "You stand in about the third row, with no belts, and try to stand through the whole ride."

Guests are securely strapped with seatbelts. For larger guests, two extenders are available that plug into the seatbelts. Normal procedure is walking discreetly offstage and into the Star Tours office to ask for an extender. But, one afternoon, the lead noticed a young rookie wrestling with a large woman. The lead walked up and asked, "Can I help you?" "Yeah!" he blurted out, for all to hear. "Get me an extender—no, get both of them! This lady's big!"

Disney vowed to make Tomorrowland's latest overhaul, in 1998, its last. As park spokesman John McClintock explained, "Tomorrow has this nasty way of becoming today." So rather than project current design styles and colors onto the future, the Imagineers instead presented the history of tomorrow, of how great thinkers and inventors envisioned the future.

Unfortunately, budget cuts forced the designers to throw out some ideas and scale back others. Apart from a colorful new paint job, the New Tomorrowland wasn't a significant upgrade. They replaced *Captain E-O* with *Honey, I Shrunk the Audience*, a 3-D show already playing at Epcot Center. They turned Mission to Mars into a pizza place. They spruced up, renamed and relocated the Rocket Jets.

America Sings, which had been closed ten years earlier, became Innoventions, a collection of corporate exhibits. Billed as a showcase for emerging technology, it's more a video arcade without the quarters. "I could have just gone to Circuit City to see this stuff," remarked one guest.

Guest (after riding Star Tours): "Where's the track?"

Circle-Vision was turned into a queue for the PeopleMover's replacement, the Rocket Rods. The New Tomorrowland needed a big marquee ride, but due to budget restraints, it had to be built using the same track as the PeopleMover. The PeopleMover would traverse the nearly mile-long track in sixteen minutes; the Rocket Rods ran it in two minutes 40 seconds.

The track wasn't suited for high-speed cars; it vibrated so badly that nearby ceiling panels came crashing down and chunks of plaster fell off the caverns of the Submarine Lagoon. And, the cars weren't suited for the winding, unbanked track. The vehicles had to slow down every time they approached a turn or entered a building. The constant speeding up and slowing down overworked the machinery, causing the software system to fail, motors to overheat, and drive systems and axles to break. One car even shot a heavy steel part into a Tomorrowland Autopia area. The cars went through tires so quickly, a maintenance worker explained, "we have to scrape rubber from the tires off the track."

Guests, meanwhile, waited in line for 90 minutes only to see the ride shut down for the rest of the day. After six weeks of breakdowns and complaints, management finally ordered the ride closed until the bugs could be worked out. They expected it to be down three to five weeks; Rocket Rods was down for over three months.

The extended rehab made the ride somewhat more reliable — especially after its lone special effect, a modest wheelie, was eliminated. Yet nothing was done about the ill-suited track.

Maintenance crews again were forced to work twelve-hour shifts, six to seven days a week to keep the ride running. After two more years, the park gave the designers one last shot at making the ride more reliable. They closed the Rocket Rods in late September 2000, vowing it would reopen in the spring. It never did. The vehicles eventually were disassembled and sold for scrap.

Curiously, the most popular feature of the New Tomorrowland was probably its most regrettable: Cosmic Waves, a fountain that

---

Guest (after riding Star Tours): "You must have a very large building that you fly this thing in."

PUBLIC BATH. The most popular attraction in the New Tomorrowland turned out to be Cosmic Waves, a fountain that sun-scorched guests turned into a shower. (Summer 1998) Photo by David Koenig

shot five-foot-tall jets of water from the ground. Designers figured guests would enjoy dodging the spurts of water. But, especially in the heat of summer, children wanted to run around and get wet.

Soon, kids were cavorting in their underwear, even naked. One child cut his bare foot on the metal grating. Others would track water across the park or slip on the pavement. Management stationed ride operators near the fountain to make sure people didn't get carried away, but, badly outnumbered, the attendants realized there was nothing they could do.

As the area turned into a public bath, it began to smell like one. "Sweat, tears, dirt, urine, vomit, feces, blood, saliva, you name it, it goes in there," explained one custodian. Cosmic Waves became known as "Toxic Waves" and the "Cosmic Bidet." Finally, maintenance responded by chlorinating the fountain to the level of a swimming pool. The stench of contamination was replaced by the pungent odor of pool chemicals.

The fountain ran less and less frequently until, by late 2001, it stopped running all together. After four years, the New Tomorrowland had little to show for itself. Even the colorful paint job had begun to fade.

7

Character Witnesses

CERTAINLY, ride operators play an integral role in creating happiness for guests. But the employees who play costumed Disney characters share the guest's experience on a deeper, more intimate level.

"As a character, you represent what Walt Disney put into his cartoons. You become that," explained one-time character Carl Trapasso. "If you want to know what Disneyland's all about, put on a character costume. You can see Disneyland the way kids see it. You see it through their eyes. It's very difficult in operations to see what the public sees; you get caught up in the attraction."

Disguised as Mickey Mouse, Donald Duck or other members of Disney's animated menagerie, cast members become instantly recognizable, instantly approachable. You're a childhood friend, a living, breathing, walking—if not talking—playmate from their dreams and imagination. A giant, cuddly teddy bear that hugs back.

Characters can emotionally connect with the guest, on a personal level. And it's not just Mickey. For Disneyland's 25th anniversary celebration, the park created several hideous humanoid characters, villains from the studio's latest movie, *The Black Hole*. Greeting guests near Space Mountain, the creatures wore dark hoods, shading their featureless reflective faces. A little girl tugged on one creature's robe. He leaned over and she whispered, "I love you." Then she gave him a gentle kiss on his cold plastic face.

Characters make a special effort to reach out to shy children, hoping that they're comforted, not frightened by a six-foot-tall animal. They especially fight their way through crowds to reach handicapped children. Eeyore, who, unlike his cartoon counterpart, walks on two legs instead of four feet, once caught the eye of a wheelchair-bound four-year-old with braces on both her legs. As the character got closer, the girl began to cry. He started to back up, thinking he had scared her, when she said, "Look, mom, God gave Eeyore my legs so he could walk." The actor wept in his costume.

The costume lets cast members fearlessly approach and interact with guests, as well as secretly spy on them. Even though the mask's eyes may be looking straight ahead, the actor inside might be looking to the right or left. Once, Brer Bear was posing for pictures in New Orleans Square when, out of the corner of his eye, he noticed a woman slapping around her small daughter. The hulking bear walked up to the girl and picked her up. She collapsed into his arms. Brer Bear hugged her tightly and finally let go, then firmly squeezed mom's hand good-bye. Without the mask, the timid actor inside never could have intervened like that.

A furry coat also attracts women. "I can't tell you how many hotel keys I was handed," a former Tigger recalled. "They didn't know what I looked like inside. I could have been a Cyclops!"

Still, playing a character (now called a "pageant helper") may be the toughest job in the park. Despite the permanent grin molded onto the character's face, the actor inside probably isn't smiling. The outfits, dozens of pounds of latex, fiberglass and fur, are uncomfortable, heavy and unbearably hot. The costumes for Gus and Jacque, the mice from *Cinderella*, have such poor ventilation, they're nicknamed "The Ovens."

One actor, suffering from heat stroke, threw up inside the King Louie costume, spewing vomit through the costume's screen mouth. Even after it was cleaned, nobody ever wanted to wear that suit again.

Sometimes the actors put out so much energy, they return backstage physically exhausted and drenched with sweat. "At night, I'd wake up with my arms outstretched, shaking hands," Jim Moore remembered. "I couldn't sleep because I'd still feel people tugging at my skin. I would wake up with the bed drenched—just dreaming about playing the characters would make me sweat."

A greater danger, though, is the abusive guest, from the overanxious child and mischievous teenager to the brainless adult. Then there are the downright sadistic, who maliciously push, kick, hit or otherwise injure the characters. "People have no respect for the characters," decried one of the Three Battered Pigs. "They think of us as cartoon characters, 'Oh, just hit 'em with a frying pan!'"

Brer Bear, reaching out to greet a crowd, shook hands with a knife. Several characters, including Mickey Mouse himself, have been stabbed. During a private party at the park, Winnie the Pooh began complaining that every time he bent down, he felt a sharp pain in his back. When he took off the costume, he saw the inside was covered with blood. Some young hoodlum had stuck a stiletto in his back and left it there, so every time the actor moved, it cut him. Eventually, the park stopped putting characters in the park during certain private parties.

One hot summer day in Adventureland, a guest took a pocket lighter to Baloo the bear. A security guard finally noticed and told him, "Hey, bear, you're on fire." "Yeah, it sure is hot in here," Baloo agreed. "No, you're really *on fire*," the officer said, racing for a fire extinguisher.

Characters learn ways to protect themselves. They'll shake hands with overzealous kids, squeezing extra tight, to let them know they are dealing with an adult not a stuffed animal. Macho male guests sometimes challenge characters when shaking their hands, squeezing as tightly as they can, so a few characters learned

---

Thumper

Common words of direction from parents to their children, sure to strike fear in a character: "Go kick him, and I'll take his picture."

an aikido martial arts technique. They grabbed their thumb instead, so the harder the guy squeezed, the more pressure he put on his own thumb.

The Baloo outfit can be used as a weapon because the actor looks through a patch on the chest and can raise up the head portion then let go, dropping the chin down on someone's head. Baloo and Brer Bear are made entirely of fiberglass, so kids who punch them usually hurt their hands.

Characters also can ward off attackers by stepping on their toes. For years, a league of Goofys secretly plotted to sharpen the taps on the bottom of their shoes (but, reportedly, never did).

While greeting guests near the second-story entrance to Space Mountain, Chip and Dale suddenly found themselves under attack by an unsupervised hellion. Unable to persuade the boy to stop hitting them, the characters grabbed his shoes and, one at a time, threw them over the side to the concrete below. They then grabbed the boy and lifted him toward the railing, whispering, "You're next..." Terror-stricken, the brat said he was just playing, so they let him break free and flee.

Yet, actors are trained that if things start getting out of hand or they feel they're going to fight back, they should find a way to excuse themselves offstage. "If it gets that bad, take a 'people break,' calm down," a character suggested. "Retaliation should never be in a character's vocabulary."

Since characters are roughed up so much, complaints against them are taken less seriously. Recently, though, Tigger was caught red-handed. He was bored, and four children were pulling on his tail, trying to get his attention. So he whipped around, sending one kid flying. Mom captured the incident on video and sent a copy to Disney headquarters in Burbank. Management terminated Tigger and began using the video for training purposes.

Traditionally, though, management offers the characters little respect—"They're nothing but a clothes rack," as a top executive referred to them.

"You had to have camaraderie because others disowned us," Terry Garrison recalled. "Ride operators started a petition to have us banned from the Small World/Storybook break area because we were sweaty and we stank. When they heard we might get our own air-conditioned break area, they gave up on the petition."

Considering the grueling working conditions and lack of sympathy, characters might be expected to do something outrageous on their last day of work. But, whether due to respect for the image or fear of Disney's trademark-protective legal department, going-away pranks have been relatively tame. A favorite last day stunt is for characters to go onstage wearing different pieces of different costumes. One cast member went onstage as the Big Bad Wolf wearing a Pig's head, while another wore a Tigger body with a Captain Hook head.

One stormy evening, after a Winnie the Pooh walked offstage in Tomorrowland ending his final shift, a co-worker in an identical costume took his place posing for pictures in the Bell Telephone building. Instead of hanging up his outfit, the former bear returned on stage to confront his replacement. After a quick mirror routine, old Pooh started chasing new Pooh across Tomorrowland through the rain.

As popular as they are today, when the park first opened, the characters were more like window dressing. There was no formal character department. An office worker, ride operator or whoever was available might be recruited to don a costume and pose for pictures or march in a parade.

But the park soon realized that the characters were attractions unto themselves. Three days after the park opened in 1955, ride operator John Catone was asked to try on a space suit and walk around Tomorrowland. Audiences loved him. "The spaceman was like a crowd control person," he said. "If 20,000 Leagues Under the Sea had a really long line, I'd go over there. Everyone wanted to take my picture, so I'd move to the next attraction, and the crowd followed me."

A park survey revealed that, on average, visitors took 13,000 pictures of him a day. Catone spent the next two years as K-1, the Kaiser Aluminum spaceman, until a new, taller suit was created.

Dressing up a spaceman for Tomorrowland or a cowboy for Frontierland was easy enough. But, especially in Fantasyland, guests expected to see Disney's popular cartoon characters. The earliest outfits looked more like homemade Halloween costumes, bearing little resemblance to the characters as seen in cartoons and comic strips. In the movies, the characters were drawn with exaggerated features, especially huge heads and short bodies. Gradually, the costumes were redesigned to look more cartoonish, with little concern for the comfort of the people inside. The actors often wore gigantic heads over the upper halves of their bodies and saw through a mesh screen in the character's hat.

Gradually, a small staff of full-timers and larger staff of seasonal part-timers were assembled. Training was far from extensive. Their instructions were to wander around a particular corner of the park and mingle. When Mark Gabriel became a character 30 years ago, "there wasn't much direction," he recalled. "They took us to the Disney University, showed us some cartoons and said, 'Have a good time.' You basically have dancers as characters now. We were animators. We had to develop characters. Everyone had their own style. You could tell who was in a costume by how they walked."

Because Disneyland now packs the park almost daily, guests increasingly must line up to meet characters at prearranged "photo locations." It's less spontaneous, but more orderly. Said photo aide Christopher Borja: "Some characters who were used to roaming around get burned out from just sitting there, while newer characters who have only done photo set-ups don't know what to do when they're set loose. It's the best of the worst. The photo set-up gets you a private picture, but you have to wait half-an-hour to an hour-and-a-half."

Break Room With a View

Years ago, the characters had a second-story break area above Sunkist, I Presume (now Bengal Barbecue), with sofas, showers and a veranda overlooking Adventureland. Naive guests, noticing the actors in their street clothes kicking back on the balcony between sets, would ask, "Hey, do you guys live up there? How much does it cost?"

After the Character Department outgrew its offices in the old administration building, the area became the male characters' dressing room, lockers and showers, called "The Zoo," with the costumes kept upstairs in "The Head Room."

The costume department has several sizes of the more popular characters, such as Donald Duck and especially Mickey Mouse, to make sure there's always a costume available no matter who's scheduled to work. You don't want Mickey calling in sick.

Once, a group of cast members hung a Grumpy outfit on a T-shaped stand, put a pair of shoes underneath it, and called over their supervisor. They told their boss that the guy who played Grumpy was really upset. "We think you better talk to him," they said. So, the supervisor went over and spent several minutes, pleading and commiserating with the empty costume, before realizing he'd been had.

The department also cleans and repairs the costumes. "During the summer, the little kids try to feed ice cream bars to the pigs and the dwarfs," one staffer revealed. "So we end up cleaning a lot of chocolate off their mouths."

The diminutive Donald Duck outfit requires constant attention. "We're always trying to clean red smooch marks off his yellow beak."

Although Mickey Mouse is by far the most popular character with the kids, one actor who played him for many years did not evoke similar reverence from his co-workers. Loud-mouthed and abrasive, the actor felt that since he was personally hired by Walt Disney in the early 1960s because of his short stature, he was guaranteed a lifetime contract. As he grew older and less mobile, he resented that girls were increasingly asked to play Mickey, and his attitude continued to slip.

A co-worker, who played Brer Bear, on his own last day of work got his revenge on the abrasive Mickey. The mouse was in front of the Main Entrance greeting guests before the park opened. The bear reached through the fence behind him, grabbed his mouse ears, and started whamming his head against the fence. "You're breaking my neck!" Mickey shrieked. "I'll kill you! I'll kill you!"

The feisty actor once was suspended for accosting his supervisor after he lost his place at the front of a parade and was nearly trampled by cheerleaders and a marching band. The supervisor said Mickey hit him with his baton, the mouse claimed he just shoved him against a wall.

One morning, the park was filming a Dream Vacation commercial with Mickey, Goofy and actors playing an All-American family. Unfortunately, the brat who played the son kept grabbing Mickey's ears and shaking his head. Then Goofy lost a contact lens, so he put his hand into his costume's mouth to retrieve it. Finally, one of the actors blew his lines, so Mickey, assuming they'd stop shooting, turned to bawl out the kid. "You sorry little s.o.b.," he snarled. "You mess with my ears and I'll kill you." But the director hadn't yet called, "Cut," so somewhere somebody has on film Mickey cussing out a kid as Goofy thrusts his arms down his own throat.

The long-time Mickey was also a dirty old mouse, with a fondness for after-hours parties and a wallet filled with photos of topless dancers. In his gruff voice, he often asked the tykes: "Hey, kid, where's your mommy?" For a while, every morning he buffed his shiny vinyl shoes reportedly to use them to look up women's dresses. He even was rumored to have a mirrored ceiling above his bed at his home in a nearby trailer park.

During the same period, Donald Duck usually was played by a hard-talking, cigar-chomping, bowlegged dwarf. Since he had difficulty walking, the diminutive actor was allowed to ride in the fire engine or on a float during most parades. Jealous co-workers would chant, "The duck walks! The duck walks!"

One afternoon, the dwarf was needed to play Minnie Mouse. He hated the assignment, but started to get into it when three sailors showed up and started coming on to him. Mr. Minnie played it to the hilt, flirting back, teasingly lifting up his skirt. At the end of his set, he walked backstage, removed the Minnie head and lit up a cigar. The sailors, though, were dying to meet the real Minnie, and pushed their way through several cast members to get backstage. "Where's Minnie?" they asked. "Dis is it!" the polka-dot-jumper-wearing dwarf replied, pointing at himself with his cigar. The three seamen walked off, deflated and disturbed.

So that the character could walk on all fours, the first Pluto costume fit two people inside. It made for a bizarre sight, however—a dog about ten feet long from paw to paw. The costume soon evolved into a single-piece, single-person outfit, complete with plastic claws on its paws and a plastic tail bringing up the rear. Pluto constantly watched his backside, because guests loved to try to tear off his tail. One night during a private party, a kid grabbed hold of Pluto's tail and yanked it off, then ran off down Main Street, waving the tail like a prized catch. Pluto and Goofy gave chase, and finally caught the boy. As the characters returned to Town Square, Pluto hammed it up, yelping, rubbing his backside and nursing his severed tail.

Pluto was one character who was never allowed to speak. Once, a man walked up to Pluto and asked, "How ya doin'?" Pluto gestured back, but the man repeated, "I said, '*How ya doin'*?" Pluto could only respond by gesturing, which infuriated the man. The guest cussed out Pluto and stormed off, calling back, "Nice talking to you!"

In the early years, most characters were permitted to talk. Then, in the early 1970s, the park began giving "voice clearance" only to "face characters" (unmasked actors whose real faces were visible). Most of the costumed actors did bad impressions of the character's voices, anyway. Pantomime also prevented them from saying the wrong thing. Recalled Goofy: "Kids would question us about a Little Golden Book incident, and you'd better be right or they'd say, 'Hey, you're not Goofy!'"

Another time, the actor quickly changed into a Goofy costume after appearing as the Big Bad Wolf a minute before. As he bounded back onstage, a boy tried to get his attention. "Out of my way, kid!" he growled. "I'm hunting for a pig!" The boy responded, "Hey, Goofy, you sound like the Big Bad Wolf!" Remembering he'd just changed costumes, the actor tried to recover with a quick "H'yuck!"

Originally, the actor inside Goofy wore a black felt veil over his head, while the character's head was built into a helmet, with the actor looking out the mouth. So, most of the time, the actor was watching people from the knees down. He had to look up to see what was going on, which made it look as if he were yawning. Co-

workers were always whispering, "Goofy, lower your head."
Today's Goofy looks through the mask's eyes.

The rest of the outfit consists of pants, suspenders, a pullover
turtleneck, vest, and size 24 shoes (actually a shoe built into a
shoe). The shoes were so long that someone could stand on them,
push Goofy back, and there was nothing he could do to keep from
falling.

Once Goofy went down in front of the castle, and a security
guard hurried to his side. Instead of helping him up, the clueless
officer remarked, "I didn't know characters were allowed to get on
the ground."

The Big Bad Wolf is a similar costume, down to the floppy
shoes. "With the Big Bad Wolf, you'd think the pigs would be at
his mercy because they were smaller and had fake arms, but actually it was the other way around," recalled wolf Don McLaren.
"They'd gang up on me. If they could get one to stand on my toes
and another behind me, I was guaranteed to go down. Then they'd
get around me and wouldn't let me up."

In reality, the early Three Little Pigs costumes were among the
most helpless and, as local chiropractors will attest, the most
uncomfortable. A bulky fiberglass head covered the actor up to his
waist. He peered through a nylon screen in the pig's cap and used
a T-bar to move the arms. Without functional hands or arms, a pig
who was pushed over had no way to break his fall—or to get back
up—and would roll around helplessly, kicking frantically, until
someone helped him up again.

Their legs and feet were particularly vulnerable since they were
protected only by long pink socks and deck shoes. Once, a guest
put his arm around one of the pigs to pose for a picture and dug the
sharp heel of his cowboy boot into the pig's calf, bursting a blood
vessel. The pig dropped to the ground and his head fell off. The
actor jumped up and sprang to attack the guy, before the Big Bad
Wolf could separate them. His calf required emergency surgery to
strip veins, and he missed six months of work. The guest's excuse?
He didn't know there was a real person inside.

The pigs had to look out for each other. In 1976, the crew,
inspired by the television show *Baa Baa Black Sheep*, organized
their resistance into the Black Pig Squadron. Underneath their cos-

tumes, the actors wore cut-off fatigues and carried walkie talkies, so they could warn a fellow pig if they noticed a potential trouble-maker sneaking up behind him. "Bandit at ten o'clock," one Piggy Boyington might say, and the other would quickly turn and bop the kid with a free-flying arm.

More often the role of guardian went to the taller, more mobile Big Bad Wolf. Usually, the wolf would just pull the overzealous tyke off the pig, but once a boy was battering a pig so mercilessly, the wolf dragged the adolescent culprit offstage behind Storybook Land. The Three Pigs followed, and all four characters took off their heads. "Now," the wolf snarled, "we're going to kill you." The boy, terrified, wet his pants, and the characters quickly shoved him back on stage.

Still, a cartoonish wolf with a long tongue hanging from its mouth is not exactly intimidating. And since he's a sneering vil-lain, many guests who beat on him consider themselves heroes. He and Captain Hook earn the most kicks to the shin. In fact, an old rite of passage was putting a rookie in a wolf costume and pushing him into a crowd of children.

Once, the Three Little Pigs and the Big Bad Wolf were leaving Tomorrowland when a huge man heading toward the castle snapped. The man sprinted over and tackled the wolf. The wolf tried to crawl away, but the man kept punching, until the three pigs pulled him back.

Years ago, a well-known actress visited the park with her young son, who was playing the role of spoiled brat. Not amused, the Big Bad Wolf walked away. The movie star repeatedly called for him to come back, but the wolf kept walking. "I'll have your job!" she barked. The wolf turned and replied, "You don't want it. I have to put up with kids like that." He continued walking and was not rep-rimanded despite the star registering a formal complaint.

One Christmas Day, a Mexican woman who spoke only limited English walked up to the Big Bad Wolf and said, "Picture with my baby." Since characters are not allowed to hold babies, the wolf politely refused. The woman didn't understand. She kept trying to force the infant into his hands and, finally, stuck the baby into the wolf's baggy pants. The baby, too young to hold himself up, slid down into the wolf's pants. As the infant disappeared from sight, the mother grew hysterical and began beating on the wolf, scream-ing, "My baby! My baby!" Supervisors soon arrived to peel the woman off the wolf and fish the baby out of his pant leg.

As a joke, co-workers would slip ice cubes and other objects down the wolf's loose trousers.

Until the late 1980s, the Seven Dwarfs costumes featured equal-ly oversized heads. Half of the actor's body fit into the head, and he peered through nylon mesh in the cap. Since the costume's long arms hung almost to the ground, hands were fastened to the sleeves with Velcro and actors controlled the arms with a T-bar. Dopey also had hinged bars to flop his big ears.

For their entrances and exits, the Dwarfs usually marched in sin-gle file, their arms hanging limply at their sides. They could swing their arms to play with the guests or each other, but soon devised a more sinister application: Dwarf Wars. The Dwarfs would square off, three against four, wildly flailing their phony appendages at each other. One combatant was hit so hard, his head flew off. As he scrambled after it, a Marine stepped out from the audience and pulled out a gun. "Let's have some fun!" the serviceman hooted. The Dwarfs froze, not quite sure what he was getting at.

Dwarfs appeared to be an easy target for abusive children, but, remember, they traveled in a pack. An overeager kid pounding on Dopey soon found himself surrounded by Sleepy, Sneezy, Grumpy, Doc, Bashful and Happy. Once, three Dwarfs noticed a boy beat-ing on Doc. They closed in on him and backed the kid into a foun-tain. They split as a security guard walked over to help the boy out of the water. "Did you get wet, little man?" the officer asked in mock sincerity.

Another pre-teen hit one of the Dwarfs as they marched offstage, so they changed direction, circled the lad, closed in, and stomped on him.

Children are less likely to fight back against the Dwarfs' other guardian, Snow White. One time, a kid was wailing on Grumpy, when Snow White hurried over and put the kid in a headlock. "Beat the crap out of him, Grumpy," she smiled, holding the kid so Grumpy could slap him silly.

Although the characters, since redesigned, are used less fre-quently now, the Dwarf unit was so popular in its heyday that it had groupies. Some female admirers got carried away. Certain Dwarfs would leave the fronts of their outfits unfastened, and entice women to reach through their beards, into their costumes and pleasure them sexually. Management eventually caught on, fired two actors and stitched up the fronts of all the Dwarf costumes.

Captain Hook had a distinct advantage in warding off aggressors. "Hook had a mean streak to him," remembered a long-ago Captain. "Luckily, he could growl and the kids would back off."

But, he did have to be careful what he did with his sword and latex hook. One afternoon, Hook was dancing in New Orleans Square with a woman in a halter top. When the Pearly Band finished the number, Hook turned away and, not realizing his hook had caught onto the woman's top, took the top with him.

Another time, the Captain's own coat flew open, revealing a book he had tucked into his waistband: *The Happy Hooker*.

Cast members really enjoyed playing Hook's bungling sidekick, Mr. Smee. "The costume was regular clothes with a soft rubber head," Paul Kabat recalled. "It had a lot of mobility, so you could do a lot of things, like go over a railing."

Guests like to tweak Smee's big bulbous nose, unaware that there's not much padding behind it. One large gentleman walked up to Smee and punched him squarely in the nose, expecting a playful reaction. Smee staggered back and collapsed against a wall. The guest was just as startled.

Hook and Smee usually cavort with Peter Pan, often played by the manliest of women or the most screamingly gay man. Before the Chicken of the Sea pirate ship was removed during the remodeling of Fantasyland, the trio staged sword fights around the "tuna

---

True Colors

A black woman once accused Captain Hook of racism. She angrily denounced the character because she thought he was refusing to play with her child. Hook finally slipped off a long white glove to reveal that his hand also was black.

boat." One time, Hook teamed up with Pan against his own side-kick. They grabbed Smee, pulled his mouth open and held him under the Skull Rock waterfall, until his rubber head filled up with water.

Tic Toc, the crocodile that pursues Hook, appeared mostly for out-of-the-park promotions and tours. The short-lived costume, which zipped up the side, was made of such heavy vinyl that it didn't circulate air, making the inside unbearable. During one tour, the suit disappeared. Its body was found later, decapitated. Likely mounted over some madman's fireplace is the head of a cartoon crocodile with a big, old-fashioned clock in its mouth.

Cast members usually can't prevent costume alterations that decrease comfort, but have stopped changes by demonstrating they would be dangerous to guests. Pinocchio wears beige tights under-neath his Tyrolean shorts, but costumers proposed fiberglass leg coverings to make them look more like wooden legs. The girl who played Pinocchio was able to prove the change would be a safety hazard; if a little finger got between the upper and lower pieces of the covering, bending the character's leg would chomp the finger right off.

Pinocchio performs with Foulfellow the wolf and Gideon the cat, rascals who have been known to trip children with their canes or put a wad of gum on the ends of their canes to fish coins from the wishing well. Maintenance suspected children were to blame and installed a steel mesh covering over the bottom of the well. But that didn't stop the thievery since the small-diameter canes could still fit between the mesh.

Although women usually play Pinocchio, one man often got the part because of his slight, almost frail build. As such, he was a favorite target of Gideon and Foulfellow. One day, while perform-ing near the castle, the villains decided to dunk their delicate pup-pet friend into the wishing well. When he was finally able to climb out, the actor scampered offstage, his tights soaked. He tried to dry

---

Guest: "Where are the fireworks?"

his vinyl shoes with radiant heaters in the break room, before the vinyl began to smoke and melt, nearly catching fire.

The park also has a latex Geppetto mask with body costume, a rarely used Jiminy Cricket outfit (probably because it's as tall as Pinocchio), and, of course, Tinker Bell, who "flies" across the front of the castle to kick off summertime fireworks shows.

Beautiful blonde Alice in Wonderland usually appears with the White Rabbit and the Mad Hatter. "The White Rabbit is a neat character, always rushing around, very hyper, always up," said Paul Kabat. "The costume has hands, and it's cuddly, so kids would hug rather than hit you. Plus, you're always walking around with a beautiful woman."

The original Mad Hatter outfit, on the other hand, was one of the most awkward, consisting of a giant fiberglass body, hat and head, with a latex face riveted on. The immobile arms were pre-formed clasping a tea cup, so the actor used his own hands to move the character's rubber mouth and nose.

To defend himself against hecklers, the Mad Hatter bent forward and bopped kids on the head with his fiberglass hat. Once, during a set by It's a Small World, a Middle Eastern cast member named Nazim was playing the Mad Hatter and bonked a boy so hard, the kid was knocked unconscious. The Mad Hatter walked over to Alice and the White Rabbit to report: "Nazim hit boy. He not move." His friends scurried over to the boy, each grabbed a leg and they dragged him behind some bushes.

That particular Alice looked gentle and gracious, but she had subtle ways of protecting her pals. "She had really long finger-nails," the White Rabbit recalled. "She would grab little kids, dig her nails into their arms, and smile as she whispered, 'Don't hurt the other characters. Do it again and I'll rip your head off.' Their parents, meanwhile, were taking pictures, thinking, 'Oh, isn't she sweet!'"

Guest: "How many times does Tinker Bell go down in a night?"

The Mad Hatter was such an uncomfortable costume that on one cast member's last day, he took the costume out near It's a Small World and smashed the fiberglass head on an exposed sprinkler head, shattering it. A supervisor nearby was in disbelief. "What are you gonna do?" the worker challenged. "I quit!"

Actors did find one advantage to that early Mad Hatter outfit— the big fiberglass teacup was perfect for panhandling. During sets in the far corner of the park near It's a Small World, they'd slip a quarter into the cup ("not a penny or a nickel, or that's all you'd get") and act like beggars, encouraging guests to throw coins into the cup. Alice would even say, "Mr. Mad Hatter would like you to give him a donation." The troupe made up to $20 a day and split it three ways. Occasionally, a lead would spot them, and make them put the coins in the wishing well. Finally, the park had the costume taken in and added a tea-colored resin to cover the inside of the cup.

Not long ago, the park junked the entire costume and made the Mad Hatter a face character.

To fill out the Alice group, the park also has a Walrus outfit, Queen of Hearts and, more often, Tweedledee and Tweedledum, identical costumes except for the name stitched on their collar. For several years, Tweedles 'dee and 'dum were not used because a top park official thought they looked too much like they had Downs' Syndrome.

Winnie the Pooh of the 1970s was designed similarly to the Mad Hatter, with inoperable hands and the actor peering through a fiberglass honey pot sitting on Pooh's oversized rubber head. Unfortunately, the original designers finished the honey pot with a copper-laden spray, then forgot to seal it, so actors spent hours a day with their faces pushed up against the toxic material.

One Pooh liked to climb up on the concrete planters inside the Main Entrance and run in circles around the trees. Management told him several times not to, but he continued. Sure enough, one day he fell off the planter and onto his head, shattering the honey pot. The crowd parted as Winnie the Pooh ran across the park with a human head sticking out of the top of his honey pot.

In 1972, Pooh threw his hat into the presidential race, with a whistlestop tour down the California coast and three special Winnie the Pooh for President Days at the park. To kick off the "Poohitical Campaign," Disney held a contest to select one child from each state to act as delegates to nominate Pooh. Local Sears department stores held drawings and flew the winning families to Disney World to appear in a Winnie the Pooh for President parade. The pint-sized representatives were given placards for a Town Square rally, and as part of the show, the Big Bad Wolf, Cruella de Vil, the Queen of Hearts, and the rest of the villains showed up to try to stop it. The kids, though, stood up for their candidate, and began beating on the villains with the placards. Supervisors had to pull the kids off, and the battered characters quickly retreated.

Cast members enjoy portraying Pooh's bouncy friend Tigger because the costume is mobile, the character inherently animated, and guests always happy to see him. The outfit is similar to a pair of pajamas, without much padding, so actors are vulnerable to pinches and squeezes. Looking through the costume's nostrils restricts them to tunnel vision. And the tail is PVC tubing in a foam sleeve attached countered with a belt to a back brace. Visitors constantly pull on the tail, so Tiggers learn to whip it around to fend off intruders. Once, a guest kept grabbing at his tail, so Tigger maneuvered him toward a small fence in front of the castle. The character held his tail over the fence, and as the guest reached for it, Tigger spun around and flipped him into the moat.

Melancholy Eeyore is the polar opposite, "the slug, gray and depressing," actor Robert Hill called him. Audiences love when an actor pumps energy into the character by dancing around, but management doesn't since hyperactivity goes against the character's

---

Tigger Hunting

A small boy inadvertently had wandered backstage near the Tomorrowland break area, just as an off-duty cast member was walking by with Tigger's head under one arm and the body thrown over his shoulder. The kid went into hysterics. "What's wrong? What's wrong?" the employee asked. The boy cried, "You killed Tigger and skinned him!"

established personality.

Still, one Eeyore in particular would make mischief more subtly. Whenever the Pooh unit appeared in the castle forecourt, Eeyore would take dry ice from the nearby ice cream vendor, and toss it in the wishing well or the castle moat, making them smoke. The swans usually make a beeline for anything thrown into the moat. One swan snatched up a piece of dry ice and swam away, steam curling out of his beak.

Over the years, other characters from the *Winnie the Pooh* storybooks have performed at the park, including Owl, Rabbit, Kanga with a puppet in her pouch for Roo, even Hephalumps and Woozles.

Every character has its own war stories. Chip and Dale were performing on a floating stage on the Rivers of America when an errant firework launched from Tom Sawyer Island fell on one character's head. The chipmunk kept dancing, oblivious that his acrylic fur had begun to smolder, glow, then melt. Finally detecting the fire, he ran to get an extinguisher and put out his head.

Orville, the albatross from *The Rescuers*, is a particularly lanky, cumbersome outfit. The actor, wearing a backbrace with a fiberglass cap, sees through a scarf around the bird's neck. He holds a metal bar to flap its wings, and flops around in huge, webbed feet. One afternoon in front of the castle, a pin that held the head in place broke, and the head started to bob. The character fled toward a Tomorrowland exit, trying to balance the head, but a woman with a double stroller blocked his path. She wanted him to greet her twins, so Orville came closer, reaching for them. The children, terrified by this creature with a bobbing head, started screaming, so Orville bent over to calm them, and his head fell off. It hit both kids in the head and landed in their laps. The actor grabbed his head, then tried climbing over the strollers to escape, only to strike the kids with his giant feet. He finally resumed his flight offstage, to the sounds of stereophonic wailing.

One night, two teenage girls walked up to Pluto, who was played by a beautiful, blue-eyed blonde. Wardrobe had sewn pouches inside the costume to keep personal effects, and she was carrying a hairbrush. The girls felt her brush and shrieked, "Omigosh, it's a guy—and he's excited!"

Robin Hood the fox had a more embarrassing tale. The actor liked to strike an "Erroll Flynn pose," with his fists on his hips and his legs spread apart. "Little John had just wandered away, and two girls walked up, about twelve or thirteen years old," he said. "They reached down and grabbed me between the legs to see if I was a boy or a girl. I was stunned, but the worst thing of it was they ran away screaming, 'It's a girl!'"

As instantly recognizable Disney ambassadors, the characters are natural recruits for out-of-town promotional trips or special appearances, including parades, stage performances or impromptu visits to children's hospitals. The first major character junket was in January 1961 when Pinocchio toured the U.S. By the late 1970s, Walt Disney Productions was sending out about 75 tours a year, including fifteen annually involving Disneyland characters. The largest was in 1978: nineteen persons spent 37 days in Japan.

Appearances such as hamming it up with Walt at Radio City Music Hall could be glamorous. Sometimes, they're more personal, such as bringing a smile to the face of a six-year-old with weeks to live. Said one character after a trip to a children's hospital: "I'm glad Mickey always has a smile on his face because inside, sometimes you're ready to cry."

More often, Disney characters don't blend well into the real world. After a late night flight to Kansas City, the cast members were waiting for their costumes in the baggage claim area, alongside a group of intoxicated businessmen. One tipsy traveler turned to a cast member picking up a massive black garment bag and asked, "What do you have in there, a bear?" He replied, "As a matter of fact, yes." Inside was Baloo. One of the bags, though, came down the ramp deflated and empty. Then came a clunking sound, followed by Donald Duck's head bouncing down the ramp. The drunk spectators, eyes glazed over, were not sure what to make of this.

A few years earlier, following a flight to Phoenix, the head for the Dumbo costume proved too big to fit through the jet doors, and the ears broke off.

A parade in Chillecothe, Missouri, was organized by a local

church pastor. The night before, he asked the characters to do a "Meet and Greet" in the lobby of his chapel-turned-mortuary, where a funeral would be held the next morning. So, the characters frolicked with the residents, around an open casket. Goofy, in his rush to catch the plane, had forgotten his suspenders at home. He noticed the straps that held spare caskets together, so he cut off some straps with a buck-knife and wore them as suspenders for the rest of the trip.

During a parade through Fremont, California, several characters noticed a church garage sale, so they jumped off their float, bought a few old books, and rejoined the parade.

Traveling to Portland, Oregon, for a special event, the group's bus passed by a house with a big "Happy Birthday, Terry and Sherry" sign out front. So, Goofy and Minnie thought it would be fun to crash the party. They rang the doorbell, holding a huge tray of leftover donuts, and ended up spending a half-hour there. They left with everyone wondering who booked the Disney characters.

Once the troupe got lost driving through a small town in the Midwest, and stopped to ask directions, in costume, at a local bar. Mickey soon found himself playing pool with a group of burly truck drivers. Goofy ended up dancing with a woman who became intent on taking him home with her.

During day trips, Disney would pay a resident in the area to allow the characters to use their home for a dressing room. Two characters and a driver went to Fresno for a parade, first stopping at the address they were given. They knocked on the door, and an elderly woman answered. "I'm here with Mickey and Minnie," the assistant announced. "Where can they get changed?" The performers changed into their costumes, left their regular clothes behind, and said they'd be back later in the afternoon. When they returned after the two-hour parade, the homeowner and her husband seemed agitated. But, after changing, the characters were so exhausted, they decided to kick back on the living room couch. Then Mickey asked, "Do you have any Cokes?" Finally, the woman blurted out, "Could you leave now, please! We had to wait here for you to come back. We haven't been able to do anything all day." Amazed at how rude their hosts were, the characters returned to the park, only to discover they had gone to the wrong house.

Leaving the protective environment of Disneyland can be dangerous for talking animals. The worst experience was a Watts summer festival in the late 1960s, which featured a Black Panthers-led parade. Mickey Mouse and Donald Duck rode in the Casey Jr. train, with Baloo and King Louie marching alongside. Midway through the parade, a riot broke out, and the crowd turned on the characters. Baloo and King Louie fled, and hid behind a Bank of America until a van could come pick them up. They returned to the train to find it and their costumes in tatters, and Mickey lying unconscious on the train.

Over the years, Disneyland has employed generic characters, such as a spaceman in Tomorrowland, to add atmosphere or, like the gunslingers of Frontierland, to stage little shows. Occasionally, Indians would attack the Disneyland Railroad.

During the mid-1980s, the Haunted Mansion recruited a live Phantom of the Opera to scare guests. Then, they experimented with a character in a suit of armor who stood in the ride's corridor of doors. "I'd pretend to be a statue, and then lash out at guests. Or, their cars would turn and suddenly I'd be there," recalled one Scary Knight. "I'd catch them smoking pot, or one woman with her blouse open. I was always getting complaints for scaring people and I'd tell them I thought that was my job. Once I scared a man with twin infants, they bumped heads and I could hear them screaming through the rest of the ride. One kid was standing up on his seat lashing out a Pirate musket at everything; I took it away from him."

When Fantasyland was remodeled in 1983, an actual Sword in the Stone was constructed in front of King Arthur's Carrousel. The Entertainment Division created a Sword in the Stone ceremony featuring Merlin the magician (with long white beard and mustache; purple gown; tall, pointed sorcerer's hat, and bag of props) and a five-piece band, the Make Believe Brass. During the twelve-minute show, Merlin searches for someone strong enough to pull the sword from the stone. First, he selects a burly "strong man" from the audience, who predictably is unable to budge the blade. Then, Merlin chooses a small child, who miraculously raises the sword and is crowned temporary ruler of the realm.

Our young Hercules has some help: the sword is locked into position by hydraulics. Originally, it was released by flicking a nearby switch in the bushes, but that was painfully obvious. Now a stage manager releases the mechanism with a garage door opener. If you listen closely, you can hear the tone off in the distance. Signals from radios and other devices also can trigger the release, so don't be surprised to see the unpullable sword slowly rise by itself in the middle of the show. Or, occasionally, the strong man succeeds in freeing the sword, forcing Merlin to crown the embarrassed adult and cut the show short.

At first, the same crown was reused at each performance—until it was discovered that one former winner had lice and passed it on to his successors. Now, about three crowns are rotated so they can be cleaned between shows.

Along with the crown, Merlin originally presented winners with a button, replaced today with a nifty medallion. Some parents, lured by such fortune and fame, go out of their way to persuade Merlin to pick their child. They line their kid up in certain spots, beg the actors before or after the show, and, if their child is overlooked, complain to City Hall. One pet peeve among Merlins is pushy parents who line their kids up to be picked, especially annual pass holders whom they recognize as having been chosen several times before.

Inside Merlin's prop bag are two homing pigeons. During the show, Merlin tosses the birds into the air, they fly over the castle, loop back over the audience, then head home. All too often the pigeons, no longer cooped up in the prop bag, litter their flight paths with bird droppings. When they drop their load while circling above the crowd, Merlin will wrap up the show as quickly as possible.

For the hawks nesting in nearby Frontierland, the pigeons' take-off is feeding time. At least once, the pigeons took flight, soared above the castle and, just as they circled back, a hawk speared one, right above the heads of a horrified audience.

As the years passed, the pigeons apparently inbred. Merlin would throw them out and they couldn't find their way back home. Or, they would circle above aimlessly, not knowing where to go, or they might drop to the ground and flop about. One sat on top of the Carrousel and remained there as it continued to spin.

The stone is located behind a large planter, where ducks sometimes climb inside and put on a show of their own. Merlin has had several audiences distracted by a duck noisily gobbling down snails in the planter or a pair of ducks getting wildly intimate.

To avoid boredom, Merlin would compete with his band members, trying to see who could make whom laugh first. Merlin might nonchalantly try to step on a musician's foot or turn quickly and whack one in the back of the head with his tall sorcerer's hat. Once Merlin performed the show without a stitch of clothing underneath his robe.

In the early days of the show, there were no microphones, so the musicians could whisper profanities in Merlin's ear to try to crack him up. Recalled band member Phil Keen: "If we made Merlin laugh, a lot of times he'd break the glue holding his mustache. Remember, it's a twelve-minute show in direct sunlight, and by the end his mustache would be flapping in the wind."

Nowadays, Merlin performs the Sword in the Stone ceremony solo. In 1994, to save money, the park canned the magician's back-up band.

Parades provide an excellent vehicle for showcasing the characters in an exciting format for large audiences. In fact, the very first event after the Opening Day dedication was a spectacular parade starring characters from Disney films and TV shows. Disneyland soon added an annual Christmas parade, long-running Easter Parade, and daily Character Parades.

In the 1970s, the Character Department began requiring that new

---

Guest: (looking for Town Square) "Where is Times Square?"
Cast member: "New York."
Guest: "Is that where the Character Parade starts?"
Cast member: "Yup."

hires be able to dance, quite a challenge when dressed in an awkward, 40-pound suit of fur. After a few characters fell off floats,
the more active performers, such as the Main Street Electrical
Parade's swinging, calliope-playing lion, Prince John, started being
tied to the float.

In 1987, someone thought it would be a good idea to kick off the
summertime parade with Mickey and Minnie on horseback, accompanied by a team of footmen. Although the horses were "parade
friendly," one afternoon they got spooked. Mickey's horse suddenly reared up, scaring Minnie's horse, and both Mickey and Minnie
were thrown to the ground. Mickey's head fell off, revealing the
female cast member underneath. Starting with the next performance, two of the footmen rode the horses and Mickey and Minnie

---

Keep Your Cool

When guests reserve spots to watch parades, ridership
drops on the attractions, freeing ride operators to work crowd
control, a sometimes challenging chore. "You really separate
the wheat from the chaff on a hot summer day at
Disneyland," said Kevin Chaney. "So more people can see
the parade, you ask the front rows to sit down. It was fun to
get a rookie to try and see how many people he could get to
sit down. Usually no one listened to him. Some guys who
were really good could get people seated halfway around the
hub, all the way back to Circle-Vision."

One woman, though, complained that the sidewalk was
too hot to sit on and asked the cast member working crowd
control what he could do about it. The quick-witted host
pulled out his flashlight, held it up to his ear like a phone,
and said, "Climate Control, can you turn up the cooling
(equipment) under the sidewalk on Main Street and turn
down the temperature in the dome?" Then, turning to the
woman, he added, "They're taking care of it now, ma'am."
"Thank you," she answered, thinking she was beginning to
feel a difference.

followed, safely perched on a float.

In 1972, Disneyland introduced its most popular parade, the Main Street Electrical Parade. Tens of thousands of miniature Christmas lights on the floats formed animated shapes and characters. Audiences were captivated by the twinkling lights and catchy, synthesized music.

After three years, the Electrical Parade was retired to make way for the Bicentennial-themed America on Parade. The parade, which ran two summers, starred famous figures from American history as normal-sized people with gigantic oversized heads. The actors peered through the characters' necks, though sometimes the giant heads would tip over and fall off.

Some audiences didn't know quite what to make of these mutant creatures. As a joke, characters would sneak into It's a Small World, and pretend to stomp around the Mexico scene, like giants terrorizing the village.

After a two-year hiatus, the Main Street Electrical Parade returned by popular demand, with even more lights, elaborate animation and dimensional floats, including a Casey Jr. circus train and giant, smoke-breathing Pete's Dragon. Every parade started with the Blue Fairy from *Pinocchio*; the float formed her giant gown with the actress inside sticking out the top at the waist. A former head of the Character Department bragged that he would ride inside the Blue Fairy's costume and fondle her during the parade.

Alice in Wonderland, similarly, poked through the top of a giant mushroom float, with a pair of artificial legs crossed in front of her. As a gag, she once rode the entire parade with a hat pin stuck in one of her phony legs.

In 1982, the Electrical Parade again was replaced, this time with a Flights of Fantasy parade featuring giant inflated balloons to commemorate the remodeled Fantasyland. Once again, the public demanded the return of the Main Street Electrical Parade and it was

---

Guest (noticing the crowds forming behind the parade ropes): "What are these people in line for?"

back in 1985.

By 1993, though, the park's Entertainment Division was convinced that the Electrical Parade's time had passed. Indeed, lacking sophistication and state-of-the-art technology, it did seem an anachronism preserved from a more innocent era. But rather than update the Electrical Parade or temporarily shelve it to allow fans to miss it again, Disneyland decided to kill it. When they announced that 1996 would be its final run, the company was stunned to discover how popular the parade really was. Families flocked to the park to catch one last glimpse. Many returned night after night, boosting the year's attendance over fifteen million, by far the highest ever. Fans reserved viewing spots along the parade route earlier and earlier in the afternoon. The park extended the parade's run all the way into late November.

On its final day, many guests entering the Main Gate at 10:00 a.m. immediately went to reserve their spot. By early afternoon, seven hours before the last parade, there was no place left to stand. And, as the final float pulled backstage to end the final performance, audience members and cast members hugged and wept.

For its replacement, the Entertainment Department combined the latest lighting technology—fiber optics—with what had been successful in other productions: from the recent Lion King Celebration, floats that spent more time stopped than rolling, the movie clip montage from Fantasmic, even the Celtic music and clog dancing of Riverdance, all wrapped into a vague story about making your dreams come true.

Light Magic featured four identical rolling stages, 80 feet long, eleven feet wide and 25 feet high. Halfway through the fourteen-minute show, retractable screens appeared in the middle of the structures to show movie clips. The fiber optic technology was so

---

Guest (noticing employees roping off the parade route): "Is there a parade coming through?"

Cast member: "No. We just painted these ropes yellow and we're hanging them out to dry."

new that when the date arrived for a special premiere for annual pass holders, the parade really wasn't ready. The park started referring to the first show as a "dress rehearsal" instead of a "premiere," in case anything went wrong.

Everything went wrong. One float got stuck on Main Street. The film projections on some of the floats didn't work. At one point, a short snippet of the theme music kept repeating itself, until the soundtrack finally was shut off—to the thunderous applause of a relieved audience.

Technical glitches aside, audiences still didn't like the show. The main Disney characters were relegated to insignificant, supporting roles and assigned to one small area, so most audience members wouldn't get to see their favorites. The stars of the show were 64 pixies with stark masks that made them look like recovering burn victims. When the pixies approached the crowd to interact with children, many kids screamed in terror. The music and dancing were monotonous, the storyline difficult to follow. No one could understand, for example, why the characters were walking around in their pajamas. Many guests were disappointed that it wasn't a parade but a stationary street show. But worst of all, it wasn't the Electrical Parade.

Pass holders were so upset that they swarmed City Hall—by the hundreds—to demand their money back. The park promptly decided, at least for a while, to discontinue special events for annual pass holders.

Cast members also held a grudge against Light Magic because, since time was so short, pass holders got to preview the show before they did.

Over the summer, the park tried to improve the show. They shortened its length. They added narration to better explain the story. The pixies stopped wearing the scary masks.

Parade watcher (explaining why he didn't have to sit down so everyone behind him could see): "Yes, but I am French! But I am French!"

The changes weren't enough. Park regulars, who referred to the show as "Light Tragic" and "Lite Magic," had made up their minds. The show lacked originality, excitement and warmth. As soon as the summer ended, Disneyland pulled the plug on Light Magic, explaining that it would be reworked and return in a few years. No one was sure if that was a promise or a threat.

8

The Disney Police

HALLOWEEN, 1994. Normally, Disneyland doesn't allow visitors to wear costumes. But for a promotional pre-opening party, the park would invite several thousands costumed visitors to enter for free before regular operating hours, then would clear out the park, and readmit the guests after they'd removed their costumes. Yet, radio deejay Rick Dees failed to tell his listeners about the cap on attendance. Tens of thousands showed up—and went wild.

A three-hour-long line of cars outside the park brought traffic on Harbor Boulevard and the Santa Ana Freeway to a halt. Some parents who weren't in costume frantically drew clown faces on themselves and their children with lipstick to get free admission. Teenagers told the ticket takers, "I'm dressed as a gang banger," or "I came as a teenager," and pushed their way through the front gates.

The park was so understaffed, managers began calling everyone who wasn't already at work to come in and help out. It was too late. The guests, many wearing masks and ignoring PA announcements to remove their costumes after 10:00, felt they could get away with anything. They grabbed merchandise off the store shelves and walked right out the door. Shocked, clerks called security, to learn dozens of incidents already had been reported and there weren't enough guards to go around. Clerks were told not to interrupt the looting or even call back unless things turned violent.

Vandals smuggled in spray paint and tagged several areas. Fights, some reportedly gang related, broke out throughout the park. Police arrested visitors by the van full.

One little hellion, dressed in a Mighty Ducks costume complete with Rollerblades, skated around whacking guests in the ankles with his hockey stick. Kids jumped out of their Autopia cars and ran around the course. Visitors cussed out the restaurant workers because the food wasn't free.

As soon as the park filled up, the front gates were closed. Still, dozens of people were arrested for climbing the fences. The guests who did pay to get in stormed City Hall to demand their money back, forming a line that snaked around Town Square and down Main Street.

Even when admission to Disneyland isn't free, an unwholesome element slips in. Shoplifters eye the stacks of expensive merchandise. Pickpockets target the packed purses and wallets. Drug users look for rides to intensify their highs.

It's the job of the park's more than 300 security officers to keep the peace. Disneyland's security force is armed with neither weapons nor police training. Their protection is a security badge and an open-channel radio system, detectable by its telltale earpiece. They're mostly there just to be seen, to deter crime as well as help guests. "We're more for P.R. than anything else," one guard explained. "We were just told to be visible, that 90 percent of our job was to be a walking information post."

To provide an imposing presence, until the early 1970s, all the security guards were male and, due to a minimum six-foot height requirement, large. Most were six-foot-four to six-foot-eight and well over 200 pounds. Their size, plus their blue uniform, earned them the nickname "The Jolly Blue Giants."

The department didn't add its first female officers until 1974. Even then, the move had nothing to do with equal rights. "They wanted us to check the toilets," said five-foot-five, 120-pound Jan Doezie, the third hired, but first to go full-time. "On my first day, potty patrol was my only function. Drinking, drugs, smoking by minors, fights, a lot went on in the women's restrooms, and they had a complete inability to deal with it. Another guest would report something, but before a guard could go in, he had to clear the bathroom, so whatever was going on was over."

Since the park tried to theme the uniforms, female officers weren't allowed to go on Main Street, because there was never a female Keystone Kop, or on Tom Sawyer Island, because there weren't any female marshals. Their first outfits were short-sleeved blue blouses with cute little blue jackets, culottes, nylons and one-inch pumps.

"I had to make some waves," Doezie said. "On graveyard, it was damp and I'd be walking around at 3:00 a.m. in these pumps. I took so many falls. I constantly was in First Aid after getting my head bonked. I finally threatened, 'I'm gonna call OSHA.' They finally let me wear pumps when the park was open, and rubber-soled shoes after hours. Next, they wouldn't let us wear pants. On an open-air scooter, you can't ride side-saddle on an open-air scooter, in the rain, in a dress."

It was especially difficult for female security officers to work graveyard shift, because not only was the rest of the security staff male, but all 400 custodians were male, as well, except for one 60-year-old nurse.

Although their duties slowly expanded, it took time for the ladies to earn their co-workers' respect. The guys constantly teased the girls, sending them on wild goose chases or into Pirates of the Caribbean's pitch-dark backstage, then suddenly turning on the animation. One evening, Doezie spotted smoke funneling from a backstage stable, and her co-workers encouraged her to report the blaze. Actually, the cold night air caused a big pile of manure to smoke. When the fire department arrived, the guys did cover for her, explaining that she had extinguished the fire just in time, seconds before it would have spread and decimated the Pony Farm.

"Being female did have one advantage," Doezie recalled. "Men wouldn't hit us. In those days, if a man tried to break up a fight, he was as likely to get decked as to get listened to. I could walk into the middle of two guys, and say, 'Cool it.' It didn't serve their egos to hit a woman. Girls, on the other hand, had no compunction about hitting me, jumping me, pulling my hair, or clawing me with their nails."

Nowadays, female officers are about as likely as male guards to be attacked. In April 1997, a female guard spotted three large Star Trader shoppers, who were carrying $100 stuffed Mickeys and Minnies, slip sweatshirts into bags. She called for backup and trailed the suspects out of the store. As they exited Tomorrowland, they noticed five uniformed officers approaching. One of the suspects took off down Main Street, another toward Adventureland, and the third toward Fantasyland. The female guard pursued the man into Fantasyland, but, growing tired, he stopped when he reached Dumbo. The officer approached, identifying herself as park security. The burly seventeen-year-old dropped his bag and hit her in the chin with his open palm, shattering a disc in her jaw.

He then resumed his flight toward Toontown, knocking over every tourist in his path. A few toppled guests joined the chase. The call over the security radio went out to give up the chase, but, because the suspect was now endangering guests, the officers had no choice but to continue. Fortunately, a police convention was in town and the park was filled with off-duty patrolmen—some of whose children were knocked over by the fugitive. The cop who finally caught him, near the Small World Toy Shop, decked him.

The culprit was arrested, cited for assault and petty theft, and released, since police at the time were unaware that he was wanted for other probation violations. He was apprehended again later and pled guilty to all charges. The injured guard required several surgeries to replace the discs in her jaw.

Meanwhile, the criminal's two accomplices escaped. "When bad guys flee, they don't care about knocking people down. We have to worry about that," noted the officer who pursued the suspect who ran into Adventureland, but gave up to help apprehend the violent man in Fantasyland.

The challenge for park security is trying to perform a sometimes dirty job as nicely as possible. Other cast members, expected to be ever-smiling, depend upon security to be the hammer. "Out of all the people who visit Disneyland, five percent are gonna be bad apples," said one officer. "Unfortunately, 90 percent of the guests we deal with are bad apples."

The guards' serious response to disturbances often takes trouble-makers by surprise. "I thought you were paid to be nice," a suspect will say. "No, these people are paid to be nice," the guard might respond, pointing to the clerks, restaurant workers or ride opera-tors. "I'm paid *not* to be nice."

Or, while detained in the security office, visitors have asked, "But isn't this the Happiest Place on Earth?" Guards reply, "The Happiness ended at that door."

Bad guys rarely go quietly. More than once, after being escorted to the security office, criminals were angry to discover the guard wasn't armed—because *they* were.

Officers had to strap one guest, wild on PCP, into a wheelchair backstage. The man ripped himself free. Two other guests were so wasted, when police arrived at the park to take them to jail, they tried to bash out the back window of the patrol car with their heads.

During a Grad Nite in the mid-1990s, two officers tried to appre-hend a brawny football high school star who apparently was on acid. When they grabbed him, the guest lifted them both off the ground. "It took sixteen security officers to get him on the ground," recalled one of the sixteen. "He was kicking his legs. We rolled him over. Five of us got hold of him, and twisted him like a pretzel to carry him off backstage. Because of this incident, super-vision was allowed to start using handcuffs."

Drug use is rampant on Grad Nites at the park, despite the park's demand that everyone arrive together on a school bus. "We'd pull 'em off the bus throwing up," a former guard remembered. "It got to the point where the paramedics wouldn't leave. Some try to swim in the river. Acid and Disneyland don't mix."

Guards also search everyone at the gate. Security searched one suspicious-looking guy and found nothing. His girlfriend had a 35mm film canister in her purse, but no camera. It was full of pharmaceuticals. They spent Grad Nite on the bus.

Since Grad Nite is limited to graduating seniors from a particu-lar school who pay their admission, dress appropriately and aren't under the influence, it's the most common time for guests who don't measure up to try to sneak in.

Usually non-paying guests climb over the fence, but they have also tried cutting through or digging under. The fence surrounding

the park has been cut through so much that, according to one officer, "there's not a 100-foot stretch left that's original fence." In
fact, years ago, two kids had tunneled underneath the fence to the
left of the Main Gate, then covered their passageway with leaves,
so they could reuse the route on later nights.

A favorite spot to climb the fence is by the kennels to the right
of the Main Gate. But while the outside of the fence, overgrown
with vegetation, appears to be secluded, on the other side is the
security breakroom.

Disneyland Railroad operators help keep watch. "On the trains,
we were the border patrol of the park," recalled a former conductor.
"The track circled the park, up on the berm, so we could spot fence
jumpers in backstage areas. Plus, they would have to cross the
tracks. We'd see them maybe in the meadow, get on the radio and
call security."

Officers also walk the perimeter accompanied by guard dogs,
while keeping in radio contact with their foreman, "Pluto One."
Security has a team of about ten guard dogs, including bomb-sniff-
ing dogs and one bite dog for riot situations. Despite its vicious
barking (usually after spotting a wild cat), a patrol dog that jumps
an intruder will probably just lick him.

For years, the security dogs were housed in an old wooden lean-
to, but in 1996, they got a fancy new kennel by the Pony Farm.
The guards are jealous. If the weather is too hot or too cold, the
dogs stay in, but the officers still have to go out.

The canines, mostly German shepherds, were originally military
dogs imported from Germany. Now most are fully trained police
dogs. Security tried using Doberman pinschers, but found "they
were chewing too many people."

The dogs are used less frequently now that the fence gradually
has been equipped with silent alarms. The devices feature motion
triggers that cycle as long as the fence is shaken, so guards can tell
if the person is still climbing.

Usually, security officers feel safe. "In the park, I never felt
threatened because it was enclosed, there was nowhere to run,"
recalled one guard. "There's a code (999) and when you hear that

code every security guard in the place responds. Your best protection is each other."

It's a different story in the parking lot. Officers have come across people with guns and knives, who may try to steal, break into or vandalize cars, and constantly find people drinking or doing drugs. Security discovered one man, tripped out, naked and locked in his car, trying to tear himself apart with any glass or sharp objects he could find.

In part, the parking lot is more dangerous because there are fewer barriers separating it from the real world. One morning in the summer of 1995, a drunk driver crashed into another car on nearby Harbor Boulevard. He grabbed his dog and fled on foot into the Disneyland parking lot. He dropped his pet off at the kennel, but was so hysterical, attendants called security. Thinking he was a mental patient, they asked police to take him home instead of arresting him. Late that night, the man returned to the park in a Suburban. He drove up to the main entrance, around the ticket booths by the kennel, and up against the Main Gate. Both the Main Street Electrical Parade and Fantasmic had just let out, so if he would have been able to barrel through the gates, he might have plowed over countless guests down Main Street. The man just wanted his dog back.

After the incident, the park considered erecting concrete dividers to make sure someone else didn't drive through the front gate. They didn't and two years later, another man trying to evade the police drove his car up by the ticket booths. Fortunately, police, guns drawn, pulled him out of his car before he got to the fences.

Occasionally, officers in the parking lot discover pets or children that people have left locked in their cars. One afternoon, security noticed a dog, seemingly dead, inside a locked car. The animal had overheated and stopped breathing. The guard broke into the car and revived the dog with mouth-to-mouth resuscitation.

Some guests are too cheap to board their pets or apparently don't trust them to the Disneyland kennels. A visitor from New York, outraged to learn that he couldn't bring his dog into the park, demanded that Disney refund not just his tickets, but his hotel fare, airfare, and all other vacation expenses. Security spent more than three hours trying to calm the man, before finally persuading him to leave his beloved pet at the kennels.

At least twice, women who couldn't stand to be apart from their dogs hid their pet in their purse. The first dog jumped out of the woman's handbag while she was waiting to board the old Flying Saucers attraction, and operators spent the next few, frantic minutes chasing her pet all over Tomorrowland. In the other instance, security spotted the lady feeding her smuggled Chihuahua at one of the restaurants.

Usually, guests are warned of restrictions at the Main Gate. Although dress and hair restrictions have loosened, guests aren't allowed in wearing masks, costumes, spiked jewelry such as dog collars, handcuffs, multiple chains (that can be used as a weapon), pants torn near the crotch, string bikinis or anything deemed offensive. Visitors wearing T-shirts with graphic sayings or illustrations may be asked to cover them up or wear them inside out. Kids cannot bring in toy guns, not even squirt guns, even though some of the shops inside sell toy rifles.

Still, inside the park you're liable to see everyone from crossdressers to the Voodoo Lady, a black woman with her face powdered white, a white wig, bright red lipstick and corkscrew fingernails several inches long.

With some guests, security is alerted whenever they enter the park. One man has covered his body with over 500 tattoos of Disney cartoon characters, including all 101 Dalmatians on his back. Guards follow him around to make sure he keeps his shirt on, because he likes to show off his personal art gallery.

Officers also keep an eye on another frequent visitor who has been known to fondle the horses on Main Street.

To prevent known troublemakers from getting annual passes, a list of banned guests was posted at the Bank of Main Street, where annual passes were processed.

One once-regular visitor had a fondness for the Tea Cups. The tall, thin young man would spend his entire day on the ride, spinning as fast as he could, a dozen trips in a row, two dozen trips, or more.

A creature of *Rain Man*-like repetition, as a teenager he would ride his skateboard up and down the street in front of his Anaheim home, the same route, back and forth, over and over again. Then

Wheelchair Scams

Since it can be difficult to maneuver a wheelchair through a queue, wheelchair-bound guests and their party are usually "backdoored," or allowed to move to the front of the line without waiting (taken up the exit and put on without waiting). Unfortunately, non-disabled guests have caught on, renting wheelchairs to get short-cuts onto attractions.

"A lot of people rent wheelchairs who don't belong in wheelchairs," said one cast member. "We'll have kids who limp from their wheelchair to an attraction, and then later see them running around with someone else in the wheelchair."

Attendants at the rental station tried to screen customers and had to see the person the wheelchair was for, but it doesn't always work.

One morning during Star Tours' first summer, all of the wheelchairs had been rented by 10:00 a.m. At Star Tours, the park had been opened only an hour and already there was a two-and-a-half hour wait. The area supervisor tracked down the lead and asked why the line had come to a complete stop. "We're running at full capacity," the lead explained, "but wheelchairs are killing me."

The supervisor asked how many wheelchairs. The lead answered, "52." The lead suspected that the long line of wheelchair-bound guests were not all handicapped. The supervisor was so angry, he walked down the line, pointed at each guest, and growled, "What's wrong with you?" Most of them crumbled. He reclaimed over 20 wheelchairs on the spot. Soon after, the policy changed so that if there were more than two in your party, you had to wait near load until your party had waited in line.

he discovered the Tea Cups, and a new obsession was born. A few months later, long-time Disneyland employee Diane Judd was visiting her mother, who lives on the same block as the spinner. Unaware of his new hobby, Judd's mother said that she no longer saw the curious young skateboarder and wondered if his parents had him institutionalized. "No, mom," her daughter explained. "They got him an annual pass. It's much cheaper."

Nicknamed "Spin Man," he rode only the light yellow Tea Cup; while not as fancy as the others, supposedly it spins the fastest. Sadly, his annual pass was revoked after he hit another guest for "stealing" his yellow cup.

One Disneyland-loving blacklistee did get a second chance. A disabled girl who could be very demanding of the cast members, she became a terror after trading in her manual wheelchair for a high-speed, electric model. She would tear at full speed through the park, running over guests' toes, yelling at pedestrians to get out of her way, and plowing through slow-moving crowds. The joke among employees was that they'd like to wax the deck of the Mark Twain before her next trip.

"When she went on a ride, we'd ride her hopped-up wheelchair," admitted one ride operator. "We'd pop wheelies and she'd get mad at us for leaving her battery on."

The girl was especially fond of 1995's "40 Years of Adventure" stage show at the Tomorrowland Terrace and attended almost every performance. At the end of the show, the costumed characters would exit offstage and children would always head after them. The disabled guest, though, took it upon herself to protect Mickey and his pals, and would push the children back or pull them back as they tried to climb up the steps to the stage. Management finally banned her from the park, but, after a lot of negative publicity, gave her back her pass. Reportedly, her behavior has improved dramatically ever since.

The park was less tolerant of another group of pass holders, nicknamed "the Prairie family" by cast members because the woman and her three daughters wore calico outfits resembling those on *Little House on the Prairie*. The small son was dressed in homemade, miniature cast member costumes: Indiana Jones, Big Thunder and Splash Mountain ride operator uniforms, a blue and yellow Fantasmic crowd control costume, and custodial whites.

The five, joined by the father when he wasn't working, visited Disneyland several times every week. They got friendly with dozens of cast members, maybe a little too friendly. In 1993, the parents believed that God had instructed their oldest daughter, age eighteen, to marry a certain 21-year-old Jungle Cruise skipper. The skipper was unconvinced.

Still, the family hung around his attraction and videotaped him at work. The daughter wrote him at least seven "disturbing" letters and found out where he lived. Concerned that the operator was being stalked, security told the family to stay away from him, threatened to revoke their annual passes and began following the family around whenever they visited the park. The operator transferred to Big Thunder Mountain, but the family found him. At least once, security escorted the family out of the park, but the stalking continued.

In January of 1994, the park, out of options, revoked the oldest daughter's annual pass and escorted her out of the park. She eventually acquired another annual pass, by using her middle name as her first name, and continued joining her family at the park. The daughter kept after the Big Thunder host and, in fact, her twelve-year-old sister began pursuing an eighteen-year-old who also worked the ride.

On April 19, 1995, five security guards and an Anaheim policeman confronted the family on a path near Big Thunder Mountain. When one officer identified himself as park security, the oldest daughter struck him. She and her sister then tried to push the other officers away, shouting and swinging their arms and fists about uncontrollably, even after being led offstage and into the security office. Disneyland pressed charges. The oldest daughter was convicted of criminal assault and battery, and her sister pled no contest to similar charges.

In retaliation, the family filed suit against the park and the five officers, claiming the guards attacked the whole family, even the five-year-old boy in the stroller, then held them against their will for three hours, during which officers ran their hands under the three girls' dresses. What compensation did they demand for these heinous crimes? They wanted their annual passes back.

After going through four lawyers, the family decided to represent themselves in court. To testify on their behalf, they submitted a list of 181 potential witnesses, including dozens of cast members identified by first name only, Peter Pan, Pluto, Mary Poppins, Chip,

Dale and the Adventureland Steel Drum Band.   After nearly two years, the family dropped its suit, in exchange for Disney agreeing to pay its own legal costs and not prosecute.

 While the uniformed officers hope to deter crime by being seen, Disneyland also has six different types of undercover security guards:

(1) Eagles, although infrequently used, are plainclothes officers who work the parking lot, looking for car thieves, drug users and other mischief makers. Before the parking lot was relocated to make room for a new Disney's California Adventure theme park,

SECURITY could keep an eye on Disneyland's old parking lot from this covert lookout booth on the roof of the adjacent Disneyland Pacific Hotel. (1999) *Photo by David Koenig.*

officers also could play spies from a lookout station on top of the Indiana Jones show building. Usually, though, the station was occupied by only a mannequin. The real officers manned a less visible station on top of the roof of the Disneyland Pacific Hotel. There, they used high-powered and night vision binoculars, a military scope, and a video camera with constant record.

Not only was the station less conspicuous, but the top of the hotel provided a closer view of the most remote end of the lot, presumably the likeliest location for a crime. In fact, one of the park's few armed robberies took place in 1995 right below the station, in the lot's King Louie section. A 52-year-old woman, her daughter and her daughter's three children were robbed at gun point of about $1,650 in cash as they returned to their car. The robber fled on foot and was never apprehended.

The victim, who as a child had been a second-string Mouseketeer, promptly filed suit against the park for providing inadequate security. For good measure, she also claimed that the children were traumatized when they were brought backstage and saw several costumed characters removing their heads.

A judge eventually dismissed the suit, partly because he found "no evidence to suggest that the incident could have been prevented." No one, it seems, had thought to mention the lookout station.

"The lookout on top of the hotel had left on a bathroom break, and that's when the robbery occurred, directly below him," said that day's relief watchman. "If you go on a break, you're supposed to have someone cover for you, but he didn't. So the woman lost the case, because no one asked to see the security logs. And, of course, Disney didn't volunteer information."

(2) Falcons, also rarely used, are positioned at the Main Gate to watch for guests trying to jump an unmanned turnstile or transfer their handstamps for re-entry onto the back of a friend's hand. One falcon would sit in a wheelchair with a blanket over his legs. Sooner or later, someone would hop the turnstiles and the officer would jump out of the wheelchair and grab them. Although guests are devising more ingenious ways to transfer the stamps, some are still caught for having the fluorescent mark backwards (when transferred directly from hand to hand) or on the wrong hand (gate personnel only stamp left hands). As a safeguard, when guests re-

enter the park, attendants now demand to see their ticket as well as their handstamp.

Occasionally, during special promotions, officers have to watch the gate to make sure guests aren't trying to cheat. During a give-away in 1985 for the park's 250 millionth guest, the park installed a giant counter inside the gate, and guests brought walkie-talkies inside the park to watch the sign and tell their friends outside when to come in.

That same year, for the park's 30th anniversary, every 30th guest won a prize, ranging from inexpensive souvenirs to a new car. One guest, though, said that by studying the giant counter and when the prizes were awarded, he could predict when the cars would be awarded. Security caught on to his scheme and kicked him out of the park one day while he was standing near the Main Entrance. He filed suit for $50 million, claiming the contest was not totally random.

For other giveaways, though, no amount of conniving would have helped. "The 300 millionth guest contest was a fix," claimed former security guard Pat Robertson. "When it got close, I saw supervisors pointing out people in line: 'Him? Her? No, no, not yet.' They chose a French girl, because at the time they were pro-moting Euro Disney. She was hand-picked."

A year later, to celebrate its 35th anniversary, the park gave away a large number of prizes, including an automobile a day. As they entered the park, guests were handed a special ticket that allowed them to pull a switch on a giant Dream Machine contrap-tion in the hub. Supposedly, if their ticket was the lucky winner of the car, the machine would make a lot of noise and music, lights would flash, confetti would shoot into the air, the new Geo would rise on a platform out of the machine, and Mickey Mouse and a photographer magically would appear, car key in hand. "But," said one sweeper, "no specific ticket won the car. They always waited until afternoon and arranged to have Mickey and the sweepers ready, because there was a lot of confetti to clean up. You could hear the machine's motor starting before anyone even walked up. Sometimes, we'd be all ready, but no guests walked up. We'd encourage people, but they'd say, 'No, I never win anything.'"

(3) Ravens blend in during private parties, such as special

Enchanted Evenings when the park serves alcohol. Guards, who act either like a guest or part of the media, watch for guests who drink too much or give minors alcohol, celebrity chasers or employees who crash private parties. The best part about being a raven is you get to eat for free.

(4) Pigeons, also known as shoppers, act like guests to make sure employees who handle money don't pocket any of it. Pigeons are not regular security guards, but temporary outside hires to make sure other employees—even security—don't recognize them.

(5) Hawks, used quite often, don't approach guests; their job is to observe and report. They especially watch for taggers, then call for other officers to detain them. If they think someone might vandalize, say, Space Mountain, they'll try to get on the same sled as them. Once, a pair of hawks followed two suspicious girls onto a Matterhorn bobsled, and during the ride, thought they were struggling to get markers out of each other's pockets. Actually, they were fondling each other.

(6) Foxes are, by far, the most common plainclothes officers. They spy on guests to catch counterfeiters, forgers, pickpockets, pedophiles and especially shoplifters. Unlike hawks, if they see something suspicious, they'll act.

Most foxes pretend that they're shopping. They frequently work the shops that attractions empty into (such as the Star Trader at the end of Star Tours), where there's the highest impulse to steal.

"For the summer, full-timers get a $300 allowance for plain clothes," one guard revealed. "You are encouraged to get nondescript clothes. Hats are encouraged, so you can pull them down over your eyes. Sunglasses are encouraged. No tank tops, no sandals. They want you to get clothes that blend in. A white shirt blends in; a pink shirt stands out."

The most effective foxes appear inconspicuous, unthreatening. One looks like a little old grandmother—with running shoes. Another productive fox, a short, pock-faced Mexican, dresses like a gangbanger, including a ponytail sewn in his hat. Once, at Tomorrowland's Premiere Shop, he was signaled by a boy, who said, "Hey, check this out," then slipped a souvenir into his jacket. After the kid left the store, the guard answered, "Hey, kid, check this out," and revealed his security badge.

Usually shoplifters offer one of the common excuses:

"Well, I thought I could pay at the exit."

"My hands were full, so I put it in the bag."

"I bought it yesterday."

"I threw the receipt away."

In court, one mother admitted that she placed an item on top of her stroller and left the Tomorrowland shop with it, but had intended to pay for it. "But our toddler was distracted by some characters and ran out of the shop, so we followed him," she testified in court. The prosecutor asked which characters, and mom replied, "We saw Snow White and the Seven Dwarfs." Later, a cast member testified that not only do Snow White and the Seven Dwarfs never, ever go in Tomorrowland, but on that particular day at that particular time, they were in the back with their heads off on a 30-minute break.

Guards escorted another suspect to the security office for stealing merchandise from the old One of a Kind Shop in New Orleans Square. The man, who walked with one leg absolutely straight, maintained his innocence, until the officers discovered he also had hidden an antique sword down one pant leg.

When confronted, suspects occasionally flee. One female fox caught a guest stealing leather jackets from the Premiere Shop. When she confronted him outside, he took off, out of Tomorrowland, around the castle, across the hub, and down Main Street. Two guards tackled him in front of the bakery, but when they got a closer look at him, they realized that he didn't match the initial description that went out over the radio. Figuring they had the wrong guy, the guards picked him up and apologized. The suspect ducked into the bakery and out a side door before they realized their mistake. The suspect quickly made it to the Jungle Cruise, which was drained for rehab. Several officers jumped into the dry lagoon, while others set up a perimeter around the attraction. A guard finally recognized the Asian culprit hiding in the grass hut village scene—he had taken off his shirt to blend in with the natives. He again fled and was finally apprehended after tripping over some steps near the Emporium.

Another evening, a large shoplifter pushed a female undercover officer down before fleeing into the crowds watching the Main Street Electrical Parade. Her partner gave chase, following the wave of cursing guests and flying strollers. The guard caught up at last near the Motor Boats. The suspect, evidently on drugs, lashed back with his fists. A second guard arrived, jumped on the man and tried to pin him. But the suspect fought his way back to his feet, threw the first guard against a railing and bit his arm. By now, no one was watching the parade; everyone was videotaping the wrestling match on the sidelines. The suspect finally was contained, with the help of a six-foot-five-inch parade watcher and several more guards.

To ensure a legal bust, foxes must follow five steps:

1. See the suspect without the item.
2. See them pick it up.
3. See them conceal it or make no attempt to pay for it.
4. Allow them to exit the shop.
5. Allow them to get a reasonable distance away (about 50 feet).

Original policy had been that if shoplifters were cooperative, they were expelled from the park. If not, they were arrested, to prevent suspects from claiming that they had been detained for no reason.

But in 1992, the security department learned about a state law, passed in the mid-1980s under Penal Code section 190.5(c), that allowed businesses to seek up to $500 from a shoplifter to cover their expenses from handling the case. To help recover the fines, the law permitted companies to file a suit for damages in small claims court. Typically, businesses mail shoplifters a letter asking them to pay the civil damage to avoid a small claims filing.

Disneyland security speeded up the process. They began asking suspects for $275 to $500 while they were still in the security office. Surprisingly, most of them paid it. After an Anaheim police officer issued suspects a citation ordering them to appear in court, the security guard gave them a form explaining that the park would seek civil damages. Many paid on the spot, unaware that they also would have to make restitution to the court, unless acquitted.

"At first, it was limited to people we arrested," one guard said. "You arrest one guy, you've paid your salary for a day. You arrest two, you're ahead. In one day, I could pay my salary for a month."

Soon, the demands were expanded, he added. "If we caught you shoplifting a $2.75 item, we would ask for $275, for my time, for the investigator's time, whether we arrested you or not. Legally, we probably had to sue them to get money, but we said, 'You just cut us a check, we'll let you out.'"

Suddenly, a department designed to serve and protect had become a profit center. The money rolled in. The department added extra officers and bought new vehicles and other equipment.

To make paying the civil demand easier, security began offering payment plans and accepting credit cards. Guards would escort suspects to an ATM or to cash control to break hundred dollar bills. If the guards demanded $275 and the suspect only had $200, they might respond, "Well, okay, we'll take it."

In suspects' eyes, the civil demand was validated by the presence of uniformed Anaheim police officers, who always were walking by, even using the security office breakroom.

Some policemen, though, felt uncomfortable and in 1995 the Anaheim police department asked the park not to ask for the civil damages in front of officers. Still, arrests became so frequent that uniformed policemen were always around.

Foreigners, in particular, were intimidated, and would eagerly write a check. Three Italian tourists, who spoke little English, were arrested for shoplifting beach towels and keychains. Security gave them the impression that to go free, they had to pay $500 apiece. Three hours and $1,500 later, they were gone. "They never told me I could pay it later," one said. "Never."

Two visitors from South America had $1,000 for a whole week's vacation. An officer protested kicking them out of the park penniless, but his supervisor replied, "They should have thought of that before they shoplifted."

Although foxes were never required to meet specific quotas for the number of arrests per day, the message became clear: "If you can't do the job, we'll get someone who can." Several officers were removed from fox duty for not getting enough arrests.

As a precaution, security eventually decided to demand money only from suspects who were arrested. So, a new policy was introduced: arrest everyone. The usual twelve foxes on duty had police writing 80 reports a day. Aggressive individuals could catch up to 20 suspects a day. Occasionally, the department would run "fox sweeps," packing the shops with undercover officers, according to

BLACK AND WHITE. Although usually kept backstage and out of sight to the general public, police began upping their visits to the Magic Kingdom in the mid-1990s to handle the increasing number of arrests for shoplifting. (1995) *Photo by David Koenig.*

one guard. "On a Saturday, with 27 foxes between two shifts, the security office looked like *Hill Street Blues*, with the all the people and chaos."

With only a single Anaheim policeman to process suspects, many were detained for hours. The stark waiting room featured a door, tile floor, and some plastic chairs. Surly suspects sometimes were handcuffed to a looped metal bolt in the floor. To handle the overflow, police held some prisoners in an old downstairs office, nicknamed "the dungeon." Although officers say they never separated young children from both parents, detained mothers were forever crying out for their children, convinced the kids would not survive without them. Other common cries were "I'm having a heart attack!" or "I'm having my baby!"

As the practice became more common and the officers more aggressive, more suspects began complaining. Loudly. They finally got the attention of the *Orange County Register*, which in September of 1996, ran a front-page story revealing "Disney Jail Asks for Cash." Former suspects related that guards demanded civil damages from them, even if they were never charged with a crime.

Days later, one suspect filed suit, accusing park security of false arrest and imprisonment. In all, six similar lawsuits were filed over the next two months. Many plaintiffs said they were detained for up to four hours in a small room, with no access to a bathroom, telephone or water. Several claimed that their children were forcibly separated from them, or that the juveniles were interrogated or threatened without the parents' knowledge. Eleven people in five of the cases alleged that they were shoved, struck, dragged or otherwise assaulted.

National media quickly jumped on the story. A reporter, cameraman and soundman for the TV news magazine *Hard Copy* tried to enter the park, hoping to stumble upon the "Disney jail" and film the brutish officers in action, maybe even provoking one to take a swing at them. The camera crew wasn't allowed in the park; they had to settle for filming from the top of a nearby structure and from the parking lot of a McDonald's across the street. Still, they spent several days assembling a story on "the Disney police force," only to have the story killed at the last minute, under pressure from the Disney Company. A few days later, *Hard Copy* competitor *Extra* ran the story.

Next, the U.S. Department of Justice launched a civil rights investigation of the policy. Disturbed by the mounting bad publicity, the park consulted lawyer and former cast member Janice Doezie. When the law first passed, Doezie, then the park's court liaison, had brought it to the attention of Ike Isaacson, then head of security. "Gosh," she said, "this looks like a great way to help cover some of our expenses."

Isaacson responded, "You know, we're not in the collections business. We're here to protect and serve. It muddies the water.

Imagine some foreigner who gets the impression that in the United States, if you break the law and get caught, you pay off someone $300. That's not a message I want to send out."

Disneyland took Doezie's advice. About two weeks after the story broke, after four lucrative years, guards were told not to collect civil damages from shoplifters immediately after detaining them. Once convicted, thieves would be mailed a bill.

Management didn't stop there. They remodeled the once-stark security office, adding fancy carpeting and repainting the walls in gentle, non-threatening colors recommended by a psychologist. They removed the looped bolt in the floor. In the waiting rooms, they put sofas, telephones and a television playing Disney videos.

Whereas before someone caught stealing even a $1 item would be arrested, now only people stealing more than $20 worth of merchandise were arrested. "Pretty soon," added one officer, "they said don't even work keychains, just keep an eye on bigger ticket items. Policy changed so you couldn't approach anyone by yourself—you had to call for backup, for fear *Hard Copy* would videotape you. Then it was don't chase suspects."

Management became hyper-sensitive that its security hosts didn't look aggressive. A guard pursued one criminal—and received a three-day suspension. "We found it's better to stay in the breakroom and get written up, than to go out and get fired for doing your job," he said. "Before it was accepted that (criminals) complained about us. Now, management says we can't get any guest complaints. They don't realize that security is designed to get guest complaints."

For fear of being reprimanded, some decided not to intervene after witnessing crime from underage drinking or smoking to people taking drugs in the parking lot and then entering the park.

In time, shoplifters were set free if they stole under $100 worth of merchandise or were visiting from another country. Shoplifting arrests, which in 1996 totalled 704, dropped in 1998 to 39.

Almost everyone in security with a law enforcement background, including the manager of the department, was forced out. At the same time, efficiency experts were studying the park, department by department, to recommend cutbacks. A passive security force that didn't do much didn't have to be as large.

"They wanted to know why (the Magic Kingdom at) Walt Disney World operates with so few security," one officer remembered. "At Disney World, there *are* fewer, but outside the park is miles and miles of lagoon; our bad guys are across the street."

Although the security force remained about the same size, the number of full-timers was cut in half. Now approximately 80 percent are part-time or seasonal.

Training also was reduced. "Originally training was 40 hours, then the foreman assigned you a senior officer," a guard said. "You hung out with him, and he taught you for a few weeks. They did away with foremen and now they take you around, give you a one-day overview."

Fewer, more passive officers on duty has opened the door to a potentially more dangerous atmosphere at the park. But cutbacks in other departments would have even more chilling consequences.

9

The Business
of Show Business

WALT'S management philosophy was a simple one: convince guests that Disneyland is the Happiest Place on Earth and convince employees that their job is creating that happiness. He would charge a fair price, so guests would be happy about how they spent their money, and provide the highest quality entertainment, so guests would not only return, but tell their friends.

He was always looking at how he could give the guests more. He continued to add new attractions and improve existing ones. "I remember talking to Walt in the break area of the Jungle Cruise," said long-ago skipper Gary Fravel. "He would sit down in the break area and have a cup of coffee. He was always asking, 'How can we plus the show?' He always wanted to know: 'What do the guests like?'"

Walt was forever walking the park, asking the hourly workers for their opinions and, most of all, listening. If the idea made sense, he said, "We'll go ahead and try it."

Because Walt wanted the guests—not company executives—to be the VIPs, everyone was on a first name basis. Managers today are more isolated from the average cast member, spending their hours backstage in the elaborate new Team Disney Anaheim (TDA) Building. "Walt hated spending money offstage," said

Disneyland University founder Van Arsdale France. "He wanted to spend it on the guests. The only reason he built the old administration building was because they needed a building for the Primeval World diorama."

Walt understood the value of high-capacity attractions; after all, he wanted as many people as possible to enjoy his creations. Yet, he also had patience for smaller, more subtle diversions, realizing that fine detail created a depth and richness that kept people coming back. And if a new attraction wasn't ready exactly how he had visualized it, Walt wouldn't open it to the public.

He cared about the park, and genuinely enjoyed it. "When we opened the Mark Twain for the press, we were going around the river, and Walt kept blowing the whistle like a kid," remembered John Catone. "We finally had to tell him, 'Walt, we're gonna run out of steam.' And we did. We were dead in the water until we could get more steam."

A few years later, Catone added, "Walt wanted to take the first trip on the Monorail. To get him off, we had to shut off the power. The same with the fire truck on Main Street. He was a big kid. He was human, a person, not some executive from Burbank."

His enthusiasm and concern were contagious. Employees were dedicated to Walt's vision and made to feel as if they were part of a family.

Managing the park on a daily basis, though, has never been a democratic process. Promotions were based as much on ability as on who you knew and continued that way for years. To serve as Disneyland's first vice president and general manager, Walt appointed C.V. Wood, a Texas businessman who had helped identify Anaheim as the best site for the park. As his assistants, Wood recruited many of his buddies from Texas, including Charlie Thompson, Howard Vineyard and Doc Lamond heading Operations, Fred Schumacher in charge of general services, and Earl Shelton overseeing master scheduling and later maintenance.

As the years went on, biased promotions and political hires continued, creating a Good Old Boy network, conspicuously lacking in females or minorities. Still, the leaders believed in Walt's ideals, and unwaveringly enforced his disciplines of show, despite changes in public opinion.

After Walt passed away, the company lacked someone with not only the vision to dream up profitable new ventures, but also the clout to defer the bankers. Financial pressure intensified after the 1971 opening of Walt Disney World in Florida drained the company's cash reserves and, two months later, the largest champion for Walt's ideals, his brother Roy, died.

To cut costs at Disneyland, supervision was streamlined into the "area concept." Instead of separate supervisors for Operations, Merchandising and Foods, a smaller number of supervisors would oversee all facilities within an area.

Naturally, politics played a part in who lost their job. "Disneyland was a workplace where politics and the caste system were always in evidence. Operations first and Food division last, and it came back to haunt us all in the winter of 1974," said former Foods supervisor Barry Grupp. "(Two Operations executives) masqueraded during the summer of 1973 as training coordinators. They worked all the food operations in the park during that time period, asked a lot of questions of employees and supervisors, and armed with a plan of attack, developed the area concept which devastated most of the Food division supervision. On successive Fridays in January, entire groups of supervisors were herded over to the Food Division office above Mr. Lincoln and told to clear out their offices. Nearly every Food Division supervisor was fired. I was told I wouldn't be adaptable to Disney's new streamlined management. I held a B.A. in business management with a minor in marketing, had excellent reviews over the years, and for all I gave Disneyland, I found myself on the outside looking in."

Still, for most, Disneyland remained a great place to work. As the years wore on, however, the family feeling that kept workers from moving on to careers in the outside world began working against the company. Many old-timers got real jobs, but stayed on at the park part-time to keep the benefits. Medical coverage isn't as important for a college student. But as employees grew older and started raising families, benefits became more important to them, and more costly to the company.

To instill a sense of distance between the leads and the employees, management began insisting that leads stay out of the rotation. "I used to get myself in trouble when I worked the ride," said lead Dick Mobley. "But I figured, if I'm in there giving breaks, my kids' attitudes are going to be better. The kids could watch me and see how I wanted it done."

In 1984, Wall Street increasingly was pressuring Disney's corporate leadership to make more money from its underutilized assets. Park management responded by threatening to cut employees' benefits and pay. About 2,000 workers, most of whom loved Disneyland, went on strike. "The strike is when Disneyland stopped being Disneyland," lamented 40-year veteran Bob Gentleman. "It's like two different Disneylands: the one from July 1955 to October 1984, and everything after. The park lost its charm. The attitude of employees changed. Guys who had worked together for 20 years haven't talked to each other since. We lost our innocence."

Some workers were saddened, others bitter that management would let the park family be torn in two. The strikers returned to their posts after 22 days, selling out future employees by agreeing to slower pay rate increases and loss of benefits for future hires. That deal, though, suddenly provided management with a huge financial incentive to replace experienced old-timers with disposable part-timers.

Days before the strike, Disney elected Michael Eisner as its new chairman, a move designed to deter corporate raiders from breaking up the company and selling it piece by piece. Ideally, Eisner would maximize shareholder value by rejuvenating stagnating divisions and adding complementary businesses and products.

Since Eisner's background was in the movie business and Disney's studio was in the worst straits, it received the heaviest attention. Day-to-day operation of the more reliable theme parks was left comparatively alone.

Pressure did increase, though, to increase profits. Eisner expected each Disney division to contribute to company-wide annual growth of 20 percent. For years it worked, as the company as a whole flourished. But steep, prolonged growth can be difficult for a 40-year-old business of fixed size, such as an amusement park. The studio can always produce more movies or the retail division open more Disney Stores, but there's only one Disneyland, already open 365 days a year.

Still, the park's focus continued shifting from show quality to the bottom line. In 1991, Eisner appointed Judson Green, an accountant, as president of Walt Disney Attractions. His predecessor, old-schooler Dick Nunis, who began at Disneyland as an hourly in 1955, was pushed out of day-to-day oversight of the theme parks, into a public relations job as division chairman.

The pressure on Disneyland heightened in the mid-1990s when the movie division started to falter. Corporate realized that the movie-going public is more fickle and unpredictable than the theme park-going crowd, which has fewer choices. A family traveling halfway across the country to visit Disneyland can't turn around and go home if the admission price is too high. And, once they're inside, they have to eat—again, at Disney prices. Corporate figured that the sure-thing theme park division could make up for the shortcomings of other divisions, it just had to be sold better.

So Eisner looked for a salesman. In late 1994, he appointed Paul Pressler, who had no theme park experience; he had been in charge of the fast-growing Disney Stores division. His goal became turning Disneyland into a Disney Store.

For many guests, Disneyland's shops were themselves attractions, providing unique merchandise they couldn't find elsewhere. During the holidays, people made special trips to the park just to do Christmas shopping.

But the new management noticed that while Disneyland carried a vast number of items, only a small number, mostly T-shirts and stuffed animals, accounted for a majority of the sales. Management assumed it would be more cost effective to carry fewer different items, especially park-specific items, but carry the bestsellers in mass quantities. Disney generic items could be produced in greater quantities at lower per unit costs and presumably would have wider appeal. After all, executives reasoned, you can sell Disneyland merchandise only at Disneyland, but Pocahontas merchandise could be sold at all six Disney parks and several hundred Disney Stores. Ideally, every shop in Disneyland would become a mini-Disney Store.

Gone were atmospheric shops, such as the One of a Kind Shop in New Orleans Square. In the Emporium, down came walls that lent a quaintness and allowed guests to wander, never sure of what they might happen upon next. Knocking down walls improved sight lines, increased selling space and accommodated more people—and made the Emporium look like a less homey department store.

Now, many guests visit fewer shops, since after a handful they realize that most sell basically the same merchandise. During the Christmas holidays, the park tried keeping the remerchandised Main Street shops open free after park hours, but the experiment fizzled—most people realized that everything at the Emporium was also at their local mall.

"Pardon the pun," noted a Disneyland shop clerk, "but we've got the apparel market sewn up. What we're forgetting is the souvenir market, for people who want to take home a piece of the park."

At the same time, merchandising turned aggressive. "Before, all the training stressed that it was a soft sell, that the merchandise sells itself," recalled hostess Deena Ippolito. "As soon as Pressler came over, it switched to hard sell. We had guidelines to romance the merchandise, to suggestively sell. If someone bought boxer shorts, we were to suggest the matching tie. I started to feel like a car salesman."

Clerks were urged to encourage children to play with toys, hoping the kids would beg their parents to buy it. Earlier, to better serve customers, hostesses would open another cash register if checkout lines got too long. Now, a hostess walking the sales floor talking up the merchandise might be yelled at for going to help out at the registers.

Meanwhile, management continued hiking food and admission prices, then, to ensure high guest counts in the off-season, began offering discounted admissions to Southern Californians. Also to lure in the locals, they began marketing affordable annual passes; the ranks of annual pass holders swelled to over 200,000.

Unwittingly, guests supported all the price hikes in their responses to visitor surveys. Management now floods the park with survey takers who stop guests to get their opinions about Disneyland: "What did you come to see? How did you feel about the prices? How would you rate your day as a whole?" Guests think that their answers may lead to improvements. Usually, though, the survey takers target single-day visitors and avoid annual pass holders, who as regular visitors would be more knowledgeable to suggest improvements.

Instead, the surveys help the park fine-tune its marketing and justify price increases. Responses reveal that most visitors think the admission and food are overpriced, yet they rate their overall experience as above average. Consequently, Disneyland can keep raising its prices and while guests won't be happy about it, they'll probably pay.

Management realized that they could increase profits not only by increasing sales, but also by cutting costs, particularly labor costs. Disney Stores operated lean and mean, with a salaried manager and a workforce of low-paid, disposable part-timers. But things were different at Disneyland. In Operations, salaried managers oversaw all operations in a land; individual attractions, shops and restaurants were overseen by unionized leads, who were paid a slightly higher hourly wage and could earn even higher overtime pay.

In late 1995, the park eliminated leads and began splitting the Operations division into 77 distinct operating units, with 77 salaried assistant managers to oversee each attraction, shop and restaurant. Subdividing Operations into smaller, measurable components also helped managers to identify any fat. And, increasing supervision on the floor could crank up worker output.

Management tried to sell the change by calling it the "Empowerment Evolution." Without leads, cast members would be encouraged to make more of their own decisions. The company predicted that autonomous employees would be happier and feel a greater sense of ownership, as of their own small business.

At the park, decisions were made faster, especially bad decisions. Because everyone was authorized to make decisions, suddenly busboys and stocking clerks were instituting their own new policies. In maintenance, newly empowered painters arbitrarily started using new colors.

The strategy had its roots in companies such as the autonomous work teams of auto maker Saturn, where increased decision making on the shop floor helped solve problems quicker and get them closer to customers. But Disneyland wasn't an assembly line, and it didn't offer one product; it offered thousands.

Traditionally, the park had operated as one big team. The restructuring splintered Operations into dozens of teams competing against each other for the park's resources. Team members only cared about their own area and stopped lending assistance when other facilities had problems. "They got rid of hourly leads and had a nineteen-year-old kid, salaried, working 60 to 70 hours a week with no overtime," said former supervisor Dan O'Trambo. "Most of the time, he didn't care because he loved the authority, the title. He was intent on making his little area the best area in the park, but it was a strain on Facilities because there were too many assistant managers you had to deal with calling you to do this, do that."

Some leads accepted promotions into assistant manager positions, but many declined, knowing that it would mean less pay per hour and more responsibilities. Many had remained leads for years because the position offered advancement without joining the ranks of suits. Many of the new assistant managers, then, were outside hires, especially from Disney Stores and Taco Bell, following a large layoff by its parent company, PepsiCo.

Direct supervision switched from a veteran who knew everything about an attraction to a newcomer who knew nothing about it. Assistant managers were managing people to perform tasks they couldn't perform. Without understanding how their attractions worked, they couldn't schedule or work their employees properly, and saw their own function as ordering people around. Often, as assistant managers' job knowledge grew, they were transferred. And their replacement would think that the way the last person managed was the way it always had been done; they were there to get someone else to do something. Frequently, assistant managers would tell their frantic, understaffed employees: "I'm not here to help you run this attraction. I'm here to tell you what to do!"

Before, leads might bump into rotations to give employees breaks or lunches. They could coach the workers on how to do things safer or more efficiently. "Now," said former lead Don Brown, "new employees get sixteen hours of training and they're on their own."

He added that previously leads always oversaw the opening and closing of attractions. "Today, a new hire could walk in and be the opener. It happens all the time, because a computer selects who opens the ride and who closes the ride. They will leave the lights on in the show, they'll open without the sound on or with the evacuation doors open. You're given a checklist, but it assumes you have a working knowledge of the attraction. And you're given fifteen minutes to complete what takes someone new an hour."

Costs also escalated. "On Pirates," Brown said, "we could send employees home early because if it got busy, I'd bump into the rotation. These assistant managers would never think about doing that. They use too many work hours because they're afraid to send anybody home."

The need for an experienced lead may never have been greater than on the evening of May 17, 1997. That evening, rookies were operating the keel boats, with no lead. Heading for the dock to pick up what would be their final passengers, they realized that the line had gotten longer. Keel boats accommodated about 32 guests, so an experienced lead likely would have had the keel boat make two trips. Instead, the operators let on all 49, overloading the upper level in particular. "You always had a lead open and a lead close an attraction," said one veteran ride operator. "They were responsible for their attraction. (The keel boat operators) were in a hurry to go home; a lead would not be; he has more at stake."

Since ballast prevented the keel boats from tipping too far sideways, drivers sometimes rocked the boat, to playfully scare the passengers or to illustrate that the boat wasn't on a rail. So as the operators hammed it up, swaying the boat from side to side against some passengers' protests, the top-heavy boat capsized.

Every passenger, including two pregnant women and several young children, was thrown into the river, many trapped inside the half-submerged cabin. One woman recalled the wrenching memory "of her five-year-old daughter being swept from her arms into the murky water." She and other passengers filed suit over the incident. They said that following the accident, only one employee jumped into the water to aid the "panic-stricken passengers." And the victims were forced to sit for 20 minutes, soaked, freezing and in pain.

Since the mid-1980s, the Facilities division was headed by vice president Dale Burner, who believed it was important to maintain the cohesiveness among his division's many trades. Workers agree that he wasn't a whipcracker, but they would do anything for him because they liked him personally. And he believed in Walt's philosophy.

"Even in Facilities, our main goal was to satisfy the guests," explained superintendent Earl Baker. "If an attraction went down, you had just a few minutes to get out there and get it back up. We were all brought in with Walt's theory. Guests pay our wages. We're here to meet their needs. The attractions have to be up, running and safe."

The Facilities division's Quality Standards were unparalleled. Each night, regular maintenance crews checked out their specific attractions with a fine-tooth comb. Larger, complex attractions such as Big Thunder, the Matterhorn and Space Mountain had entire crews that every night inspected each vehicle and every inch of track. Over the years, each part of each attraction was analyzed to determine its life expectancy, so a preventive maintenance crew could replace parts well before they were expected to fail. If an axle was supposed to last five years, they'd replace it in four. As well, a defect crew addressed specific flaws, and apprenticeship programs helped workers fine-tune their skills.

"There was a bit of an overlap, but it's always good to have two sets of eyes look at things," said a former Coaster Team mechanic. "It was a good set up. The group got to know several attractions well."

Projects and rehabs were planned a year in advance, parts pre-ordered and available the instant they were needed. Things ran so smoothly that in 1991, *Preventive Maintenance* magazine recognized Disneyland Facilities as the World's Best Maintenance Organization.

"If they needed one sprinkler head, we'd put in three. We did a little bit more than what it took," says former maintenance manager Jim Haught, who later joined Knott's Berry Farm. "A supervisor at Knott's told me I was too particular. I told him I was from Disneyland, and he said, 'Well, Disneyland's first class, and we're second class.'"

Facilities also was very show conscious. Your work had to be mechanically sound *and* look good. You couldn't even leave fingerprints.

Disneyland's way of doing things was effective, safe and... expensive.

To cut costs in Facilities, the park refused to grant increases in labor or material budgets through the 1990s, despite adding the large Toontown area and high-tech attractions such as Fantasmic and the Indiana Jones Adventure, which are complicated and time consuming to maintain.

As time went on, the department could have used more workers; management decided it needed fewer. Yet to legally terminate workers, businesses are required to have documentation supporting their actions. So, in early 1995, Disney called in efficiency experts McKinsey & Co. Consultants spent eighteen months studying every facet of the park, gathering information on what work each employee did.

"The McKinsey group came into Disneyland to look at its business philosophy," said Baker, who worked closely with the group as a Disneyland Facilities superintendent. "They were actually there for restructuring and downsizing, although they wouldn't use the word downsizing. Their focus was to go around and identify everyone in management, find out what they did, when they did it, and look at market value wages versus Disneyland wages. People close to retirement age were offered an early retirement package, then the layoffs started coming."

The McKinsey group viewed the maintenance division's collection of expert craftsmen and cautious procedures not as strengths but weaknesses. To them, the park was not getting enough out of its staff because the workers were overly specialized and performed redundant duties. The consultants' suggestions would be drastic, and certain to meet resistance from someone like Dale Burner.

In January 1997, Burner was replaced as vice president of Facilities by T. Irby, a retired two-star Army general. A military man, he would carry out the plan, no questions asked. As his second in command, Irby brought in Guy Davis, a long-time military associate.

About a month after his arrival, Irby rallied the troops together in the auditorium of the TDA Building. In an address to about 650 managers and workers, Irby announced that he had been hired to correct the mistakes of prior management. "I'm not here to eliminate jobs," he announced. "I am here to make this place called Disneyland a better place. Do not be afraid of losing your job."

Irby noted that during five assignments in Vietnam, he never once lost one man. And poor performance would be the only reason for him losing one of his men at Disneyland. There would be no layoffs, he said, only restructuring. People would be moved to where they best suited the company's needs. "We're going to discover how we can better utilize the people we have for the millennium," he said.

Irby began testing the workers immediately. He would walk the park and make a punch list of items he thought needed repainting or replacing. He put it out once a week, and wanted it done immediately. Workers had to be pulled off preventive maintenance and rehabs to do the list. Splash Mountain was in the second week of a four-week rehab, and work stopped. When Irby wanted to know why work on Splash Mountain had stopped halfway through a four-week rehab, supervisors explained that the repairmen were out doing his list, because it had an end date. The rehab didn't have an end date.

Then came the bombshell. Years ago, most of the maintenance staff worked after park hours, out of the view of guests and without guests in the way. Gradually, the workforce became more evenly spread among first shift (days), second shift (evenings) and third shift (after midnight). "Especially during the winter, when attendance was low and the park operating hours shorter, we'd just put up a barricade and go to work," one worker explained.

In mid-June 1997, Irby announced that 80 percent of the maintenance crew would be moved to third shift, with only skeleton crews left on first and second shifts. Instead of five eight-hour days a week, everyone would work four ten-hour days. And if they didn't like it, Irby said, they could find another job.

Some workers were livid, others just shocked. Certainly more people were needed on third shift, but 600 people? It didn't seem to make any sense. Roofers were moved to third shift, even though the moisture in the night air wouldn't let the coatings dry. Paint wouldn't dry, either, yet painters went to third shift, and forced to paint in wet conditions and artificial light, which created shadows and changed colors. At night, pink might look like orange. Backstage workers, including the cycling shop, millwork shop, sign shop and decorating department, went to third shift. Landscapers went to third shift.

"When you go to third shift, you gain efficiency in some areas. You gain freedom of movement," admitted construction field superintendent Bob Penfield, who retired a month after the move, as the last Disneylander who worked Opening Day. "But you lose some efficiency, because you're working in darkness, cold, shadows, wetness, and the workers are inherently tired. And it can affect the safety of some jobs."

On its face, the move didn't appear to lower labor costs—workers on graveyard were paid an extra 75 cents an hour. Many, instead, suspected that the real reason for the change was to make veteran workers quit, so they could be replaced by someone for less pay and with no benefits.

"With third shift, the amount of work hours kills you, as well as getting used to the hours on your days off," Penfield added. "If I was on a special project, it's a limited time. I knew I had only a few more hours or days or weeks. But someone who for 20 years has worked days and all of a sudden faces working graveyard for the rest of his career couldn't take it. A lot quit right away."

No doubt about possible downsizing remained the Monday after the graveyard announcement, when one by one eleven top maintenance supervisors were escorted into the TDA Building by security and given a half hour to clean out their desks. Included were some of the most senior, most devoted supervisors, several there since the 1960s and early 1970s. Combined, the eleven had 200 years of experience at Disneyland, experience that in ten to fifteen years would have proven costly to the company in retirement benefits.

They were given vacation pay, sick pay, two weeks' in-lieu-of-notice pay, four weeks' severance pay, and an enhanced severance package (two weeks' pay for each year worked), if they agreed not to sue. They all signed.

They were told that their positions had been eliminated. For

many, only their titles were eliminated. "Mr. T. eliminated everyone's position on one side and then he went over here and restruc-
tured, creating new positions with new titles," said Dan O'Trambo,
one of the eleven. "There were four new directors instead of area
managers, managers in place of superintendents, and assistant managers instead of supervisors."

Management split some of their responsibilities among other
supervisors, hoping to overwhelm them so that they would be
doomed to fail, justifying their dismissal. That day, director
Michael Kitchens informed superintendent Earl Baker that his
three supervisors had been fired. In addition, Baker would have his
wages frozen and be demoted to supervisor, in effect replacing all
three of his supervisors. "I guess it's gonna be you and only you,"
Kitchens said.

Earlier, Baker had been allotted nearly $1 million a year to
maintain the new fleet of parking lot trams, $500,000 in costs and
$470,000 for sixteen workers. Unfortunately, park executives'
bonuses are based, in part, on how far they can come under their
budgets, giving them incentive to not spend money where it is
needed. The trams began arriving in August of 1997, but no new
workers. Baker was told eight, not sixteen people would be hired.
Three weeks later, he discovered that his director had thrown away
the requisitions he submitted for the eight new people. The director asked him to fill out new requisitions, now for only four people.
After three months, the park had ten new trams and 100 new trail-
ers, in all $17 million worth of equipment, still without even oil or
filter changes. Finally, officials said they would hire two people.
"You might as well give me none," Baker responded. "It can't be
done with two." Desperate, he told every service station worker to
stop what they were doing and work on the trams. Soon after, Irby
called Baker to his office and berated him for not meeting expectations, in particular for not maintaining the new trams. Baker
explained about the reassigned workers, then added, "The work is
piling up and one day it will bite you." Irby replied, "I'm not concerned about the other attractions. I'm concerned about those
trams." Four weeks later, tired of being lied to, Baker resigned.

Some of the supervisors, told their positions had been eliminated, knew there were other job openings in the company. Most

were told: "I don't know what you're talking about." After inquiring about well-publicized openings for area managers, O'Trambo was told that since he had only a two-year degree, he wasn't even qualified to be a supervisor. An area manager spot had just gone to an ex-Marine, a brown-noser with no high school diploma who years before had been demoted for poor performance.

In fact, Irby replaced most of the supervisors with retired military people willing to accept lower pay and no health or welfare benefits because they already received it from the government. Typically untrained in the area they oversaw, these new assistant managers served as nothing more than administrators. An assistant manager overseeing the mill, for example, didn't know anything about carpentry, lumber or grading.

A supervisor who didn't understand the park's thirteen different disciplines of crafts would have no idea how to formulate a budget or coordinate his workers. Before, a supervisor would size up a problem and say, "I need a welder, a painter and someone from the staff shop." Now, without knowledgeable supervision, workers had to figure things out by themselves. And most crafts people didn't want to deal with the other trades—they just wanted to do their work.

With less supervision, lazy employees welcomed the opportunity to give less effort. But even once-conscientious workers began slacking off, tired, discouraged, and turned off by being bossed around by an outside hire with no job knowledge or experience. As one carpenter grumbled: "Nine months ago, they hired in all these military people who didn't know anything then and they don't know anything now."

Employees stopped doing the little things that made Disneyland great. "Workers want to see T. Irby fail, and I suspect they are going to do things to make T. Irby fail," one insider reasoned.

Local doctors reported treating an increase of Disneyland maintenance workers for high blood pressure or other ill effects from the transfer to graveyard, and for emotional effects from the disruptions to their family life. Several employees took stress leave. To help them, Disneyland hired a family counselor and conducted group counseling sessions, which produced such insightful suggestions as "Use caffeine to stay alert" and "Make sure to videotape daytime family activities so that the night shift worker can obtain enough sleep, but also stay connected to the family."

Aware of the growing resentment, Irby trained video cameras on his car parked outside his TDA office, to make sure a disgruntled worker didn't vandalize it or plant a bomb inside. Later, some suspected sabotage after a 50-ton hydraulic crane tipped over onto the Matterhorn and damaged the nearby Alice in Wonderland attraction office. In truth, during the 3:00 a.m. renovation project, the operator had extended the crane well beyond the angle and height allowed by the size of the load. As the crane began to tip forward, a welder and an iron worker jumped onto a rising outrigger to add counterweight. The welder jumped off, just before the outrigger and iron worker smashed through the mushroom-shaped office, a foot away from the dispatch console. As the outrigger lifted the mushroom higher, the iron worker finally jumped off, falling about eight feet and breaking his right ankle. The crane toppled onto the Matterhorn, an outrigger narrowly missing the Monorail beam. The park assigned a guard to watch the crane 24 hours a day for five days. After an investigation, OSHA fined the park $7,465 for various violations.

In the middle of the night, the park became crowded. With all the crafts working at once, everyone got in each other's way. If a machinist was testing a ride by running it, an oiler couldn't oil it.

Since everyone worked four ten-hour days, the crew was split into two. Only one day a week, Wednesday, was everyone there. "That's not a good way to do things. You're short handed six days, and one day there are too many people," says machinist Mike Goodwin. "I used to check the Matterhorn each night, walking the track and checking things. It would take a minimum of three men, four men preferred, eight hours. Now you can't turn that around and say, 'We'll have one guy on the Matterhorn six nights and ten people one night. I used to say, 'It takes one woman working nine months to make a baby. You can't have nine women working one month to make a baby.' You're taking a chance. Someone else is gonna get hurt."

The efficiency experts, though, didn't understand why. After noting on the Indiana Jones ride that no seatbelts failed for three straight days, they decided that seatbelts didn't need to be checked every day. "They're saying it's an acceptable risk," Goodwin said. "That's the only thing holding a kid in that car. It's like a pilot saying, 'Hey, we haven't crashed in a while, let's skip the preflight.' They weigh the cost of limbs and life versus profit."

Soon after, the eleven supervisors were fired, about 50 hourly workers were terminated, again with the excuse that their positions had been eliminated. Several were older workers or had medical problems, making their benefits more expensive to the company.

Over the following months, workers continued to retire, quit or be laid off. According to Baker, in less than a year the number of hourly employees in Facilities was reduced from 763 to 610. The Maintenance Services department, which covers driving forklifts, packing trash, digging trenches, installing pipes, mopping up oil spills on animatronic rides, cleaning up after other repairmen, maintaining the crafts shops, and countless other support functions, went from 39 people down to five.

McKinsey & Co. had completed "time studies," calculating the percentage of each worker's day spent doing his actual job. A welder, for example, might be found to spend 5.9 hours welding or performing related tasks. Evidently, they reasoned, there were too many employees and not enough work; so they suggested eliminating workers and cross-utilizing those who remained to pick up the slack.

Behind closed doors, one director informed his staffers that they had not met the quota Irby had set for terminating people. "We're about fourteen percent behind," the director announced. "We've got to step it up. See who can be cross-utilized to double up duties."

With fewer specialized craftsmen, productivity suffered. An assistant manager might randomly assign jobs to generic workers: "You, you, and you, today you check on that."

The McKinsey group also studied how much projects cost to be done in-house compared to how much an outside contractor would charge. Increasingly, repairs that had been handled in-house were assigned to outside contractors willing to do the work for less money. However, done by outsiders, many such projects would cost more in the long run. When it came time to refinish and reseal the walkways on Main Street, management brought in outside contractors to steam clean, strip and repaint the sidewalks. Within a month, the paint was peeling. "We had tried that years ago and it didn't work," an old-timer recalled. "You can't paint concrete and have twelve million people walk over it. They didn't listen to the few people who knew better." Management grudgingly decided to replace the sidewalks with interlocking bricks like those Imagineering had used for the New Tomorrowland.

Soon after, the E.P. Ripley, engine Number Two on the Disneyland Railroad, needed an overhaul. It took management six months to decide what to do; instead of doing the repairs in-house or hiring the local expert who had done the work before, they located a company in New England with a cheaper bid. It was not only expensive and time consuming to ship the train across the country, but the repair firm reportedly lacked experience in the type of work necessary. They installed the plumbing wrong. They didn't have a track or a compressor to test the engine. The cost skyrocketed. A year later, the train finally returned to Disneyland—and went straight to the roundhouse, where Disneyland's crew spent a full month correcting the outside contractor's mistakes.

Overworked and undermotivated, crews fell hundreds of man-hours behind on preventive maintenance schedules, in some cases completely abandoning them. "Now," a worker explains, "you run it till it falls apart."

Mostly show items suffered: faded facades, giant swatches of peeling paint, rotting wood, broken-down animatronics. Repair requests went unanswered for months. A torn screen in the Haunted Mansion went undetected for months. Rarely would all the Tiki Room birds perform. A Jungle Cruise elephant had to be airlifted out by helicopter after its head broke. Outdoor lights across Main Street, which used to be replaced before they burned out, stopped being replaced altogether.

With similar cutbacks in custodial, the once-pristine park looked faded and dingy, not much different from the real world outside.

The attractions, without sufficient maintenance, began breaking down more frequently. Unfortunately for guests, during operating hours only a barebones repair staff remained. Irby named the breakdown crews Maintenance Response Teams, but they jokingly referred to themselves as a Fast Action Response Team, or "FART." Each team consisted of a supervisor and about ten hourlies, including an electrician, mechanic, plumber, computer technician, air conditioning repairman and others who might be needed in quick-fix situations. Anything non-urgent was delegated to third shift.

But with usually just one of each craft on site, when more than one facility broke down, delays grew longer and longer, as the skeleton crew frantically raced from attraction to attraction. Sometimes, if an attraction went down on a busy morning, they'd just leave it closed for the rest of the day.

Attraction downtime skyrocketed an estimated 300 to 400 percent, although park management can cite dubious figures to dispute that. Each attraction's downtime is defined by an Operational Readiness Index: the hours an attraction is actually open divided by the number of hours it is supposed to be open. An ORI of 90, for example, means the ride is running 90 percent of the time it should be and down (or "101" due to breakdown or delayed opening) ten percent of the time. As such, running rides at reduced capacity (a "105") and scheduled rehabs don't count against an attraction's ORI.

To cover their tracks and disguise bad ORIs, management just redefined ORI. "Now what has happened is what used to be called a 101—whenever an attraction didn't run—has been reconfigured so unless an attraction is powered completely down, it's now reduced capacity, instead of down," a manager revealed. "They changed the terminology so it has now made it look like downtime has decreased when actually attractions are down more than they've ever been."

For example, since the Matterhorn's two sides had separate tracks and separate queues, they had been treated like separate attractions with separate ORIs. Now, if just one side goes down, it's considered a 105 (reduced capacity). It's only deemed a 101 if the entire attraction is down.

Furthermore, attractions that seriously fail are moved into rehab, to give the illusion of an efficient operation. In April 1998, the Peter Pan attraction was shut down after the track cracked and reportedly almost fell out of the ceiling. Immediately, the ride was sent to early rehab, because rehab doesn't count as downtime.

Shortly before, a fracture was detected in a supporting bracket on one of Dumbo the Flying Elephant's arms. On closer inspection, cracks were detected on about six supports. "Before, we would have caught it after one," said a current supervisor. "Granted, there are safety devices, but I've seen them break before, and people got hurt."

Other problems worsened due to less frequent checking. The concrete Monorail beam came loose from a pillar near the Indiana Jones attraction and began rocking, but no one had time to fix it. Finally, after several days, the beam was moving so badly, a machinist foreman demanded the ride be shut down.

The aging Mark Twain was in possibly the worst shape. Repairmen had been covering up wood rot for years. Moisture was allowed to collect beneath the boiler and nearly rusted through the bottom. Its rehab would last for months.

In the meantime, the guests paid the price, as lengthier, more frequent breakdowns resulted in excruciatingly long lines. Lines also grew longer because not only were fewer attractions open, there were fewer attractions, period. For years, whenever the park added a new attraction, it took away an old, usually lower-capacity attraction. But with the 1998 renovation of Tomorrowland, Circle-Vision became a queue, Mission to Mars became a restaurant, and the Submarine Lagoon became an abandoned lagoon. Pressler, in fact, had vowed not to close the Submarine Voyage until he had a replacement. Five months later, with no replacement planned, the subs closed.

An assistant manager defended the closure despite the subs always having a line of people waiting: "How do you know all those people in line weren't there because they said, 'Hey, here's a short line. Let's go here!'?" (Certainly, some guests may have lined up for the Submarine Voyage because the wait was shorter than at other attractions, but isn't that an argument for adding, not subtracting attractions?)

Four weeks later, employees learned that the canoes were closing for the season, instead of running on weekends. Ride operators suspected that the labor-intensive canoes were doomed to the same fate as the subs. So, on the ride's final evening, after their final trip, the closing crew jumped into the Rivers of America. After they climbed out, they paraded across Frontierland and down Main Street, oars in hand, sopping wet and whooping it up. Guests who noticed cheered them on. As they approached Town Square, they were ushered off stage by security. All were reprimanded.

Historically, guests could avoid long lines early in the morning and late at night, when crowds were lightest. Management even devised a solution for these hours of less-than-packed queues. In the fall of 1998, management began keeping the park open later on weekdays—but not necessarily the attractions. Although not publicly announced, more than 20 attractions, including favorites Pirates of the Caribbean and Storybook Land, would open hours after the park opened or close hours before it closed. The Haunted Mansion and Autopia, for example, opened two hours late, while the Jungle Cruise and all of Toontown shut down two hours early. Guests, left with fewer available attractions and longer lines were in essence funneled to the shops and restaurants.

Management fully expected to upset guests, beforehand distributing to cast members a list of stock answers to guests complaining about the early ride closures. After apologizing for Big Thunder being closed, employees were to suggest that guests instead might want to "take a crack-shot at the Frontierland Shootin' Arcade!"

Days later, flooded with phone calls, letters and negative comment cards, the park partially reversed the policy and kept some of the rides open later.

Ironically, in the early years, Walt forbid lessees from closing up their shops early because he disliked the look of closed facilities. In fact, one of the first lessees to vacate was the proprietor of a baby shop in the castle, because he refused to stay open on Christmas.

"I always believed that when the park was open, everybody should be open," said Bo Foster, who operated the Sunkist Citrus House on Main Street for 30 years. "It wouldn't look right if some were closed. Those days are gone. There's nothing done just for show."

To further reduce labor costs in Operations, management eliminated positions on attractions. Reduced were the number of operators who checked to make sure seatbelts were fastened on the Matterhorn. Eliminated was the Load Two position on Haunted Mansion, so there was no one to check that passengers had boarded safely. Eliminated were positions inside theater shows, such as Tiki Room and Country Bear Jamboree, who had watched for medical emergencies or show malfunctions.

Some moves, such as reducing Toontown's two Jolly Trolleys from double to single cars, then eliminating one of the trolleys altogether, merely reduced capacity and increased wait times. Sometimes there would be only one loader on Pirates, meaning every other boat was dispatched empty—which cut capacity by two-thirds.

"They strip staffing to the bare bones, then wonder why we're getting guest complaints," grumbled an attractions host of 20 years. "We are so stressed out of our minds, we have no time to think. We're all winging it."

Management reduced the number of workers who gave breaks, explaining that they wanted more equality among divisions. If a clerk could work eight hours with two fifteen-minute breaks and a half-hour lunch, so should ride operators. "But on rides, every position is a safety position," argued attractions host Chris Perley. "We had been given more breaks to keep us fresh and alert. We're operating machinery that, if we make a mistake, can seriously injure someone. In merchandising, they're operating cash registers. In the worst case, they give someone the wrong change."

Come Christmas Eve 1998, the park was packed with guests. With the Mark Twain docked for emergency repairs and the keel boats and canoes mothballed, the only boat ride left on the Rivers of America was the less-frequently used Columbia. Management already had eliminated Mr. Squishey, the below decks position, and scheduled the breaker to arrive later in the morning. They scheduled the bare minimum of three operators to open the Columbia, but one cast member was running late. So, assistant manager Christine Carpenter agreed to fill in, despite never being trained on the attraction. Assigned to the West Side two months earlier, she trained on seven rides in ten days. As part of the abbreviated indoctrination, she learned to dock the Mark Twain, but never performed the task by herself and never on the Columbia. Christmas Eve morning, Carpenter took the dock position, and the Columbia set off for its first trip of the day.

Since the massive tall ship has no brakes, drivers stop the boat by shifting into reverse as they near the dock. Then, when the boat stops, the dockhand tethers it to the dock by throwing a rope over a metal cleat on the boat. Occasionally, dockhands threw the rope before the boat fully stopped, straining the bolts that held the cleat to the ship. Over the last five months, operators called in at least three requests for maintenance to repair loose cleats on the Columbia. The work orders, marked "safety issue," were completed quickly, yet the general consensus among the troops that the average work request is ignored remained. So, in early December, operators noticed a loose cleat and rotting wood around the cleat on the Columbia, but didn't report the problems because, one confessed, "normally they aren't repaired."

After the first trip that morning, the driver approached the dock too fast and the untrained dockhand didn't know that you never throw the rope if the boat is moving too fast. Years before, Disneyland used traditional natural fiber ropes, that would snap if pulled too tightly. But in the early 1990s, the park switched to stronger nylon lines. Synthetic lines also could break under greater tension. At least once, though, in 1997, an overextended synthetic line reportedly yanked a cleat off a submarine and shot it over the heads of guests waiting in line.

That morning on the Columbia, the synthetic line didn't snap; it tore the nine-pound cast iron cleat from the ship's hull and slingshot it back toward the crowd. The cleat ripped through Carpenter's foot and ankle, then struck 33-year-old tourist Luan Phi Dawson in the face and neck and his 43-year-old wife, Lieu Thuy Vuong, in the face. Carpenter and the two guests were rushed to the hospital.

Meanwhile, cast members formed a human fence in front of the dock to shield the ghastly scene from other guests. Park management ordered employees immediately to clean the dock, covered with blood and body parts—and never called police. Officers, who

DEATH SCENE. For weeks after the fatal accident, screening shielded the site, the Mark Twain/Columbia dock. The Mark Twain docked there while maintenance completed repairs. (February 1999) *Photo by David Koenig.*

heard about the accident from the paramedics, didn't arrive on the scene for five hours—by which time Disneyland had thoroughly cleaned the site, gathered and sorted all evidence, and selected and briefed potential witnesses.

Dawson, his skull fractured and brain hemorrhaged, never regained consciousness. Forty-eight hours later, the hospital disconnected him from life support, the first person ever killed at Disneyland while just standing in line.

10

Crossroads

IN the weeks surrounding the Columbia tragedy, the Disney executives behind the cutbacks all received big, fat promotions. Judson Green became chairman of the theme parks division, forcing Dick Nunis into retirement. Paul Pressler got Green's job as division president, and park vice president of Operations Cynthia Harriss took over as head of the Disneyland Resort. The message was clear: public relations black eyes, unhappy customers, declining employee morale, none of it mattered as long as profits and attendance remained strong. Ironically, the week after the Columbia accident was Disneyland's most heavily attended week of the year.

After preliminary investigations cited inadequate training as a contributing factor, newly promoted vice president of Operations Mike Berry vowed to increase training and reinstitute leads. Sure enough, management quickly rewrote all attraction training manuals and instituted new training requirements. Staffing increased to previous levels. Maintenance also seemed to improve after 200 workers returned to days and evenings after a year on graveyard.

Unfortunately, the changes seemed short-lived. Within a year, a new wave of Disneyland ride accidents began hitting the press. Part of the reason why the incidents received so much attention was a new law, engendered by the Columbia tragedy, that forced theme parks to report serious accidents to authorities.

At the same time, the company seemed to be devoting most of its energy, resources and attention to opening a second theme park, Disney's California Adventure, in Disneyland's parking lot.

More importantly, Disney's stock price was stagnating, encouraging the executives to slash budgets with renewed vigor. And while policies at the park may have changed, at least on paper, the same managers remained. Managers concerned more with numbers than anything else. Managers conditioned to change sound policies just to show their bosses how clever they were. And managers who ignored the old rules out of convenience.

Certainly, some of the mishaps were due to guest misbehavior. A girl injured her foot after abandoning her Roger Rabbit car in the middle of the ride. A 15-year-old fractured his foot on Alice in Wonderland. In a freak accident, a six-year-old's finger was torn off after it got stuck in the trigger of a toy rifle in the Tom Sawyer Island fort.

Yet operator error or inexperience was a factor in other instances. A new hire nearly lost her thumb while incorrectly tying off a raft. An inexperienced ride operator prematurely dispatched a boat on Pirates on the Caribbean, while passengers were still loading. Guests, including a man cradling his baby, went flying and one woman got her leg smashed between the boat and a dock railing. Four weeks later, another new hire launched a Pirates boat with guests still unloading. Again, passengers, including a mother with her 16-month-old daughter, toppled and another woman caught her knee between the boat and dock.

A four-year-boy suffered brain damage after falling out of a spinning Roger Rabbit taxi and being run over by the next car. Employees allowed the boy to sit next to the open door side of the vehicle and, according to the victim's family, never fully lowered the lap bar.

Weeks earlier, nine passengers were injured on Space Mountain when faulty bolts on their rocket snapped and the vehicle screeched to a halt. Clueless operators then left the bloodied victims stranded in the darkness as they tried to figure out what to do.

Finally, in May 2001, just when it seemed like nothing else

could go wrong, a giant oak tree collapsed in the middle of Frontierland, crashing down on dozens guests and flattening a popcorn cart like a soda can. Ambulances rushed 27 visitors to the hospital, as news helicopters circled overhead.

"Now a tree is attacking the guests? Believe me, a lot of us are scratching our heads about this one," remarked one employee. "With all the mishaps going on, some cast members are wondering if this is a sign that the park is protesting in the way it is being treated. With the constant penny-pinching, and the neglect it is going through, many of us think that it is saying, 'I've had enough!'"

Did it take something falling from the sky to wake people up? The turning point did come, with the opening of California Adventure—but not because the new park was a return to quality theme park design and operation. Heavens no. The company, figuring that guests would patronize anything that had Walt's surname on it, created Theme Park Lite, a modest, half-day affair. Disney was so sure guests wouldn't notice, initially it offered no two-park "hopper" passes and suspended all sales of annual passes for both parks.

The turning point came on February 8, 2001, when California Adventure proudly threw open its gates—and the public yawned. Days of sparse attendance turned into deserted weeks and months. Desperate, the park introduced deeper and deeper discounts. It altered, added and subtracted attractions and entertainment. It even revived the Electrical Parade. Still, the new park was hard pressed to find many people willing to pay full fare.

The guests were finally catching on. Maybe the Disney name wasn't the ironclad guarantee Walt had convinced us that it was.

Walt, more than anyone, knew that Disney's greatest asset was its reputation. More valuable than any movie, theme park, or even Mickey Mouse, the Disney name was a known commodity, a stamp of approval, a promise of quality. Other studios started from scratch to sell every product, but Disney products carried an inherent endorsement earned from years of making good on its promises to provide quality family entertainment.

Later Disney management began selling off that goodwill for fleeting gains. They never considered what might happen if they lost their customers' trust. They never contemplated how long they could continue to attract new customers and prospective employees while betraying the traditions that made Disney great.

"Nowadays you only do what you have to do," sighed one old-timer. "Walt demanded perfection."

Consequently, Disneyland is held to a higher standard, which current management does not take as a challenge to pursue excellence. "The biggest monkey (today's managers) have on their backs is the memory of Walt, living up to that," agreed another veteran.

A third added: "They don't like traditions. They're in the way."

But, argued a current manager with minimal theme park experience, "we can create *new* traditions. It always bugs me when people don't like something new and say, 'Walt would be turning over in his grave.' Walt's gone. No one can know what Walt would think."

Nonsense. Walt spent his whole life telling everyone what he thought about everything. That's not to say that his every idea was a winner that could never be improved upon. The key is cultivating not detonating Disney's quality image.

It's not too late. Disneyland can ensure high short-term profitability as well as long-term survival. The solution is three-fold:

(1) Regain the parkwide team spirit. Disneyland no longer has a president who personally knows his few thousand employees. It can never be a little family again. That doesn't mean cast members can't be made to feel part of a team again. First, the high turnover must stop.

Park management must listen to employee complaints and concerns. "Employee morale is down the toilet," groused one sweeper. "Nobody cares. I don't care. It's parkwide, because they treat you like crap."

Agreed a devoted, yet downtrodden, co-worker: "It's hard to choose to be happy when you're stuck in a place that constantly asks you to take on more work and then is hellbent on reducing your paycheck, all while the parent corporation rakes in record money. What is the incentive to perform? Out of devotion to the guests? Why should the rank and file be devoted to the guests any more than their leaders? Why would we look positively on cuts, when we know they're for the ultimate purpose of getting a handful of people outlandish bonuses?"

Ironically, some of the most spirited workers are new hires. "They have the pixie dust for a year or two, but they can sense something's wrong," said a veteran. "There's very little sincerity left in the park. It's a business. I know they have to make money, but there doesn't seem to be the balance. Walt realized if you make the employees happy, it would trickle down. The guests pick that up. Now we're as replaceable as Dixie cups."

The park should eliminate the distance between bosses and employees. Encourage teamwork not competition. Be honest. Don't *say* you value your employees. *Show* them. And not by handing out huge bonuses, but by providing good pay and working conditions, making reasonable expectations, and rewarding good performance.

(2) Remember that Disneyland is a show not a shop, one that should be run by a showman not a shopkeeper. Guests go to a store to be sold to, but they go to a show to be entertained. After they pay their admission, guests may buy food and souvenirs, but that's not why they're there. Present the Disneyland experience with that in mind. You can maximize profits without grabbing for the customer's wallet at every opportunity.

Shockingly, at Disney's California Adventure, far more money was budgeted for shops, restaurants and a hotel than for attractions.

Previous management recognized the importance of staging a good show. But the new corporate bosses, explained an old-timer, "got rid of the old blood. There's nobody left out there with any park history. We created amusement parks, we developed what an amusement park is today. They don't want any Disney people. They don't want to hear old ideas."

Disneyland could use fewer people with retail backgrounds and more with theme park experience. Get a few of them back. And ensure a knowledgeable management team in the future by again promoting from within.

(3) Return guests to their rightful place as Priority One. Remember why they're there and what they want and expect. Change can be good—if the changes are improvements and not arbitrary decisions made just because a new manager wants to show he's doing something.

For now, casual visitors probably don't notice many effects of the cutbacks. They register as aberrations the occasional frowning cast member or the trash floating in the long-abandoned Submarine Lagoon. Yet California Adventure's chilly reception may indicate that customers are beginning to catch on and become more discerning. Inevitably, if the prices at Disneyland get much higher, if upkeep remains shoddy, if the hard sell becomes harder so that stores outnumber attractions, or, worse, if more people get hurt, visitors will stop coming.

Cut fat, not substance. Admit mistakes. Reinstitute procedures that worked better than their replacements; most of those 40-year-old policies had a reason.

Walt's immediate successors ran into trouble because they failed to realize they had to spend money to make money. Give guests more, not less. As Walt said, "Plus the show." Expenses will increase, but guests will stay happy and the money will continue rolling in for a long, long time. Customers, shareholders, executives, employees, everyone will live happily ever after.

Notes

Q – Quote
I – Interview by author
L – Lawsuit filed against Disneyland

Note on Sources: Unlike my first book, which identified every source, this time I allowed several cast members to remain anonymous. All are current security guards, supervisors or management hopefuls who thought inclusion of their names might jeopardize their jobs or chances for promotion. Unlike the other cast members I interviewed, all of them sought me out, concerned about current problems at the park. All stories they provided were verified by others.

Chapter One
(Page 18) Stack of applications *Q*: *I* Gentleman
Casting *Q*s: *I* Conk
Beautiful People: *I* Hayes
Broad in beam: *I* Wilson
Foods *Q*: *I* Beaumont

(19) Work harder *Q*: *I* Fujimura
Better conditions *Q*: *I* Trapasso
Cultural difference *Q*: *I* Ezell

Night and day *Q*: *I* Boynton

(20) Falling IQ *Q*: *I* Spindler
Won't read signs *Q*: *I* Catone
"Guestions": Disneyland Line 8-15-73

(21) Human factor, repetition *Q*s: *I* Wilson

(22) Unpaved lot, old trams *Q*: *I* Gentleman
Penal colony *Q*: *I* P. Lewanski
Field rats: Disneyland Line 3-11-76
Abandon infant, weather *Q*, medical parking: *I* P. Lewanski

(23) Kleenex, Pop Tarts, Burger queen: *I* Judd
Gate questions: *I* Yan

(24) Olympics: *I* B. Levine, I P. Lewanski
White car prank: *I* B. Levine
Super 8 movies: *I* P. Lewanski
Store questions: *I* Yan, Magic Kingdom Gazette 4-86

(25) Shops: *I* Foster, *I* H. Johnson, Disneyland Line 7-24-80
Where's the market?: Jungle Drums 8-7-79

(28) Horses: Disneyland Line 5-27-94; Streetcar horses work two days on and one day off during the summer, but just two to three days a week in the off-season.
Jet *Q*, Michelle, in Opera House: *I* Beeman
Clock Shop: Magic Kingdom Gazette 4-86

(29) Baked bean slick: *I* Aramaki
Train operators: Disneyland Line 9-28-90
Primeval additions: *I* M. Keiser
Triceratops' top: *I* H. Levine
Are you Disney?: Magic Kingdom Gazette 4-86

(30) World's Fair kinks: *I* Conk
Spasms from Monorail: *I* White
Abe's bends: Disneyland Line 10-29-75
Lincoln himself?: *I* Archer

Chapter Two

(31) Dark ride track: *I* Glisch
Tripper: *I* Catone, who says he devised the system himself.

(32) A fifth Fantasyland dark ride, Pinocchio's Daring Journey, was added during the 1983 remodeling of the area.
Scared kids, working Tea Cups: *I* Archer
No brakes: Times 8-30-96, *I* Archer
Flying pigs: Magic Kingdom Gazette 4-86

(33) Tea cup injury: *L* DoSanjh 1994
Giant dishwasher: *I* Wickstrom

(36) Storybook weed *Q*: Disneyland Line 4-29-76; Storybook Land can accommodate up to nine boats at one time, each with a maximum capacity of fourteen guests.
Outboard motors: *I* Catone
Closing crew, Walt's bias: *I* Archer

Woman's spiel *Q*: *I* Catone
Break ticket takers: *I* Mobley

(37) Storybook babes *Q*: *I* George
Weedwhackers: *I* Goodwin
Sunbathing rat *Q*: *I* Judd
Need kids to ride?: Magic Kingdom Gazette 4-86

(38) Skyway swingers: *I* Nutt, *I* Stanley
Round trips: Disneyland Line 7-7-77, *I* Nutt
Phones: *I* Archer

(39) Skyway excuses: *I* Archer

(40) Disciplining spitters: *I* H. Levine, *I* Stanley
Retaliators: *I* Archer
Fantasy Island?: *I* DeForest

(41) Wind meter: *I* DeForest
God Switch: *I* Stanley
Broken arm: *I* Trapasso
Lawsuit: Register 4-18 & 19-94, 9-24-96, Times 4-18-94, OCN producer

(43) Skyway lower ridership, *Q*: *I* DeForest

(44) Lookout Mountain: *I* Archer
Holey mountain: Disneyland News 7-85

(45) Matterhorn's two sides: *I* Hayes; Side A's one significant dip is known as "Dolly's Dip," named after Dolly Regene Young, who was killed there 1-3-84 (see *Mouse Tales*, p. 174).
Rearendings, safety light: *I* Mobley
Bobsled lawsuits: *L* all Municipal and Superior Court cases involving the Matterhorn.
Speed pacers: *I* Goodwin, *I* Mobley
Wet *Q*: *I* Goodwin
Stop watches: *I* Zimmer

(46) Computer brakes: *I* Mobley
Rehabs: *I* Goodwin, Disneyland

Line 10-25-96; In 1996, the Matterhorn underwent major rehabs twice.

Breakdowns: *I* various

Small kid ride?: Magic Kingdom Gazette 4-86

(47) Electrocution: *I* P. Lewanski

Belt checking after death: *Mouse Tales*

Purse on track: *I* Judd

Water bucket: *I* Hedman

Mad, Mad World: Magic Kingdom Gazette 4-86

(48) Small World stats: Disneyland Line 9-16-76 & 7-5-91; The World's Fair version featured 204 dolls; by 1991, the head count had grown to 350.

High capacity: Earlier attractions like the Disneyland Railroad and Monorail offered high capacities, but are not continually loaded, one vehicle immediately after the other, like on Small World.

Backed up boats: *I* Goodwin

Capacity incentive: *I* Mobley

(49) Three straight trips: *I* Landis

Sweeper network: I Chaney

Trolley?: I DeForest

(50) Toontown limbs, chutes, Nut House *Q*: *I* Hunsaker

Chutes: *I* Perley

Slide injury, replacement: *L* Head 1995

Boat stairs?: *I* various

(51) Wet pants: *I* Perley

Misspelled Donald: *I* various

Gags: *I* DeForest

Chapter Three

(52) Adventureland Walt *Q*: *Disneyland* TV show: "A Trip Through Adventureland" 1955

Early Cruise: *I* Archer, *I* Fravel, *I*

George, *Disneyland* TV show 1955

(53) Goatees, earrings: *I* Johnson

Guns: *I* George, *I* Steele

Eliminated: MousePlanet's Disneyland Information Guide 1-22-01; During the firearms' final few years, politically correct management instructed Jungle Cruise skippers not to shoot *at* the hippos, but to fire into the air to scare them away.

Headless hippo: *I* Garcia

Damage: Jungle Drums 7-14-79

Bathroom on board: Jungle Drums 6-23-79

(54) Shoots himself: Jungle Drums, *I* G. Brown

(55) Signals: *I* Gordon, *I* Hunsaker, copy of ride's SOP

Derail *Q*, shoot the rapids: *I* George

Shootouts, retaliation: *I* various

Silent Japanese: *I* George

(56) Serious *Q*: *I* Fravel

Waterfall joke: *I* Spindler

Spiel changes: Copies of ride's spiel from 1960s, 1980 and 1995

Ad lib policy, competing: *I* various

(57) Native sing-a-long: *I* Seymour

Leg hairs: *I* Vogelvang

Jokeless spiel: *I* Green

Comes with costume *Q*: *I* Hunsaker

Blind ticket taker: *I* Chaney

Supervision *Q*, breastfeeding remark: *I* Maloney

Too many jokes: *I* Gordon

(58) Sumo *Q*: *I* George

Demanding *Q*: *I* Ezell

Spiel hater *Q*: *I* Flores

Elephant. Snake. Hippo: *I* Chaney

Transfer from Foods: *Q*: *I* Trapasso

(59) 18-year-olds *Q*: *I* Fujimura

Inebriated operator: *I* Flores

Insecticide?: Jungle Drums 6-23-79

(60) Goofing off *Q*, water gags *Q*: *I* Fujimura
Water pranks: *I* Maloney, *I* Seymour
Extinguisher ambush, boat sinks: *I* Fujimura
Party hats on hippos: *I* Seymour
Gorilla pin-up, dressing up Trader Sam: *I* Maloney

(61) Simba in hiding, room setting gags, flea pickers: *I* Hunsaker
Missionary: *I* C. Miller
Safari climber: *I* Turner
Popcorn: *I* Maloney
Spider, skull head: *I* Fujimura
Hyena sex, rhino exam: *I* Maloney
Pet hyenas: *I* anonymous

(62) Elephant shower: *I* Kaml
Rerouted rail: *I* Seymour
Stubborn skipper: *I* Fujimura
Clamping down *Q*: *I* Ezell
Kaml's final day: *I* Kaml, Register 8-27 & 9-10-96, Times 9-3 & 5-96
Electric socks: *I* Zimmer

(63) F ticket: Jungle Drums 1979
Kaml rumors: *I* various

(64) Narrations, summer of '95: *I* DeForest, *I* Hunsaker, *I* Kaml, "Jungle Cruise Survival Guide"

(65) Long line: *I* Flores

(66) Theming *Q*: *I* Kaml
Narrations philosophy: Kimbrell memo 7-28-95
Delivery *Q*: *I* Kaml

(67) Walt Jr. *Q*: *I* DeForest
Supervisor memo: Kimbrell memo 7-16-95
Stamps?: Jungle Drums 6-23-79

(68) Kimbrell on Andrew Dice Clay, sissies: *I* DeForest

Compliment tally: Kimbrell memo 8-16-95; Within eight months, Narrations had received its 100th compliment. At Circle-Vision, the spiel centered on a mechanical mural depicting the destinations reached by sponsor Delta Airlines. It was replaced in 1996 by a display of state flags.

(69) Ties cut *Q*, terminations: *I* Hunsaker
Capacity changes: *I* Kaml

(70) Summer of '97: *I* Gordon, *I* Green, Register 10-11-97
New Cruise *Q*: *I* Green

(71) Gordon's ouster: *I* Gordon

(74) Green's ouster: *I* Green
Pressler compliment: *I* Green, confirmed by other skippers on the dock at the time.

(75) Personal expression *Q*: *I* Kaml
Current atmosphere: *I* various current skippers (*Q*: *I* Steele)
Treehouse positions: *I* Archer
Is this Treehouse?: Jungle Drums 7-4-71

(76) Visitors: *I* Archer
Leaky coconuts: *I* Zimmer
Swiss don't live in trees: Archer in Disneyland Line 2-26-76

(77) Experts: *I* Archer
Tiki cast of 225: Disneyland Line 5-3-84
Stomping: *I* Spindler; Soundmen continued staffing the Tiki Room basement and other control rooms full time for years after the systems became more reliable due to a former provision in their union contract.
Birds don't fly away?: Disneyland Line 5-3-84

(78) Pump up the thunder: *I* Seymour

Firecrackers: *I* Flores
Dry windows: *I* Archer
Spades *Q*: *I* Flores
Haunted Treehouse: Jungle Drums 8-7-79

(79) Brokers, *Q*, Tikigate: *I* Flores
Lost girl: Jungle Drums 9-72

(80) Park uncovers scam: *I* Haught

(81) Indy set-up: Register 2-24-95; At maximum capacity, Indy can accommodate 15 twelve-passenger vehicles at one time, with #16 as a spare.
Bleeding knuckles *Q*: *I* DeForest
Almost fell out: *I* Mumford

(82) Indy's rough ride: Times 12-30-98, 1-11 & 31-99, Register 12-30-98, *L* Katic 1995

(83) Brain injury, profile removed: *L* Jacob 1995, *I* Sterns
2nd Indy case: Register 6-24-00

Chapter Four

(84) Mule behavior: *I* Haught, *I* Trapasso
Clothesline: *I* Trapasso
Bridge *Q*: *I* Beeman

(85) Jarvis *Q*: *I* Mendez
Saddle slips: *I* Pena
Blood on trail *Q*: *I* Trapasso
Mule union, cowboy *Qs*: *I* Mendez
Wool jacket: *I* Trapasso
Real horses: Magic Kingdom Gazette 4-86

(86) Wranglers: *I* Mendez, *I* Trapasso
Shooting Gallery difficulties: *I* Haught (*Q*), *I* Mendez
Electronic guns: Disneyland Line 4-11-85
Bird shooters: *I* Maloney
Restroom ticket?: Disneyland Line 8-15-73

(87) Sand, water: *I* Mendez, *I* Reger

Nature's Wonderland stats: press release 6-60
Sound problems *Qs*: *I* Gerlach

(88) Grad Nite *Q*: *I* Flores
Train jumpers: *I* Trapasso
Talk to guests: *I* various
Great attraction *Q*: *I* Fravel
Dirty hanky: *I* Haught; There are several legends about how the group got its name, but this is the best one. Some say the red handkerchief was never an official part of the costume.

(89) Membership drive: *I* Mendez
Big Thunder accidents: *I* Goodwin, *I* Maloney, *Mouse Tales*
Higher tension *Q*: *I* Seymour
Right-of-way *Q*: *I* Rainey
Duties: *I* Seymour

(90) Wheelhouse: *I* Seymour
Steam fitter: *I* Mendez
Urinating: *I* H. Levine
Popcorn incident: *I* Flores
Mint juleps: *I* Archer, *I* Foster
Navajos: Times 8-30-96

(91) Drinkers: *I* Catone, *I* Haught
Complainers: *I* Haught
White Indians: *I* Haught, *I* Turner
Hard work: *I* Pena, *I* Turner
Real water, don't drink it: *I* Chaney

(92) Difficulties: *I* Messick
Air bags, negative buoyant: *I* Chaney; The first canoes were made of wood, the second generation were wood covered by fiberglass, the third were all fiberglass weighing 2,500 lbs. each and accommodating 16 guests, and the fourth generation canoes are made of Kevlar, weighing 2,000 lbs. each and accommodating 20 guests (Disneyland Line 6-11-93).
Jump in: *I* Pena

(93) Keel boats, rapids, *Qs*: *I* George,

I Mendez, *I* Nutt; The keel boats were shelved in 1994 due to their low capacity, then refurbished and returned to the river 3-30-96 for a little over a year. In 12-01, Disney sold the Bertha Mae on eBay for $15,000.

Treasure Island: Magic Kingdom Gazette 4-86; Treasure Island also originally was supposed to feature a permanent home for the Mickey Mouse Club.

Historical sites: *Disneyland: The Nickel Tour* (Bruce Gordon and David Mumford, Camphor Tree, 1995)

(94) Seesaw fall: *L* Stevenson 1958
Barrel bridge fall: *L* Serradell and Duarte 1974
Merry-go-round fall: *L* Makoutz, Jr. 1969
Barbed wire: *I* Wolf

(95) Runaway: *I* Haught
Docking rafts: *I* Catone, *I* George
Raft prank: *I* Herrera
Wet feet, hit piling: *I* Mendez
2 Bs and C?: Jungle Drums 6-23-79; Supposedly, requests for this type of "horse trading" were common (*I* Y. Lewanski).

(96) Columbia duties: *I* Seymour
Cannon: *I* Hackbarth, *I* Maloney
Chimp: *I* Hackbarth
Not a pirate ship: *I* Seymour

(97) Narrations-type changes: *I* Kaml (*Q*), Disneyland Line 8-9-96
Where's B?: Disneyland Line 8-15-73

(98) Fantasmic fallout: *L* Jones 2-19-95, which cites First Aid records for incidents on 7-15 & 10-31-92, 1-9 & 2-14-93
Pink elephants: *I* Robertson
Pirate injury: *I* various

Equipment graveyard: *I* Robertson
When's Fantasia?: *I* DeForest

(99) Skiing: *I* Turner
Target practice: *I* Maloney
Bare rear: *I* Flores, *I* Maloney
Rollerskater: *I* Turner
Cannonball: *I* H. Levine
Bear lawsuit: *L* Martin 1972

(100) Aneurysm: Times 7-24-94, Register 7-25-94; purple photo confirmed by witness. The camera was first used 1-31-92.

Lost finger: *L* Eubanks 9-7-96, Times 1-31-99; Eubanks lost his finger, as well as his case, after Disney argued that riders are instructed to keep their hands inside the vehicle at all times. Suspiciously, before accident photos were taken, maintenance workers had cleaned up the scene and tightened the screw.

Flash mountain: *I* anonymous, Times 1-97; remake confirmed by unnamed programmer.

Where's Disneyland?: Magic Kingdom Gazette 4-86

(101) Silent trip: *I* Yang

Chapter Five
(102) History of Pirates: Disneyland News 7-85

(104) Bayou: *I* Haught
Rearending lawsuits: various, including *L* Illions 4-23-67
Early riders soaked: *I* Haught
Do you work here: *I* various; A common question asked of just about any employee, no matter how obvious their costuming.

(105) Too heavy in front: *I* Zimmer
Leaks: *I* Goodwin, Pirates log book
Captain's Quarters rainfall: Pirates log book 12-18-74

Shootout showers: *I* J. Moy
Pumps: *I* Goodwin
Buzzing: *I* Zimmer
Sensors: *I* Goodwin
Fluid leaks: *I* Zimmer
Chain-lift, downstairs flooding, free-floating lawsuits: *I* Goodwin

(107) Boy falls: *I* Zimmer
Danger *Q*: *I* Fujimura
Knee injury: *L* Forte 1967
Thrown guest, guard falls: *I* Fujimura

(108) Pregnant fall: *I* Fujimura; The first drop is 52 feet long, the second 37 feet long, but both are at a 21-degree slope. For the record, the upramp is 90 feet long at a 16-degree angle.
Security cameras: *I* Mendez
Maze: *I* various
Maze races *Q*: *I* Chaney
No narration: Log book 8-13-74
Bleeping sign: Log book 6-25-75

(109) Cook's tours: *I* Zimmer, Log book (various entries, including 7-14-74, 9-21-74, and 6-28-75)
Stoners: Log book 7-31-76
Cockroaches: *I* Goodwin
Carrots of Pyrobbean?: Disneyland Line 8-15-73

(110) Extinguishers: *I* Chaney
Last day prank: *I* Fujimura, Log book (7-27-75)
Mylar table: *I* various

(111) Flooded pits: *I* Haught; After the Rivers of America was drained in early 1970, it would not undergo another "dry rehab" for 14 years.
Haunted Q: *I* Gentleman

(112) Smile, look terrible (Zimmer *Q*): Disneyland Line 7-22-76
Freak out: *I* anonymous
Ear plugs: *I* Gentleman; It's easy to

spot the elevator attendants who aren't wearing ear plugs; they inevitably slip their fingers into their ears a split-second before the lights go out.
Vomit: *I* J. Moy
Nun?: Disneyland Line 7-22-76

(113) Pepper spray: *I* Robertson, confirmed by second security officer

(114) Elevator molester: *L* Rogers 96
Mischief: *I* Gentleman, *I* Mendez
Slap *Q*: *I* Fujimura

(115) Utility positions: *I* M. Keiser, *I* Mendez, *I* Zimmer
Ballroom window size: Disneyland Line 12-13-72
Shot glass: *I* M. Keiser (*Q*), *I* Mendez
Women leaders: *I* Mendez
Halloween party?: Disneyland Line 5-28-69

(116) Eight-foot drop: *I* Mendez
Vandals *Q*: *I* Goodwin
Dangerous conveyor belt: *I* Haught, *L* various
Stuck stockings: *I* Zimmer
4th of July party?: Magic Kingdom Gazette 4-86

(117) Hitchhiker photos: Disneyland Line 7-22-76
Artists return: Disneyland Line 11-13-86
Art spots: *I* C. Miller
Portrait races *Q*: *I* Stout
He paid his way: Disneyland Line 5-28-69

(118) Union *Q*: *I* C. Miller

Chapter Six
(119) Early Autopia: Magic Kingdom Gazette 4-86; The mini-police cars mostly acted as escorts, giving rides to undersized kids, and were later repainted as

regular cars. Walt had his own car, too—the Disneyland Autopia Special, painted metallic maroon with red and white upholstery, and the only car with a gearshift.

(120) Recklessness: *I* various
Curved bars: *I* Archer
Hooked bumpers: *I* Mobley
Ungoverned: *I* Stanley
Pebbles: *I* Judd
Where do I go?: *I* Levine

(121) New hires: *I* George
Blood Alley: *I* Archer, *I* George
Child driver: *I* Hayes
Junior Autopia: *Nickel Tour*; After two years, the Junior Autopia was expanded into the full-sized Fantasyland Autopia.
Headlights?: *I* Levine

(122) Abandon ship: *I* Archer
Screaming kids: *I* D. Keefe
Claustrophobia training: *I* George
Descriptions: *I* Chaney, *I* Seymour, *I* Zimmer
Fumes Q: *I* Stanley
Sub to hotel?: *Magic Kingdom Gazette* 4-86

(123) Sicknesses: *I* Chaney
Euro *Q*, diaper: *I* Zimmer
Reading/eating: *I* Keene, *I* Mobley, *I* Seymour
Cavern signs: *I* Baldwin
Mermaid on board: *I* Keene

(124) Spiel gag: *I* Keene; Setting the pre-recorded spiel to start at the wrong scene was also a common prank on the Disneyland Railroad (*I* G. Hamlin).
No. 9, whistle: *I* Baldwin
Leaky lagoon: *I* Cashen, *I* Penfield, *I* White
Rehab *Q*: *I* White; White provided the 8 million gallon figure, while other sources estimate the

lagoon's volume between 6.3 million (Disneyland Line 1-31-80) and approximately 9 million gallons (Disneyland Line 6-10-94).

(126) Monorail joke: *I* Perley; The other attraction that at first was personally owned by Walt Disney was the Disneyland Railroad.
Monorail speeder: *I* Perley, confirmed by Anaheim police
PeopleMover dull: *I* Gentleman
Injuries: *Mouse Tales*
Monorail to Knott's?: Disneyland Line 5-28-69

(127) Climbing out *Q*: *I* Baldwin
Intrusion systems: *I* Perley
Rocket Jets record: *I* Baldwin; There's a difference between the Fantasyland and Tomorrowland rides—the Rocket Jets and Astro Orbiter vehicles tilt slightly as they elevate, the Dumbo vehicles do not.
Jets elevator: *I* Ralston

(128) Santa hat: *I* H. Levine
Groucho glasses, slob: *I* Keene
Join critters: *I* Ralston
Join Carrousel: *I* Mobley
She's real!: *I* Judd
Freak out: *I* Perley
America Sings soundless, drunk storks: *I* Hughes
Phone off hook: *I* H. Levine
Unarmed: *I* Hughes
Obscene jerk: *I* H. Levine

(129) Space Mountain computer: E-Ticket Fall 1998, *I* Goodwin, *I* Mobley, *I* Wilson; The system, initially operated by one PLC and one true computer, was upgraded in 1988.
Enter the exit?: Magic Kingdom Gazette 4-86

(130) Malfunctions: *I* Goodwin, *I*

Trapasso, *I* Zimmer
Things We Hate: Space Mountain log book 7-18-85 (condensed from a list of 38 items)

(131) Catapults: Disneyland Line 9-15-77
Design flaw, loading *Q*: *I* Zimmer
Hand-picked crews: *I* Wilson, *I* Zimmer
Begging for Matterhorn: *I* Zimmer
Chaos *Q*: *I* Wilson
Front seat *Q*: *I* Hayes
Pregnant *Q*: *I* Y. Lewanski
Legless vet: *I* Judd

(132) Circle-Vision errors: *I* Perley, *I* Wilson; The original Circarama movie was filmed using eleven cameras, while later Circle-Vision movies used nine cameras.
Bell out: Disneyland Line 9-15-83

(133) Phone employees, crabs: *I* Judd
Farter: *I* Judd, *I* Wilson
Shrinko?: Magic Kingdom Gazette 4-86

(134) Ear plugs: *I* Perley; E-O could match any Circle-Vision film error for error, including on-camera stagehands, a roll of duct tape on a space ship console, objects such as spears that disappear from shot to shot, and a dancer whose top falls down.
E-O *Qs*: *I* Hayes
Inner Space nickname, sparks: *I* Pritchard
Son won't wave: *I* Baxter
Written guarantee?: *I* Archer

(135) Monsanto *Q*: *I* Mobley
Grad Nite *Q*: *I* Goodwin
Tally sheet: *I* Serber
Close encounters: *I* Baxter

(136) Speeder cracks: *I* Goodwin
Best seat: *I* Hayes
Surf *Q*: *I* H. Levine

Belt extenders: *I* Chaney
McClintock *Q*: Register 5-98
Where's track?: Disneyland Line 12-24-86

(137) Rods problems: Register 7-11 & 14-98, *I* various current cast members
Ceiling panel falls: *I* Rowland
Scrape rubber *Q*: *I* anonymous
Large building?: Disneyland Line 12-24-86

(138) Sweat *Q*: *I* unnamed sweeper
Chlorine level: Times 8-26-98

Chapter Seven

(139) Character *Q*: *I* Trapasso, who worked as both a character and a ride operator.
Humanoids: *I* Moore

(140) Eeyore's legs: *I* Garrison
Intervention: *I* Moore
Cyclops *Q*: *I* Garrison
Ovens, Louie barfs: *I* Hill

(141) Sleep *Q*: *I* Moore
Frying pan *Q*: *I* Borja
Shake hands with knife: *I* Garrison
Stabbings: *I* confirmed by most characters
Pooh stabbed: *I* Gabriel
Bear on fire, go kick the character: *I* Garrison

(142) Aikido: *I* Gabriel
Baloo fights: *I* Gabriel, *I* McLaren
Hurt hands, taps: *I* McLaren
Shoe toss: *I* Hughes
People break *Q*, video: *I* Borja
Rack, disowned *Q*: *I* Garrison

(143) Costume switch, double Poohs: *I* Gabriel
Spaceman *Q*: *I* Catone

(144) Training *Q*: *I* Gabriel
Photo set-ups *Q*: *I* Borja
Break room balcony?: *I* Hill

(145) Fake Grumpy: *I* Hill
Cleaning costumes *Qs*: Disneyland
Line 4-28-77
Surly Mickey: *I* Borja, *I* Garrison, *I*
Hill, *I* Kabat, *I* McLaren, *I* Moore.
Actually, I spent many hours
speaking with this Mickey and
found him charming, but the opinions expressed in the text are
unanimously those of the more
than a dozen people I interviewed
who worked with him during his
25 years at the park.
Brer Bear's last day: *I* Hill

(146) Suspension: *I* Castle
Dream Vacation: *I* Garrison;
Although he did not confirm that
this is the same Mickey as in the
other anecdotes, it seemed to fit
nicely into this book here.
Dirty old mouse: *I* Borja, *I* Garrison, *I* Hill, *I* McLaren, *I* Moore;
While he was famous for the line
"Where's your mommy?," he was
just as likely to use such varia-
tions as "Hey, kid, which one's
your mommy?," "Bring your
mommy over here," and "Do you
have an older sister?"
Wallet photos: *I* Moore
Buffs shoes, mirrored ceiling: *I* Hill
Duck walks: *I* Hill
Where's Minnie?: *I* Garrison

(147) Pluto loses tail: *I* McLaren
Pluto cussed out: *I* Hill
Goofy *Q*, pig hunting: *I* Garrison

(148) Heads up, Goofy: *I* McLaren
Goofy grounded: *I* Garrison
Wolf *Q*: *I* McLaren
Pig sliced: *I* Gabriel

(149) Squadron, wets pants: *I* Hill
Shin-kickers: *I* Moore
Rite of passage: *I* Hill
Wolf attacked: *I* McLaren
Spoiled brat: *I* Garrison; The movie

star was Barbra.
Baby in pants: *I* Garrison, *I* Hill

(150) Trouser pranks: *I* Hill
Dwarf wars, Marine: *I* Gabriel
Doused by Dwarfs: *I* Hill
Stomping, headlock: *I* Hill

(151) Dwarf fondling: *I* Hill
Hook *Q*: *I* Kabat
Halter top Hooked, Happy Hooker:
I Garrison
Smee *Q*, hit in nose: *I* Kabat
Pan's orientation: *I* Hill
Hook's black hand: *I* anonymous

(152) Smee dunking, Tic Toc: *I* Hill
Pinocchio alteration: *I* Moore
Coins from wishing well, Pinocchio
dunked: *I* Hill
Fireworks?: *I* DeForest

(153) White Rabbit *Q*: *I* Kabat
Nazim: *I* Hill
Alice *Q*: *I* Garrison
Tinker Bell goes down: *I* Beeman,
who says he was fired for
responding, "I didn't know she
was that kind of a girl."

(154) Hatter's last day: *I* Hill
Panhandling: *I* Garrison, *I* Hill
Downs': *I* Borja, *I* Moore
Copper pot, Pooh on planters: *I* Hill
Poohitical Campaign: *I* Garrison,
Disneyland Line 9-20-72

(155) Tigger: *I* Garrison
Flip into moat: *I* Gabriel
Eeyore *Q*, overly energetic: *I* Hill
Skinned Tigger: *I* Garrison

(156) Dry ice, other Pooh characters,
Chip & Dale: *I* Hill
Orville: *I* Moore
Pluto's excited: *I* Garrison

(157) Robin Hood: *I* Kabat
First tour, biggest tour: Disneyland
Line 8-2-79
Crying *Q*: Cheryl Bruton in

Disneyland Line 4-24-86
Airport: *I* Moore
Dumbo's ears: *I* Gabriel

(158) Out-of-town incidents: *I* Moore

(159) Watts parade: *I* Gabriel
Indian attacks: Disneyland Line 8-7-80
Phantom, Scary Knight *Q*: *I* Moore
Merlin: *I* Borja, *I* Keen

(161) Crack up *Q*: *I* Keen
1st Character Parade: Disneyland News 7-85
Dance requirement: *I* Garrison, *Mouse Tales*
Times Square: Jungle Drums 7-4-71

(162) Horse fall: *I* Yan, confirmed by unnamed source
Chaff *Q*, Climate Control: *I* Chaney

(163) Giants in Mexico: *I* Moore
Fairy fondler: *I* Garrison, *I* Hill
Alice pinned: *I* Hill
Why waiting?: *I* DeForest

(164) Electrical finale: *I* Ippolito
Light Magic: Register 5-18-97
Pass holder night: *I* various unfortunate guests in attendance, including Dana and Sylvia
Painted ropes: *I* DeForest

(165) I am French: *I* Yang

(166) Light Magic closes: Times 10-15-97

Chapter Eight

(167) Halloween: *I* various, including Hunsaker (gate crashers, refunds) and Ippolito (shoplifting); History would repeat itself five years later when violence broke out during another Rick Dees/KIIS-FM promotion that offered guests 5-cent admission to Knott's Berry Farm for Cinco de Mayo.

(168) P.R. *Q*: *I* Wolf
Jolly Blue Giants, female officers, *Q*s: *I* Doezie

(170) Shattered jaw: *I* officer involved in pursuit, surgeries confirmed by the victim
Bad apples *Q*: *I* Doezie

(171) Guards' responses: *I* current security officer
Armed suspects: *I* M. Keiser, *I* Wolf
Out of wheelchair, using their heads: *I* M. Keiser
Football star: *I* officer involved in arrest
Throw up *Q*: *I* Robertson
Drugs in film canister: *I* M. Keiser

(172) Patched up fence: *I* Robertson
Tunneling under: *I* Haught
Fence by kennels: *I* various
Border patrol *Q*: *I* M. Keiser
Security canines: *I* Homola, *I* Robertson, *I* Wolf
Chew *Q*: *I* Homola
999 *Q*: *I* Wolf

(173) Cut up: *I* Doezie
Drive thrus: *I* Robertson
Doggie CPR: *I* Aramaki

(174) Flying Saucer dog: *I* Baldwin, *I* Haught
Smuggled Chihuahua: *I* Haught
Items not allowed in: *I* Robertson
Crossdressers, Voodoo Lady: *I* Judd, *I* Robertson
Tattoo guy: Register 10-26-94
Horse fondler: *I* Judd
Spin Man: *I* Judd, *I* Robertson

(175) Wheelchair *Q*: *I* Yang
Screening: *I* Hendrickson
Star Tours repossession: *I* Chaney

(176) Handicapped terror: *I* Yang
Waxed deck, stage show: *I* Alanis
Pop wheelies *Q*: *I* Judd

Prairie family: *L* Paulson 1995, *I* Robertson, *I* Yang, discussions by phone with Mr. and Mrs. Paulson

(178) Eagles: *I* Robertson, confirmed by current officer

(179) Mouseketeer robbery: Register 12-95 & 8-22-97; Times 9-1-95 & 5-30-97
Lookout *Q*: *I* anonymous
Falcons: *I* Robertson, confirmed by current officer

(180) Gift-Giver Extraordinaire Machine: Disneyland Line 1-3-85; Disneyland's 250 millionth guest arrived 8-24-85.
Walkie-talkies: Bruce Gordon, at 7-95 presentation in Garden Grove
Lawsuit: *L* Killackey 1985
Fix *Q*: *I* Robertson; The 300 millionth guest, a 28-year-old French woman making her first trip to Disneyland, arrived 9-11-90.
Dream Machine: Disneyland Line 1-19-90
Sweeper *Q*: *I* Robertson

(181) Ravens, pigeons, hawks, foxes: *I* Robertson, confirmed by current officer
Plain clothes *Q*: *I* anonymous

(182) Excuses: *I* Robertson
Dwarf alibi: *I* Doezie
Sword, into bakery: *I* Robertson

(183) Flees through parade: *I* officer involved in pursuit
Legal busts, civil demand: *I* Robertson, *I* anonymous officers
At first limited *Q*: *I* anonymous

(184) Police presence: *I* various, confirmed by Register 2-21-99
Quotas, sweep *Q*: *I* Robertson

(185) Waiting room, dungeon: *I* Robertson, confirmed by current officers

(186) News coverage: Register 9-15 & 20 & 27-96; 11-3 & 4-96; 12-6-97; As it played out, of the six cases filed in 1996 by suspected shoplifters, one was awarded $65,000 (she later found her receipt for a hat). Most of the others lost.
A woman who said she was trying to return a toy her young daughter had walked out of a store with couldn't keep her story straight; the jury believed the security guard, who said that the woman, upon noticing the girl had taken the toy, put it in a bag and continued walking away from the shop.
Another woman claimed she was being prosecuted supposedly for "stealing" a Gap sweatshirt her son had brought into the park; she was convicted, instead, for swiping three t-shirts.
Hard Copy: *I* Robertson, my own experience being interviewed for the segment; The show's reporter claims that Paramount, producer of *Hard Copy*, gave in after pleas from Michael Eisner, who before joining Disney had worked for Paramount.
Policy rethought: *I* Doezie, confirmed by current officer

(187) Complaints *Q*: *I* anonymous
Arrest statistics: Register 2-21-99

(188) Criticism, training *Qs*: *I* current officer

Chapter Nine
(189) Plus the show *Q*: *I* Fravel
We'll try it: *I* Catone
Administration bldg. Q: *I* France; The 800-foot-long TDA Building is known to hourlies as the "Hot Dog Building"—it's mustard yel-

low and relish green on the outside and filled on the inside with weenies.

(190) Twain, Monorail *Qs*: *I* Catone
Texans: *I* Eno

(191) Anti-Foods *Q*: *I* Grupp
Benefits: *I* Mobley

(192) Rotation *Q*: *I* Mobley
Strike *Q*: *I* Gentleman; More in-depth coverage of the strike appears in *Mouse Tales*, p. 68-77.
20% growth goal: Disneyland Line 9-13-96

(194) Walls come down: Disneyland Line 7-5-96
Pun *Q*: *I* Haller
Hard sell *Q*, tactics: *I* Ippolito
Survey questions: These are paraphrases of actual questions asked to me by survey-takers on recent visits to the park.
Survey responses: *I* Hirsch

(195) Empowerment Evolution: Times 4-14-96

(196) Asst. managers *Q*: *I* O'Trambo
Tell what to do *Q*: Internet posting by Al Lutz

(197) Changes *Qs*: *I* D. Brown
Keel boat mishap: *L* Davis 5-17-97, *L* Martin 5-17-97 (panic *Q*)
Keel boat *Q*: I anonymous current employee

(198) Likable Burner: *I* unanimous consensus
Goal *Q*: *I* Baker
Overlap *Q*: *I* Goodwin
Sprinkler head *Q*: *I* Haught

(199) No fingerprints: *I* Goodwin
McKinsey *Q*: *I* Baker

(200) Irby's opening remarks: *I* Baker, *I* O'Trambo, confirmed by others in attendance

Punch list, winter *Q*: *I* O'Trambo

(201) Graveyard shift: *I* Baker, *I* Goodwin, *I* O'Trambo, *I* Penfield, *I* Russo
Efficiency, hours *Qs*: *I* Penfield
Mass firing: *I* Baker, *I* Goodwin, *I* O'Trambo, *I* Penfield, *I* Russo

(202) Restructuring *Q*: *I* O'Trambo
Kitchens meeting, trams: *I* Baker

(203) Military promotions and hires: *I* confirmed by all
Size up problems: *I* O'Trambo
Carpenter *Q*: anonymous, reported by Penfield
Fail *Q*: *I* anonymous
Stress: *I* Penfield, *I* Russo
Suggestions: Register 5-21-98

(204) Crane mishap: OSHA report, Register 11-9-97
Short-handed, Indy *Qs*: *I* Goodwin

(205) Reductions, time studies, quota: *I* Baker
You check on that: *I* O'Trambo

(206) Outside contractors *Q*: *I* Penfield; The two-year pavement replacement project began in the fall of 1997 in the hub.
Railroad overhaul: *I* Cashen, confirmed by current employees
Falls apart *Q*: *I* Goodwin
Repair requests: *I* various
Show specifics: eye-witnessed, Register 4-5-98

(207) Downtime rises: *I* Baker, confirmed by current supervisor
New terminology *Q*: *I* anonymous

(208) Cracks on Peter Pan, Dumbo, *Q*, Monorail: *I* current supervisor
Twain: *I* various
Vow to save subs: Register 4-5-98
Closure announced: Times 7-30-98
Closure defended: *I* Emporium asst. mgr. "Terri"

(209) Canoe closure: I anonymous current ride operator

Late openings and early closings: Register 10-3 & 7-98, Times 10-3 & 7-98

Baby shop lessee: I H. Johnson

All should be open Q: I Foster

(210) Positions eliminated: eye-witnessed, confirmed by current employees

Strip staffing Q: I Helwig

Safety Q: I Perley

(211) Columbia accident: Register 12-25 & 27 & 28-98, Times 12-25 & 27 & 28 & 31-98

Lack of training: OSHA report; Disney publicly insisted that Carpenter was fully trained to operate the Columbia, possibly because the park possessed paperwork showing that she had "signed off" on the Mark Twain. Yet, according to the OSHA report, "although there are similarities between the docking operations of the two ships, the speeds and size of forces involved are quite different."

In addition, reported OSHA, the "injured employee stated that she had never performed a docking operation of any ship, all by herself, prior to the accident. During her training on Mark Twain, somebody was always with her to help and she never had any training on the Columbia's operations, as it was not operating that day."

Nevertheless, Disney P.R. stood by its claims that she was properly trained. Ironically, in the spring of 1998, about eight months before the accident, several old-timers had given me this prediction: before too long, cut-backs at the park would result in a serious injury that management would try to blame on an hourly employee.

Normally aren't repaired Q: Tom Bugler interviewed in OSHA report

Work orders: OSHA report included copies of work requests 26422, 24583 and 26512 for repair of a loose cleat on the docking side of the Columbia.

Rope switch: I various

Sub loses cleat: I anonymous current Tomorrowland ride operator

Employee response: I Perley, current cast members

(212) Causes: OSHA report, Register 3-26-99, Times 3-26-99; Vuong and Carpenter survived, but endured lengthy hospital stays in critical and serious condition, underwent multiple operations, and reportedly suffered permanent disfiguring injuries, Vuong to her face, Carpenter to her foot and ankle.

Chapter Ten

(213) Promotions: Register 12-12-98 & 1-15-99

Heaviest attendance of year: I Hirsch, citing figures obtained by The Register

Berry's vow: Times 1-28-99; Disneyland began requiring that all employees, including managers, receive full hands-on training before working any attraction and instituted specific changes to the operation and docking of the Columbia, such as using bells and standardized markings along the river as signals during docking, bringing the boat to a complete stop before mooring it, and hand-

ing the line down to the dockhand
to tether it to the mooring post
(Times 4-14-99).

(214) Alice hurts foot: Register &
Times 12-22-00
Rifle finger lost: Times 1-24-01
Tying off raft: *I* anonymous
1st Pirates accident: *I* with cast
members, including Wes Elskamp
2nd Pirates accident: *I* with cast
members, Register 1-31-01
Roger Rabbit victim seated on open
side, claims about lap bar:
Register 12-30-00
Space Mountain crash: Register 8-
2-00
Bolts faulty: *I* Coaster Team
mechanic, who alleges crew had
been forced to reuse old bolts.
Stranded: MousePlanet's Disneyland Internet Guide

(215) Tree falls: Register & Times 5-
5-01
Attack tree *Q*: *I* anonymous

(216) Perfection *Q*: *I* White
Monkey *Q*: *I* Gentleman
Traditions *Q*: *I* D. Brown
New traditions *Q*: *I* Emporium asst.
mgr. "Terri"
Morale *Qs*: *I* anonymous hourly
employees

(217) Pixie dust *Q*: *I* Gentleman
A showman not a shopkeeper: An
excellent treatise on Disneyland's
problems posted on the Internet
under the pseudonym "Jack
Danger" used this same analogy.
Old blood *Q*: *I* Penfield

Index

Adventure thru Inner Space, 115, 133, 134-135
Adventures of Ichabod and Mr. Toad, 31
African Lion, 52
African Queen, 52
Alice (costumed character), 153-154, 163
Alice in Wonderland (attraction), 32, 41, 204, 214
Alice in Wonderland (movie), 31
America on Parade, 163
America Sings, 128, 134, 136
America the Beautiful, 132-133
Archer, Earl, 33
Astro Jets (see Rocket Jets)
Astro Orbiter (see Rocket Jets)
Autopia, 45, 119-122, 134, 137, 168, 209

Baa Baa Black Sheep, 148
Baker, Earl, 198-199, 202, 205
Baloo, 141, 142, 157, 159
Bashful, 150
Beaumont, Eric, 18
Beeman, Robby, 28, 84
Berry, Mike, 213
Big Bad Wolf, 143, 147, 148-150, 155
Big Thunder Mountain Railroad, 72, 75, 89, 129, 176-177, 198, 209

Black Hole, The, 139
Blue Fairy, The, 163
Bobsleds (see Matterhorn)
Borja, Christopher, 144
Boynton, Doug, 191
Brer Bear, 140, 141, 142, 145
Brown, Don, 196-197
Burner, Dale, 198-199

Canal Boats of the World, 34
Canoes, 90, 143, 149, 151-152
Captain E-O, 133-134, 136
Captain Hook, 96, 143, 149, 151-152
Carousel of Progress, 103, 127-128
Carpenter, Christine, 210-211
Casey Jr. Circus Train, 35, 39, 40
Catone, John, 20, 37, 143, 190
Chaney, Kevin, 162
Chip and Dale, 142, 156, 177-178
Chip 'n Dale Acorn Crawl (Nut House), 50-51
Chip 'n Dale Tree Slide, 50
Cinderella, 140
Circle-Vision 360, 64, 68, 132-133, 137, 162, 208
Clay, Andrew Dice, 68
Columbia, Sailing Ship, 64, 96-97, 98, 99, 210-214
Conk, Gary, 18
Cosmic Waves, 137-138
Country Bear Jamboree, 99, 210

Crockett, Davy, 84, 93
Cruella de Vil, 155

Davis, Guy, 199
Davy Crockett Explorer Canoes (see
  Canoes)
Dawson, Luan Phi, 211-212
Dees, Rick, 167
DeForest, Mike, 67
Disney, Roy, 191
Disney, Walt, 11-12, 17, 19, 20, 29,
  31, 34, 36, 44, 52, 56, 67, 90, 93,
  96, 102-103, 132, 139, 145, 189-
  191, 198, 209, 215-218
Disneyland Hotel, 122, 126
Disneyland Pacific Hotel, 178-179
Disneyland Paris (Euro Disney), 180
Disneyland Railroad, 25, 29, 120,
  159, 172, 206
Disney's California Adventure, 178,
  214, 215, 217-218
Disney World, Walt, 129, 188, 191
Doc, 150
Doezie, Janice, 168-170, 186-187
Donald Duck, 49, 51, 139, 145, 146,
  157, 159
Donald Duck's Boat, 50
Dopey, 150
Dotts, Bob, 110
Dumbo (character), 157
Dumbo the Flying Elephant (attrac-
  tion), 32, 127, 208
Dutch Boy Color Paint Gallery, 119

Eeyore, 140, 155-156
Eisner, Michael, 192-193
Enchanted Tiki Room, 18, 64, 65, 75,
  77-80, 81, 87, 99, 206, 210
Epcot Center, 136
Extra, 186
Ezell, John, 19, 58

Fantasia, 51, 98
Fantasmic, 97, 98, 164, 173, 176, 199
Flights of Fantasy parade, 163
Flores, Ray, 58, 88
Flying Saucers, 174
Flynn, Erroll, 157
Foster, Bo, 209

Foulfellow, 152
France, Van Arsdale, 11-12, 190
Fravel, Gary, 56, 88, 189
Fujimura, Ken, 60, 107

Gabriel, Mark, 144
Garrison, Terry, 142
Gentleman, Bob, 22, 111, 192
George, Jack, 37, 55, 93
Geppetto, 153
Gerlach, John, 87
Gideon, 152
God, 41, 118, 140, 177
Golden Horseshoe Revue, 88
Goodwin, Mike, 45, 116, 204-205
Goofy, 49, 142, 146, 147-148, 158
Goofy's Bounce House, 50
Gordon, Chad, 71-74
Grand Canyon diorama, 29
Great Moments with Mr. Lincoln, 30,
  64, 81, 87, 103, 191
Green, Josh, 70, 72, 74
Green, Judson, 193, 213
Grumpy, 145, 150
Grupp, Barry, 191
Gus, 140

Happy, 150
Hard Copy, 186-187
Harriss, Cynthia, 213
Haught, Jim, 86, 198
Haunted Mansion, 63, 65, 103, 111-
  117, 206, 209, 210
Hayes, Elizabeth, 134
Hersek, Paul, 65, 97
Hephalumps and Woozles, 156
Hill, Robert, 155
Hill Street Blues, 185
Honey, I Shrunk the Audience, 136
Hunsaker, Sam, 51, 69

Indian Village, 84, 90, 99
Indian War Canoes (see Canoes)
Indiana Jones Adventure, 44, 66, 70,
  81-83, 176, 199, 204, 208
Innoventions, 136
Ippolito, Deena, 194
Irby, T., 199-200, 202-206
Isaacson, Ike, 186-187

It's a Small World, 46, 47, 48-49, 70,
    103, 105, 163

Jackson, Michael, 133
Jacob, Zipora, 82
Jacque, 140
Jiminy Cricket, 153
Jolly Trolley, 49, 50, 210
Judd, Diane, 37, 133, 175-176
Jungle Cruise, 18, 19, 52-75, 97, 99,
    177, 182, 189, 206, 209
Junior Autopia, 121

Kabat, Paul, 151, 153
Kaiser's Hall of Aluminum Fame,
    119
Kaml, Larry, 62-64, 65-67, 74, 97
Kanga and Roo, 156
Keel Boats, 93, 99, 197, 210
Keen, Phil, 161
Keiser, Mark, 115
Kimbrell, Bruce, 65-73, 75
King Arthur's Carrousel, 32, 159,
    161
King Louie, 140, 159
Kitchens, Michael, 202
Knott's Berry Farm, 126, 198

Lamond, Doc, 190
Levine, Heidi, 136
Lewanski, Paul, 22
Light Magic, 164-166
Lion King Celebration parade, 164
Little House on the Prairie, 176
Little John, 157
Lookout Mountain, 44

Mad Hatter (costumed character),
    153-154
Mad Tea Party, 32-34, 174-176
Magic Kingdom (Florida), 129, 188
Main Street Cinema, 30
Main Street Electrical Parade, The,
    162, 163-165, 173, 182-183, 215
Mark Twain, 64, 80, 89-90, 93, 95,
    96, 99, 176, 190, 208, 210-212
Marx, Groucho, 128
Mary Poppins (character), 177
Matterhorn, 18, 36, 38, 39, 44-48, 65,

110, 125, 129, 181, 198, 204, 207,
    210
McClintock, John, 136
McLaren, Don, 148
McNell, Frank, 88
Mendez, Rolf, 85, 93
Merlin the Magician, 159-161
Mickey Mouse, 49-51, 139, 141,
    145-146, 157, 158, 159, 162, 180
Mickey's Toontown, 50-51, 199,
    209, 210
Midget Autopia, 121
Mike Fink Keel Boats (see Keel
    Boats)
Miller, Colette, 118
Mine Train Ride, 87-89
Minnie Mouse, 49-50, 146, 158, 162
Mission to Mars, 127-128, 129, 136,
    208
Mr. Toad's Wild Ride, 32
Mobley, Dick, 135, 192
Monorail, 29, 30, 121, 122, 125-126,
    190, 208
Monsanto's Hall of Chemistry, 119
Moore, Jim, 141
Motor Boat Cruise, 122, 183
Mouseketeers, 179

Nunis, Dick, 193, 213

Omnibus, 28
Orange County Register, 74, 186
Orville, 156
O'Trambo, Dan, 196, 202-203
Owl, 156

Pack Mule Ride, 84-86, 88
Peter Pan (costumed character), 151-
    152, 177
Pete's Dragon, 163
Penfield, Bob, 201
PeopleMover, 126-127, 134, 127,
    174
Perley, Chris, 210
Peter Pan (movie), 31, 36
Peter Pan's Flight, 21, 32, 207-208
Phantom of the Opera (costumed
    character), 159
Pinocchio (character), 152-153, 157

Pinocchio (movie), 31, 163
Pirates of the Caribbean, 60, 65, 103-
   111, 112, 114, 169, 209, 210, 214
Playboy, 60
Pluto, 49, 147, 156, 177
Pressler, Paul, 74, 193-194, 213
Prevention Maintenance, 198
Primeval World diorama, 29, 103,
   115, 190
Prince John, 162

Queen of Hearts, 154, 155

Rabbit, 156
Rafts to Tom Sawyer Island, 58, 93,
   95-96, 214
Rain Man, 174
Rainey, Milo, 89
Rescuers, The, 156
Riverdance, 164
Robertson, Pat, 180
Robin Hood (character), 157
Rocket Jets, 127, 136
Rocket Rods, 137
Roger Rabbit's CarToon Spin, 50,
   214

Saunders, Mark, 120-121
Scary Knight, 159
Schumacher, Fred, 190
Seven Dwarfs (characters), 150-151,
   182
Shelton, Earl, 190
Shooting Gallery, 39, 86, 209
Skyway, 38-44, 47, 125
Sleeping Beauty Castle, 31
Sleepy, 150
Small World (see It's a Small World)
Smee, 151-152
Sneezy, 150
Snow White (character), 150, 182
Snow White and the Seven Dwarfs
   (movie), 31
Snow White's (Scary) Adventures,
   32
Song of the South, 100
Space Mountain, 46, 89, 129-132,
   134, 139, 142, 181, 198, 214
Splash Mountain, 100-101, 176, 200

Stagecoach Ride, 84, 86
Stanley, Tim, 122
Star Tours, 81, 135-136, 137, 175,
   181
Star Wars, 135
Steamboat Willie, 51
Storybook Land Canal Boats, 35-37,
   64, 69, 70, 209
Stout, William, 117
Streetcars, Main Street, 28
Submarine Voyage, 122-125, 208-
   209, 211
Swiss Family Robinson, 75
Swiss Family Treehouse, 65, 75-79

Tarzan, 77
Tea Cups (see Mad Tea Party)
Tiki Room (see Enchanted Tiki
   Room)
Thompson, Charlie, 190
Toy Story Funhouse, 64
Three Little Pigs, The (characters),
   141, 143, 148-149
Tic Toc, 152
Tigger, 140, 142, 143, 155
Tinker Bell, 153
Tom Sawyer Island, 93-95, 99, 156,
   169, 214
Toontown (see Mickey's Toontown)
Toontown Trolley (see Jolly Trolley)
Trapasso, Carl, 139
Tweedledee and Tweedledum, 154
20,000 Leagues under the Sea
   (attraction), 143

Vineyard, Howard, 190
Vuong, Lieu Thuy, 211

Walt Disney World (see Disney
   World)
White, Jerry, 125
Walt Disney Story, 29
White Rabbit, 153
Wilson, Kent, 21, 131
Winnie the Pooh, 141, 143, 154-156
Wolf, Dennis, 94
Wood, C.V., 190

Zimmer, Mark, 112, 123

The Original...

MOUSE TALES

A BEHIND-THE-EARS LOOK AT

DISNEYLAND

By David Koenig   Foreword by Art Linkletter

Critics love this first-ever inside look at the "Mouse House:"

"★ ★ ★ ★ !

A sometimes hilarious, sometimes shocking but definitely unforgettable tome on the history of America's most beloved vacation destination ... a fun book ... told with a jocularity that brings tears of laughter ... (a) wild ride!"
– *Ocala Star-Banner (Ocala, Fl.)*

"Delightful reading ... the second best thing to do if you cannot visit the Magic Kingdom is to read this book. You will find it fascinating."
– *Velma Daniels (syndicated columnist)*

"A valuable addition to popular culture and to Disneyana."
– *Booklist*

"An unofficial history in which hundreds of hilarious events also prove that the 160-acre site near Los Angeles can be as goofy as a crazy cartoon."
– *New York Daily News*

"An amusing and nostalgic trip down Main Street that is entertaining and informative."
– *Santa Cruz Sentinel*

"I've read just about everything that has ever been in print about Disneyland, but I hadn't read most of the things David chronicles in his book! This is original stuff ... this book is a must."
– *Amusement Business*

"... scrapes the fairy dust off the theatrical facade to reveal that what Walt Disney envisioned as a place free from the evils of the real world can be all too real."
– *Los Angeles Times*

"A fast-paced, objective and often hilarious look at the world-renowned theme park ... the book peels away the Disney-manufactured facade and uncovers secrets previously stored behind-the-scenes."
– *Daily Pilot (Orange County, Ca.)*

"... revealing ... entertaining ... This is the book that the folks at Disney don't want you to read, (but) even those of us who are Disneyholics would enjoy reading it."
– *San Antonio Express News*

(Trade Paperback $13.95)   (Hardcover $25.95)

Order directly from the publisher using the form on the last page.

Order Form

Quantity   Amount

_____ **More Mouse Tales: A Closer Peek Backstage at** _____
Disneyland (softcover) @ \$14.95

_____ (hardcover, *personally autographed by the author*) _____
@ \$24.95

_____ **Mouse Tales: A Behind-the-Ears Look at** _____
Disneyland (softcover) @ \$13.95

_____ (hardcover, *personally autographed by the author*) _____
@ \$25.95

_____ **Mouse Under Glass: Secrets of Disney** _____
Animation & Theme Parks (softcover) @ \$14.95

_____ (hardcover, *personally autographed by the author*) _____
@ \$23.95

Total for book(s) _____

Postage: Add \$2 for first book, _____
\$1 for each additional

Sales Tax: **California residents only,** add 7.75% tax _____

Amount enclosed (U.S. funds) _____

Ship Book(s) to:

_____

_____

_____

IF THIS IS A LIBRARY COPY,
PLEASE PHOTOCOPY THIS PAGE

BONAVENTURE PRESS
P.O. Box 51961
Irvine, Ca. 92619-1961